ALSO BY ANNE ROIPHE

■

Digging Out
Up the Sandbox
Long Division
Torch Song
Generation Without Memory
Your Child's Mind
    (with Dr. Herman Roiphe)

Praise for

LOVING=
KINDNESS

"Powerful...provocative...will not fade quickly from memory."

—New York Newsday

.

"In *Lovingkindness*, Anne Roiphe has made a contribution to the literature of mothers and daughters, of the war between generations, rightly offering no simple answers, but instead giving us a heroine who is willing to face herself, her own life and responsibilities, with the same relentless intelligence she applies to everyone else."

—Philadelphia Inquirer

.

"A graceful writer...has managed to weave those philosophic issues that concern her into a tapestry of warm, real life."

—Cleveland Plain Dealer

.

"*Lovingkindness* takes the mother-daughter theme that has so dominated feminist literature and turns it on its side...will have meaning for anyone who has ever been faced with the need to let go of a child, to pay attention, but to allow it freedom."

—Fort Worth Star-Telegram

more...

"By turns caustic and lyrical...the story rings true, especially in reflecting the heartache that ensues when a child repudiates parents, culture, and homeland."

—Publishers Weekly

■

"Confronting a feminist mother's nightmare...this intense personal story is a cliffhanger."

—Ms.

■

"A wise, deeply felt first novel about the conflict between mother love and personal pride...fluid, spicy, unsentimental."

—Kirkus Reviews

■

"It's a wonderful story and what makes it so potent is the mix of tough questions and strong story."

—Betty Rollin, author of Last Wish and First You Cry

■

"A bittersweet, sometimes wry yet empathetic telling of the conflict of generations, each seeking its own truths, each struggling with the other's truths."

—Oregonian

■

"Heartfelt in its examination of the mother-daughter bond."

—Library Journal

LOVING KINDNESS

ANNE ROIPHE

WARNER BOOKS

A Time Warner Company

WARNER BOOKS EDITION

Copyright © 1987 by Anne Roiphe
All rights reserved including the right of reproduction in whole or in part in any form.

This book was published by arrangement with Summit Books, a division of Simon & Schuster, Inc., 1230 Avenue of the Americas, New York, N.Y. 10022

Cover design by Carin Goldberg
Cover photograph by Jennifer Baumann

Warner Books, Inc.
1271 Avenue of the Americas
New York, N.Y. 10020

W A Time Warner Company

Printed in the United States of America

First Warner Books Printing: February, 1989

10 9 8 7 6

I WAS at my desk by my window in my bedroom when a sparrow appeared on the sill. It peered into the room and then hunched its shoulders and ducked its head into its chest, keeping its beak turned slightly so that one of its eyes stared directly into mine. I saw a dark space opening behind the black pupil, the space reached out over the bird and included the entire sky, obliterating the tree by my window, the street below and the rooftops across the way. I looked away, back at the ordinary objects in my room. For a moment I thought that I had seen my grandfather's eye blinking at me. No doubt I was still upset over the phone call I had received from my daughter Andrea the night before. I had not heard from her for five months. She is twenty-two and this is permissible. The silence was even a kind of relief; although a part of me is always straining to hear her voice, attend to her, another part of me welcomed the pause. It made it possible to forget for a while. Days would go by and I would hardly think her name, hours would pass without my considering her fate, short and long term. I did not miss her at all. I was grateful for her silence. I knew she would not altogether disappear. I knew that she would call and there would be a request for money, for a plane ticket, the story of a broken friendship, a failed course, a discovery of a new place to go and a new

intention that I would attend cautiously, skeptically and with
a weight in my belly that has grown so large that I am now
like a pregnant elephant whose term must surely be ending.
This phone call.

"Mother?" she said.

"Yes, Andrea, where are you?"

"In Israel, Mother."

"Yes," I said, "have you been to the old city yet?"

"Yes," she answered. "I'm living there."

"Are you working?" I asked, and then answered myself,
"You can't be working, you're without papers."

"I'm living with some very good new friends," she said.

I had heard this one before. "That's fine," I said.

"I'm studying too," she added.

Never a child to study, a spirit that danced to the tune of
the immediate, the hot and the neon-colored. I was puzzled.
"Are you studying Hebrew?" I asked.

"Yes, and other things. Oh, Mother, I am very happy."

"I'm very happy to hear it," I said, uncertain. Her
happiness could be as much a cause for concern as her
unhappiness.

"I am going to stay a while longer," she said. I waited.
We were coming closer to the point of this phone call. "I
am staying at the Yeshiva Rachel, I am different from when
you last saw me." I was silent. The phone call was collect.
The distance was far, but I knew I shouldn't respond too
fast. "Mother," she said, "don't be upset. I love you, I
made my own decision, by myself. I am peaceful. I honor
you, of course," she added.

This was the most upsetting phrase of all. I had never
heard it or its sentiment from her before and I knew just
what it meant.

"Good-bye," she said.

"Wait," I shouted as if it were my responsibility to carry
my voice across the sea. "We have to talk. How do I reach
you? Do you have a phone, an address? Do you need
money?" Suddenly I was begging.

"Good-bye, Mother," she said cheerfully, sweetly.

There was something too kind in her tone. It made me sweat. I was always waiting for some definitive, end-of-the-line call. We've found your daughter in a ravine outside of Las Vegas with her throat cut, we've found your daughter dead of an overdose in a pickup truck with a Hell's Angel, we've found your daughter naked hallucinating on the L.A. freeway. I had anticipated a lot of phone calls. I had not thought of the Yeshiva Rachel.

RACHEL—what was the Yeshiva Rachel? I called a friend and a friend of the friend told me, a new yeshiva, for women only, to teach them some Talmud, to teach them how to keep kosher. "But she doesn't cook at all," I said.

"They will teach her," the friend of the friend who knew all about it said. "They will turn your daughter into a real Ba'altshuva, a returned, one of the found." I counted her still among the lost. "They will find her a husband," she said, "they will encourage her to have twelve children."

I laughed. Andrea had never picked up a shirt from the floor. She had never thrown a tissue into the wastebasket. She had never taken care of the kitten I had bought to encourage her to make the connection between obligation and affection.

She would not, I was sure of it, would not tend and clean and wipe. This will last two weeks and then she'll be off, I thought. And then what? I was distracted and unable to work.

"Maybe Andrea will turn out like Bruria," said my friend.

"Bruria, who was she?"

"A Jewish feminist from Rabbinic times."

I knew the name.

* * *

I WENT to the library and looked up Bruria. The
account was brief but not undramatic:

Outside of Jerusalem the small town of Yavneh hung
close to the massive sand-covered mounds that rolled on for
miles down to the Red Sea, where wadis and cliffs and
trickles of water and stones of brown and gold baked, while
Gd, exhausted from the heat, closed his eyes and slept. It
was to Yavneh that the rabbis had escaped with the Torah,
and it was there that Bruria went to the well, tended the
animals, folded the wash and studied the law.

Bruria's father loved his daughter and he secretly taught
her all he knew and she was as quick and as deep as any
male, or so it was said. She was so smart that her father
would consult her when the rabbis disagreed and tangled
themselves in conflicting opinions. The Romans followed
the rabbis to Yavneh and demanded that the Jews abandon
the study of Torah, forgo the Talmud. They made an example of Bruria's father because he was admired, because he
had enemies, because the holiest man is always a tasty
victim. . . . They wrapped him up in the pages of his beloved
text and under his feet they set a fire. The Hebrew letters
left the page and floated upward back toward the crest of
Mt. Sinai, back to the hand that gave them. Bruria watched
her father burn, returned to her husband's house and continued to study the Talmud. There were whisperings against
her because it had been said by Rabbi Elier Ben Harkeness
that it would be better to burn the Torah than to teach it to a
woman. *Was her father's punishment a Jewish joke?* Bruria's
children went out to play and as they were building a fort of
pebbles and sticks they fell ill. A neighbor found them
stretched out in the dirt and brought them home to Bruria.
In hours her two children were cold and stiff. She covered
them with blankets, and with pious legal reasoning con-

vinced her husband to accept Gd's choice. But the rest of us are wondering if a mother's learning was poisonous for the child. Was the mother's sharp mind an offense to a deity who preferred his women ordinary, modest, without unusual brains or fervor? Was the death of the children a test she had passed or failed?

A certain rabbi suggested to Bruria's husband, who was himself a well-respected scholar, an eminent figure in the rabbinical assembly, that Bruria was of contemptible character and would give herself to an attractive male under the right circumstance. Bruria's husband at first rejected the allegation but then agreed (peer pressure, perhaps) to have a young rabbi attempt to seduce his wife. Unfortunately, rumors spread. No one knew if Bruria did or did not give up her virtue under the siege of this fake seduction, but the learned men and their eager wives of this small community all believed that she had fallen, and she was forced to flee and her husband too left, and the disgrace, the shame, the lesson that learning does not nurture obedience, that in the woman sex will always overpower reason, has lasted through the centuries. Job's children were restored to his side. Bruria's never reappear. No voice in the wind consoles her and the damages are never undone. Job is a fable woven into the sacred text borrowed from the heathen countryside. Its happy ending is not Jewish. Bruria's tale is plausible Jewish history. The dead children are lost forever.

ANDREA'S YESHIVA was named after Rachel . . . was this a feminist position or was it a trick, a way of teaching women a little and luring them in only to return them to their rightful place? Was this a dark Jewish joke about matriarchs?

The friend of a friend found the address for me. The mail is very slow, she warned me. It can take as many as forty

days for a letter to arrive in Jerusalem, she said. What does
the name of your yeshiva signify? I wrote Andrea. Tell me
about Rachel and what you think of her. I had learned that
Andrea, who was never much of a correspondent and preferred the collect phone call, would be more likely to reveal
herself if I approached indirectly. On the other hand, the two
of us had been sparring so long that we each knew the
other's indirections. She did not answer my letter, or my
letter got lost.

DEAR ANDREA, I wrote, I am very concerned
about your stay at this yeshiva. Of course you
are an adult and are completely free to make your own
decisions. You made them anyway even when you were a
child, but I am puzzled. You never expressed any interest in
religion before. I believe you had a sign over your mirror
that said, God sucks. A little blunt, but an understandable
feeling in this modern world. I did tell you that we are
Jewish, but I never made a fetish of it. I never told you that
these were the only people that you should be concerned
with or that any one group had an exclusive on moral or
immoral behavior. I did take you with me to the feminist
seder and you thought it was ridiculous. You thought that
the Egyptians had been given a bad press, to quote you
exactly. I don't for a moment believe that you have to stick
to every passing thought of your by no means successful
adolescent years, but this seems like a peculiar change of
face. Please write and tell me what you are thinking. If by
the time this letter reaches you, you are already on the road
far from the Yeshiva Rachel, tell me what the experience
was like. I am curious. I love you as always and would be
glad to send money if I knew what your plans really were. I
am fine and am working on a new collection of essays and
reworking my fall lecture series. Love, Mother.

I read the letter over four times before I sent it. It sounded stiff, as if I were writing to a stranger, as if I hadn't woken in the night a thousand times and rushed to her side when her dreams were evil, when her stomach cramped, when her fever rose, when she cried out in fear of the next day. I was writing to her now as if we didn't remember, either of us, how she had called out over her shoulder, almost casually, when she had gone off the last time, "I'll never forgive you. . . ." I had no idea for what, and yet I knew exactly: everything. I read the letter again. It was clean enough but without inspiration. Andrea reduced my intelligence and ruined my style. I coud not be eloquent when my fears were at high tide. Mme. de Sevigne was a woman of another century and her daughter had not been to several psychotherapists, her daughter had not experimented with certain dangerous substances and been removed from several high schools. Her daughter had not humiliated her. Her daughter had never worn an iron cross around her neck and had never put a safety pin in her nostril. True, the pin had been removed well before this last journey of self-discovery. I reread the letter and sent it. Three weeks later I received a reply, or perhaps it was not a reply:

Dear Mother, Please call me Sarai, I have changed my name to one in keeping with my new life. I will not answer or read any letters addressed to Andrea. I honor you, of course. Love, Sarai.

ANDREA had been the name I had selected sometime in the fourth month of pregnancy. A name I thought most beautiful, evoking Greek islands set in pale blue pools and promising surprise and elegance, visits to shrines and mountaintops, olive groves and white walls, sun beating on clean steps of houses whose windows opened on waking babies and dark-eyed women who were staring at the sea. Andrea was a name to imagine with, not like Sarah, which reminded me of barren old ladies whose desires were granted too late to bring real satisfaction, a bitter old lady who banished her rival and the child of her rival. Sarah was the name of the matriarch whose namesakes darted through the landscapes of the Ukraine gasping for air. I wanted my daughter to have a name that wouldn't hint at limit or confinement. Andrea/Sarai—I find it hard to concentrate on my work.

I REMEMBER Andrea at the beach the summer I was writing my book on the spinsters of New England. She was brown and long-legged, and on the rainy days she sat at the kitchen table and drew pictures of crabs and clams, seaweed and butterflies. She would lean her head down over the paper and her legs would bang against the kitchen chair and I hung all her drawings in the house. I tacked them up on the pine walls and I taped them on the refrigerator door. They were elaborate crayonings with shadows and layers. If I leaned over and kissed her while she worked, she would brush me aside as if a fly had settled on her cheek. That was the summer she sold lemonade at the edge of the boardwalk with her friends and the summer she read all thirty-four volumes of Nancy Drew. That was the summer she and her friends made up plays. Each performance contained a wicked witch who was burnt, melted down, crushed in the garbage disposal or killed by a falling star. Andrea would announce the play, her cheeks flushed, her lips trembling. There would be illustrated programs placed on the seats of each adult. We clapped, we called for encores. We laughed in the right places. The plays rarely lasted longer than four minutes, but they were hours in the preparation. The audience was satisfied, eager for more, amazed by each device of plot or costume.

I watched her at the edge of the ocean, laughing that laugh that mingles joy with terror as the waves came up over her ankles as she ran back and forth like a sandpiper at dusk. That was the August when thousands or perhaps it was millions of starfish washed up on the sand and were drying in the sun. Andrea organized a crew to pick up the starfish and toss them back into the waves so that they could live longer. The children worked long hours at the rescue of the starfish, filled buckets and buckets with the pink pulsing forms who had no words to thank, no brain to register salvation. I tried to explain to Andrea that all the beach was made of dead creatures, that nature was indifferent to the particular forms it had created and was willing to let each go in turn in service to another. Andrea did not believe me. She felt each starfish had a right, had a purpose, had a destiny of its own. Only a two-day storm that shifted the currents of the sea, bringing an end to the starfish harvest, stopped the frenzied efforts of the children, tight-lipped, combing the shoreline in defiance of the natural order.

In the mornings I would wake up with her body resting against mine. She smelled of salt and sun. Once in her hair I found a tiny shell. I gave her the shell and told her to keep it in a safe place so it could bring her luck. Later that day she found a large clamshell polished clean in the sun. She gave it to me and said it would bring me luck. I still have it by my bedside. It used to serve as an ashtray and then when I gave up smoking, because Andrea begged me, I kept it. Who knows exactly what brings you luck?

Andrea found a stick in the dunes. It had been the home and the sustenance of some life form that had left markings along the dried-out curve; curious indentations, like Sanskrit, like cuneiform, like the hieroglyphics of a dwarfed species. Andrea told me that the stick was a message from the dolphins, who wished to contact us to improve human life. I watched her hold the stick in her hands and wave it at the fish in the sea. "I have your message, I have your message," she shouted at the white froth that rolled up the wet

beach. Her nose had freckled and burnt and peeled, and she
had taken off the top of her bathing suit because she didn't
need it anyway. As the wind blew up off the sea I scanned
the horizon for sharks the way I always did when I felt that
my happiness must be exposing me to immediate peril.

That was the summer I felt sorry for the spinsters of New
England. I tried not to let my pity slip onto the page. I
wanted to present these women of the nineteenth century
who devoted themselves to good works, to the library, to the
hospital, to the church, to their sisters' families, to their
elderly bedridden parents, as heroines of a new order, like
woodchucks announcing the coming spring. I tried to present their lives as knit of stern ideals, proper behavior,
repression to the right degree. I tried to see them as the
freest members of their icy social order, but every time I
would look at Andrea, asleep in her bed, Nancy Drew on
her pillow, red-and-white sneakers on the floor, I would
grieve for my straight-backed upright ladies, who had missed
the brightest bondage of them all.

MY GRANDFATHER had come from Bratslav to
New York some years before the century turned.
He had been a young man willing to work hard, and a
pushcart with trousers soon became a loft with twenty girls
sewing seams, which in turn metamorphosed into a factory
and then two factories and a sales force and an office with
secretaries and switchboards. His sons, who had gone to
college before entering the business, spoke without an
accent and they wore no beards and they went bareheaded
through the streets and they played golf on Saturday and
laughed at the old man and his black coat and his hat and
the curls that hung down beside his cheeks and all the things
he wouldn't do because it was forbidden and all the things
he would do because it was bidden. A common tale of old

ways lost and new ways taken, of the young striking out for new territory and the old beginning the journey but not completing it, of centuries of clashing, of the enlightenment wooing, of Hellenism seducing, of possessions undreamed of in the old town where the door handle on the Mikvah was constantly coming off in the hands that turned it. When they moved the firm to its new office building in the garment center amid the sounds of jazz and jive and honking horns and racks of clothing bumping steel frames one against another, they made the old man chairman of the board and sent him down to Florida to live. I saw him on his occasional trips to New York. My mother did not want him coming in the elevator and standing in the lobby of our building. We would visit him at his sister's in Long Island. "I should have gone to Palestine instead of to New York. I was a fool, a young fool," he said to me. "Look what has become of you, my family, in New York," he said. "In Palestine they have brought Rabbi Nachman's chair, piece by piece, and put it in its place, where he will come after the Messiah." There were tears in his eyes. "In Bartslav I personally knew the Bartslav Hasidim, who told the stories told to their fathers by the famous Rabbi Nachman. I knew those men who remembered those stories as well as I know the hand in front of my face.

"Better stories than your 'Lone Ranger,' better than your 'Inner Sanctum,' and much better than your 'Dr. Christian.' Those were stories that made the stars come into your mouth so you could taste them."

A story could do that? My grandfather, who died one winter in Miami wearing his black coat and his black hat and his tallis in his single room on the beachfront where I had never been but imagined him sometimes staring out the window at the pelicans diving into the turquoise waters, believed that a story could do that. "Tell me a story," I had said.

"No." He had stared at me as at a newly discovered stain on the tablecloth. "Not for you."

* * *

I HAD BEEN named Annie after my dead grandmother, Ann. My grandmother's picture was in
a jade frame near my mother's bed, a plump woman whose
pineapple-sized breasts strain forward against a string of
pearls at her throat. Her lips are parted; the photographer
asks, she obliges. Her hair is a cap of white curls and her
cheeks are full as if stuffed with chocolate. And in her eyes,
memories of soft sheets and embroidered napkins held close
and treasured. My mother lights a gray wax candle that fills
a thick milky glass and places it beneath this picture each
year at the anniversary of her mother's death. The doctors
chasing a malignancy through the membranes and the tissues had set my grandmother's bones on fire by using
excessive radiation . . . a new toy whose limits were in 1935
only a matter of opinion. Often I thought of the bones
smoldering like the late-night logs of a campfire, glowing
embers, occasional sparks and light that flickered in the
shadows. My mother told me that she had gone to a
fortune-teller who read the cards at the Palm Court of the
Plaza Hotel, and under the fronds, sitting at a table near the
violinist, the fortune-teller had said that if a special tea was
brewed and brought to the invalid's bedside, health would
be restored. My mother dipped into her jewelry box and
brought out diamond earrings and gold bracelets and purchased the tea, which proved less than effective. Which is
why I, born several weeks after the funeral, was given the
name Annie, an unpromising plain name with no reference
to art or literature or lineage, no historical reference, except
perhaps to Anne Boleyn, who had not pleased and lost her
head, an alien association anyway for a child whose relatives took their history in the collective rather than the
individual form, a people for whom historical events were
rarely spectator sports. The name Annie was an odd choice.

I had a Hebrew name but my mother forgot what it was; like my appendix, it served no function and was excised.

I sat on the carpet outside the door to my mother's room, in the dark hallway beside the linen closet whose shelves held the monogrammed sheets, the lace tablecloths, the lace-edged guest towels, the pillowcases of silk, the bedcovers fringed with gold thread. I would sit waiting for the maid to bring my mother her breakfast on a tray, a tray complete with a rose in a china vase, the morning paper and a pink napkin in which nested rolls and toast. I often waited several hours as my mother slept on and the kitchen maid scrubbed the bathtubs and the cook ordered dinner from the market and my nanny wrote long letters home to her relatives in Bavaria. In the hallway I waited, still and silent. Even after I had learned to read, in that hallway I did not read. I needed all my energy to wait, to will her awake, to will the door to open, the maid to come, the window blinds to be pulled and my mother to sit up in bed and let the smell of sweat and perfume, the smell of nail polish, cold cream and nicotine, the smell of sleep and dreams, of tissues aging and stretching, of stomach gas and waste and face powder and body powder to mix and float out the door into the hallway and let me in. The hallway was decorated with red velvet wallpaper with indentations of vines that climbed from ceiling to floor. I would lie on the carpet and put my face next to the crack at the bottom of the door. I would just see the morning light that was seeping into the room beneath the heavy drapes. I could see the base of my mother's bed and the flowered ruffle of her spread as it brushed against the floor. I could stay in that position a long time. I learned patience. I learned how to still the beating of my heart and the twitching of my limbs. I learned how to float with time as if on a raft in a becalmed sea. My mother's late sleeping habit had the effect of teaching me how to lie like a lizard waiting for a passing fly. It also taught me how to love through a closed door.

My mother woke each morning with puffed eyes. The

night had been disappointing. Her lace nightgown, the satin bed jacket, would be all askew. Her painted fingernails would be chipped. She would reach for her Camels before she rang for the maid. On the floor would be the solitaire game she had played to bring on sleep. Aces and king, fours and fives, hearts and diamonds, were slung about carelessly as if she hadn't spent hours trying to make the order come out right, as if she hadn't held on to the shiny pictures of sailboats or cats that decorated the deck in her hand and stroked them up and down, to give them luck before dealing out each hand. In the morning on her way to the bathroom my mother stepped on her cards as if they were no more than drops of light reflected from her mirror.

Sometimes she would let me in the bathroom with her. I would sit on the toilet as she soaped in the tub. A small woman with soft folds all over her body, her legs were waxed, her hair was set twice a week. There were thousands of bottles of creams on the sink and still she always looked rumpled, her mascara had a way of running down her cheeks like mourners caught in summer rain. There was always some lipstick on her teeth and she had certain complaints she was more than willing to share with me. They usually concerned my meticulous father, who had a predilection for attractive women, good clothes and fine leather attaché cases. Despite the fact he had married an heiress whose family company had put his name on the annual report, he had regrets of his own . . . or else why were his lips drawn into such a tight line, why were his hooded eyes always turning away, why did he sit silently at the dinner table and why was he always polishing his shoes and going off for long walks or staying late hours at his club, where women were not permitted past the outer vestibule? My father had a hundred white handkerchiefs with his monogram on each. His shirts were perfectly starched and his ties were of dark blue silk. He had a camel's hair coat that was so soft that if a child put her head near the pockets she might expect to hear the heartbeat of the animal who had given his skin. My father stood straight and tall and he had a cable-knit tennis sweater and his whites were always pressed.

Every few months he would succumb to headaches. He would lie in the library in his purple dressing gown with the maroon velvet collar. The shades would be down, the drapes drawn and the room still. Get out, he would yell if anyone came to the door.

He was not a free man this known, unknown fact—of his obligations to others, of his more humble past, where passage on the boat had been steerage, where he had been cast among the peasants and the Jews by a blind and dumb fate—disturbed his sleep. Rue drilled through his brain as if looking for buried treasure and the result was headache, banging, pulsating, nerve-crumpling headache. When it was over he would get dressed, shower and go off to his office. His eyes remained chips of stone, hidden under his heavy lids, slanted as if a roving Mongol had violated a Jewish maiden on the slopes of Odessa generations earlier.

Sometimes I would stand at the window of my room. Gretchen, my nanny, would be knitting silently. It was war time and she was worried about her relatives, who lived in the villages outside of Munich. It was possible they were hungry or cold, and she knitted them scarves and mittens and prayed for them each Sunday at the Church of Our Lady of Perpetual Mercy in Yorkville. In the evening light, I could see a reflection of the room in the window. My chair, my table, everything painted with red hearts and little birds, were duplicated exactly in the mirror image. Beyond the reflection the awnings on Park Avenue stood like the guards at Buckingham Palace as the streetlights went from green to red and back, and under the avenue the hidden trains rumbled on their tracks, headed to Harlem, to the place at Ninety-sixth Street when they would rise from the depths and roar past the gray-faced tenements toward escape. As I stood there transfixed between the real room and its echo in the window, I had a feeling that began low in the stomach

and settled like a handcuff on the heart that I could fall
between the two. The hearts on the wallpaper in both rooms
would begin to spin and I would hold myself very tight
because I knew that Gretchen did not like fancy. I must
manage to stay on the safe side of the reflection, in the right
room, the one with a real floor, by my wit, by my skills at
discriminating between illusion and reality. Even the best of
carpeting could cover an immense hole. I walked carefully.

DEAR ANDREA, Changing your name will not
change who you are or where you come from. It
is a superficial gesture, like dyeing your hair blue or fixing
your nose; I realize you never had nose surgery but you must
by now be learning that changing the surface has very little
effect on the substance. Your name for better or worse has
been with you since the first moments of your birth. It was
given to you with only the best intentions and I find among
the impossible things you have done in your short life, and I
will not list them all here, the new naming among the most
absurd, unfriendly and peculiar. I don't recognize the name
Sarai, I don't accept you as Sarai and I will not. If you
really are on a new turn of life that involves honoring your
mother, then you will immediately change your name back
to the one that I selected when you were no more than
plasma and glue. Does it bother you that I am the one who
gave the name? Does this fact compromise your most
precious independence? Most people in the world carry on
with the name given at birth and most certainly do not feel
yoked to the previous generation like beasts in the field
forced to plow the same row over and over again. I am not
trying to control you. I wasn't trying to hold something over
you at your birth, either. The hospital staff insisted on
having something to print on the birth certificate and you
were unable at the time to give them your opinions.

I can understand your interest in things Jewish. I have talked to many of my friends and it seems that a lot of young people are discovering their roots in the cultures and civilizations of the past. However, your grandparents were not the religious sort. They stopped going to synagogue as soon as they were old enough to defy the old man and his old-fashioned expectations. They did not think that a friendly force from the heavens had paid his passage over or protected him from the rapists and thugs in the czar's army. They spoke Yiddish, yes, but they were anxious that the next generation speak only the president's English. Don't have pictures in your head of a grandpa weaving over the Talmud, shoulders wraped in tallis, dust on his skullcap. That is somebody else's picture (mine in fact, and I don't go all to pieces over it, either). Your grandfather, my father, wanted money. He wanted to be respected in the new world. He wanted to own fine silver and jewels. He wanted security; a lot of security. He wasn't heroic or particularly gifted in spiritual matters. He didn't waste his time at the corner shul entreating, pleading, promising, feeling guilty and unworthy. Your great-grandfather had a loyalty, yes, to a town and some Hasidim who told strange stories, and he was pious enough but not so pious that he didn't start the business that his sons carried on. What is the point of going back two generations, sliding down the historical ladder, slamming doors of opportunity behind you, as if someone hadn't struggled hard and long to open those doors for you? My father, who had no patience with mystics and babblers in foreign tongues, would hardly be overcome with joy to see you poring over old books with cryptic sayings by sages so long dead that they can be misquoted at will. Your religious roots are so distant they might as well be with Abraham in the desert, or Adam in the Garden, a connection, yes, but not a particularly personal one. By those standards you are also related to the ichthyosaurus. You are not feeling under any compulsion to exercise your prehistoric wings, are you?

I doubt the sincerity of your religious impulse. Are you

sure you just don't want someone to tell you what to do? Don't you really think that those laws that determine what you can eat with what, when you can eat and what you say before and after, what belongs together, what should be separated, are infringements on your natural choices? Don't you determine for yourself your own personal ethical behavior? Is lobster really an immoral creature of the deep? Do you really need the opinions of other centuries on your dining table? Don't you feel weighted down, free spirit that thou wert, refusing to learn algebra, refusing to be home at midnight, refusing to eat anything but Hostess cupcakes? Has someone done a lobotomy on you? Did you take so many drugs that you can no longer stand alone without your strings being pulled? Who are you, anyway? Love, Mother.

I REREAD the letter and realized it was less than persuasive. It was simply angry. Was anger all right in this situation? Would it cause me to lose more than I could gain? Why did I feel betrayed? Why had Andrea always made me feel abandoned? I decided not to send the letter, to rewrite another day, to wait patiently and hear more. I tried to picture her by the Damascus gate, standing among the tourists, changing money with Arab boys, clutching handfuls of silver earrings and ropes of colored beads. I tried to imagine her near the white stones of the city wall looking up at the Mount of Olives across the ravines of graves, tombs that seemed to fall or crumble all about the mountainside as if the natives didn't know that death should be discreet, hidden, placed in orderly rows in distant suburbs or behind shrubbery on highways that led to airports. Andrew once told me she wanted to be cremated to save the land for the living. It was a blithe statement from one who didn't intend to die, but there at the yeshiva they would teach her that cremation was impure, against the law, might prevent the remains from gathering together and rising when the Messiah finally arrived. Was it possible that Andrea, who only a short while ago believed that sexual restraint was a disease against which one needed frequent innoculations, could turn into one of those pious women in long dress with high neck and long sleeves, with a scarf tied over her hair, with eyes demurely downcast, in sensible shoes with laces and thick stockings? Andrea wore red spike heels when I last had seen her. I had remarked that they looked like she was working the street. She had told me that I had lost touch with reality and belonged in an institution where they would mash up my food and take away my television privileges if I didn't behave. I loved that about Andrea: the sass, the rudeness, that was her gift. I liked the way she spoke up for herself. She was never conned by our ordinary ways of nodding back and forth. Once, when she first turned punk and shaved the back of her head and put on an old man's coat whose lining followed her like her shadow, she met me at a conference I was attending at the Roosevelt Hotel. We were going to the dentist together. (Some activities require support.) I told her I was embarrassed by how she looked. People on their lunch breaks were staring at us. She told me with her fake pout that she understood my feelings perfectly, there were parts of town, around Sixth Street and Avenue C, where she would be mortified to be walking with me. My wool coat with the beaver collar, my gray flannel suit, would be so out of it everyone would turn around to gape. Any child who understands cultural relativism can't be all bad. I kissed her on the spot and she pretended not to be pleased she had pleased me.

My mother had taught me to spit if I saw a nun on the street because without some magic I too might become a disappointed woman. My mother must have thought virginity was catching and we were in the midst of a chastity epidemic. But I used reason as my prophylactic. As I sallied forth out of the house I examined each superstition carefully on its own terms. This had left me with the normal dread of the unknown, the drift of those who cannot forgive God for the condition of life and so banish Him to the outer fringes of consciousness, where He becomes defanged, declawed, hollowed out and incapable of causing fear and trembling; also incapable of curing fear and trembling. My mother, on the other hand, wore the dress that had brought her luck at the canasta table yesterday to today's game. She never encouraged the evil eye by boasting about her winnings, she avoided black cats, walking under ladders, using the number thirteen and she always had the manicurist paint her nails from left to right because she had never yet become terminally ill on a day on which she painted her nails in the correct direction. Considering that some peoples have cut out the hearts of their enemies as sacrifices to their gods, a little directional nail painting seems harmless enough. Could Andrea believe in the evil eye?

Eventually a letter came:

Dear Mother, I am planning to stay longer at the Yeshiva Rachel. I hope that you will be pleased that I am studying hard. I am certain that I belong here where our people came after years of wandering in the desert to fulfill their part of the covenant. I too am under the covenant, it embraces me and folds me in its truths tenderly. I am your daughter, grateful at last that you gave me life, although you could have brought me up closer to Gd and more in harmony with the soul of Israel. I suppose you were distracted and fooled by the seeming cleverness of the material world, by the seducers and the betrayers who promised you truth through clever media and wicked images. I'm sure you did your best and meant well. I forgive you for your mistakes. I still have hopes of making you proud of me. I remember all the times you told me not to be afraid of dogs, of thunder, of the hamster who had died in his cage. You comforted me and one day I hope I can comfort you. Love, Sarai.

I read the letter several times. I finally tore it up, but not before I had unintentionally memorized it. It intruded on my thoughts; unwanted and unbidden it would rise to remind me of Andrea and her newest predicament even as I was working on an essay. Even when I went out to dinner with friends and even as I lay in my bed at night trying to find a comfortable position that would leave me free of Andrea and able to sleep peacefully.

ONCE I HAD hurt my lower back and was forced into bed for several weeks. I had hired a housekeeper but she left at six o'clock. One night I called out to Andrea, who was watching television in the living room, for a glass of water. "Later," said Andrea, "in the commercial."

After a half hour I called out again. She didn't answer me. She was talking on the telephone. "Andrea," I screamed, "help me." There was no answer. I got out of bed and crawled along the floor slowly. I could feel my hair damp at the back of my neck. I could smell the nightgown I had been wearing too many days in a row.

I found Andrea curled up by the phone. She put one hand over the mouthpiece. "Do you want your water in a bowl or a glass?" she asked.

I had frightened her by not standing up, I had frightened her by needing her. My thirst was gone.

UP AND DOWN West End Avenue I see them, young couples pushing strollers stuffed with little boys whose small heads are topped with velvet yarmulkes anchored wth a hair clip of the kind they used in the beauty parlor where my mother went twice a week to have her hair set and colored. I see them on Saturday, men working with men, women with proper dresses, hats and gloves, walking on Riverside Drive. They are cleaner than the joggers that

pass them by, they are intent on discussion unlike the
Columbia students who lie on the park benches with their
arms around each other as their papers blow over the grass.
I see the grandfathers, the ones with white beards and black
coats, who sit in the sun in the afternoons as the bicyclists
race past. Their heads are always larger than their bodies.
Their arms are thin and their wives are thick. These are
women whose spines have been bent carrying plates to the
table, folding and bending and counting the silver and
polishing the candlesticks and waiting for the return of the
men and the children. They wear their skirts long and their
jackets are cut in the style of another country. They duck
their heads back and forth like the pigeons that move
without fear around their solid shoes. They too watch the
young people pushing strollers and they smile at the little
boys who are wearing yarmulkes and offer them cookies
from the depths of scuffed black pocketbooks.

I see them gathering each Saturday morning outside the
synagogue at 100th Street. A large number of bearded
young men and young women, some in jeans, babies carried
in body slings and prayer shawls hanging from out of
corduroy jackets—"Good Shabbes," "Good Shabbes," they
embrace each other, crackling with energy. They are walking with the Sabbath queen while I am just walking. When I
go past I hurry. They give me the same chill as if I had
approached a group at a party only to have them all fall
silent and look away.

I see two rabbis at the corner of Broadway and 110th
Street disputing a point. Their heads are bent forward, their
bodies rock back on their heels. They are disagreeing and
their cheeks are pink with the pleasure of it. The large
blaring radio carried by a dark-skinned boy in Nike sneakers
bothers them not a bit. The flock of girls in tight jeans and
orange plastic barrettes in their hair, speaking a Spanish
they did not learn in school, disturbs them not at all. The
black man with dreadlocks proclaims that the president has
stolen his welfare check. A young man with a dirty face,

tattered clothes and eyeglasses mended with chewing gum leans against the wall and turns his face toward the sun as if he were on the deck of a tuberculosis sanatorium high in the Alps. A girl with unwashed hair and a raincoat pulled tight over her long cotton skirt holds out her hands and begs each passerby for change. The rabbis go on arguing. A young Oriental man carrying a violin case brushes past, hurrying down the subway steps. A child takes an apple from the fruit stand as his mother glares intently at the bins of broccoli and cauliflower and the buckets of carnations and baby's breath wrapped in clear plastic. I used to look at the entire scene with equal interest. Since my phone call from Andrea I watch the Jews and see them in the foreground as if the rest were only there to decorate, to emphasize, like the flowered vines on old illuminated manuscripts. I am watching differently these days.

I see young women Andrea's age, walking with a backwards tilt and the quiet inward look of mothers-to-be. I think of Andrea's three abortions—yes, three. The first was at seventeen and I was full of sympathy. It would have been hard for a girl whose biology outstripped her caution to have taken advantage of all the advice I had given. I had bought her a book, *Our Bodies, Ourselves.* She claimed to have read it. I told her to call my doctor when she felt she was ready to involve herself. I knew from looking at the fullness of her breasts, which she covered in a T-shirt several sizes too large, from the movement of her legs as they stretched and bent, that she was physically ready, but how to say so without seeming to push? I waited and watched carefully. I had other aggravations. I couldn't enter her room because of the clothes that had been heaped on the floor. She stared at me at dinner like a person in a dream. She told me nothing but whispered into the cradle of the phone. She lost her school books and slept late in the morning. I was not surprised when abruptly one evening she walked into my study and announced that she was pregnant and wanted three hundred dollars in cash by noon the next day. I went with her. I didn't reproach her. The experience alone I believed was chastening enough. I waited in a large room with boyfriends, husbands, and a few other mothers like myself. We avoided each other's eyes and read the magazines placed on the coffee table from cover to cover. I took out my notebook but was unable to work. I was certainly chastened. I gave thanks that abortion was legal; that a child did not have to have a child, that the procedure was simple and safe. Yet as the time passed and Andrea did not emerge from the inner sanctum I felt a fluttering in the muscles of my chest. I was losing my first grandchild. I would not be sentimental. It had no cortex, it had no liver function. Its legs were yet unformed, its features vague and its capacity for independence nil. I would not make too much of the little that was soon to be less. The waiting room lacked air, the walls were unnecessarily dingy, the ship prints were tasteless. I perspired. The baby I had given birth to was at that very moment not giving birth. It needed marking, but we have no ceremonies for the small deaths, the little disasters.

Andrea emerged and was quiet. She did not speak the entire taxi ride home. She lay down on the couch and watched reruns of *The Brady Bunch* and *Little House on the Prairie*. I brought her a Coke and reached out to stroke her hand. She pushed my hand away. I understood, of course. She did not want to feel like a baby herself. I went into my bedroom and lay on my bed, waiting for the heavings of my stomach to settle down.

The second abortion I was only told about later when a forged check with my name on it appeared among the more innocent items sent by the bank. I did not want to know the story, but Andrea, contrite, sincerely concerned that I would feel taken, ripped off, did manage to paint a picture of a drummer who was a friend of hers whom she'd met at this cafe where she had a temporary waitress job. His band had gotten its first booking and at four in the morning when they were knocking down the equipment something happened that should not have and there was no time to go home and get the essential precautions in place and besides he said he would be careful and then the lead singer had suddenly passed out on the floor and the bar owner was trying to get them all out in a hurry and turned off the lights and the singer was breathing strangely and they had to take him to St. Vincent's and in the excitement somehow the drummer lost his control and there it was. She was really sorry and assured me that this was the last time. She was only eighteen. Her hair was shaved on the sides and the brush in the middle was dyed with pink streaks and her hands were braceleted in black leather embedded with silver studs. She looked like a Renoir subject, soft and rosy—a Renoir trying to be a motorcycle. I told her she had to be more responsible. I looked at her with disgust. I told her she had behaved like a common thief. But what does one do about forgery between parent and child? She told me she felt humiliated and that she didn't think it was fair that only women got pregnant. She told me she had cried the day after when she passed a baby sitting in a stroller with orange juice spit up all over his face. She looked frightened and her fear frightened me. She left a sketch on my desk of a baby carriage and in the carriage a mongoose sat with its mouth open, drooling. I made her herbal tea and asked her to take vitamins because she looked pale. She stayed two nights in her room and at night I watched her sleep. I counted her eyelashes. I touched the covers carefully. In short, I was useless. I decided to keep my checkbook with me at all times as my own form of protection.

The third abortion I found out about only because I received a call from a hospital in Jacksonville, Florida, asking me if I was prepared to cover the expenses of an Andrea Johnson who had a pelvic inflammation following an abortion. Yes, I was prepared to send them a certified check by Federal Express covering all expenses. I had not spoken to Andrea for several months. I thought she was in Missouri with a young painter she had seemed very attached to. They were going to live at his sister's while he went to art school.

Andrea seemed foggy from medication when I reached her in room 503. She was extremely sorry that I had to hear from her this way. She was very apologetic about upsetting me. She sounded very young.

"Shall I come?" I asked.

"Not at all necessary," she whispered.

"Is anyone with you?" I asked.

"I left Mike in St. Louis," she said, "but Paul is here. He is very sweet. He brought me to the hospital when my fever got very high. He said it didn't matter what it cost."

I didn't point out that was because he wasn't paying for it. I decided to fly south. By the time I reached the hospital from a taxi directly from the airport Paul seemed to have taken off for Miami. Andrea was alone in bed, clean-scrubbed and very pale. Her hair was short but no longer streaked. She looked like a child again. I brought her magazines. I sat at the edge of the bed and watched *The Rockford Files* with her. I suggested she come home and perhaps apply to some college in New York. She looked at me as if I were a strange life form beamed aboard Captain Kirk's star ship. "When you're better," I asked, "what would you like to do?" She shrugged and sank down under the covers. "Don't tell me," I said, "please don't tell me how you got pregnant, what happened to Mike or Paul, or how you happen to be in Jacksonville." She told me anyway.

I rented a car and drove through the streets of Jacksonville looking for the highway to the beach. I wanted to see the waves and the white sand. The streets were littered with fast-food places, Burger King, Pizza Hut, Wendy's, McDonald's; no one in all of Jacksonville goes to the market, comes home and cooks dinner. I drove for fifty miles without seeing a house, a yard, a sign of ordinary people walking around except on golf courses. I couldn't find the highway to the beach, where I imagined hibiscus growing wild in the sand and herons stalking crabs along the curve of the receding wave. I went back to the hospital and told Andrea I thought she should come home and recover in New York.

"Thank you," she said, and sounded so sad that I turned my face away. She should not have thanked me as if she were a waif abandoned on the sidewalk to whom some stranger had just offered a bowl of milk and a night's shelter. What had happened that she should thank me for asking her to come home? That alarmed me. I wasted no time thinking about grandchildren that had not come to be.

I withdrew from the feminist symposium to be held at The New School in the fall. I was tired and for the first time in years convinced that the certainties, the political actions, the fight to legalize abortion, to raise the consciousness of American women was on a backslide, that we would lose what we had gained and enter a thousand more years of repression. I was also convinced it was not the fault of the saner ones among us. Our current unpopularity was partially the result of the unbridled hostility, the uncompromising, the unsmiling, the child-hating ones in our midst. Where was I? Any idiot could see that feminism as a way of giving women a chance to use their brains as well as their sexual equipment was now confused with godlessness, lesbian activity on campus and a life of loneliness and separation from all the other natural goals of women and men. If the president of the United States had been elected because he was seen on TV linked to puppies and families piling out of station wagons on their way to eat hamburgers and little boys fishing with their fathers and mothers on prom night pinning up the gown and Thanksgiving turkeys being carried to Grandma's house by laughing teenagers in a haywagon . . . well, then we as feminists were seen as the makers of the singles column, the proprietors of the singles bar, the deniers, nay sayers, and the ones who didn't love babies in bonnets or respect our armed forces, who were saving us from the tyranny out there. We had lost the war of propaganda and it was because we made people appear unhappy, we pointed out how people made each other unhappy in unbalanced domesticity. We had been indiscreet. It is not nice to tell people that they are not happy. In America one is not supposed to notice the down side. We were responsible for making it hard for those who watched Johnny Carson to believe that all was well. They turned a deaf ear to the messenger. That only made us shout louder and become irritating. And then, of course, there was Andrea, brought up to admire her body, to accept her biology, no facts hidden, no disgrace or limitations in girlhood, and she was falling, free falling, hang gliding, dizzy, scared. Strategies needed reshaping. It was not a time to be giving lectures.

I WENT to dancing class in 1950 with girls and boys from the right kind of homes. The boys wore white gloves and the girls wore stockings and velvet dresses with lace collars. We learned to fox trot, lindy hop and waltz. We also learned to wait to be asked to dance, looking calm and confident, giggling to one another as if unconcerned about the battalions of males on the other side of the room. We were supposed to attract them (to help them speak; most of the boys had trouble saying anything). We were supposed to make promises so that they would call us up and invite us out for a movie and a soda. We were not allowed to let them touch us in certain places. We were not to give anything that we would regret in the morning. We were not to ruin our reputations. It was hard to figure out just how much was the right amount of promising. I tried so hard to keep my accounts balanced. I wanted to be good and desired at the same time. My girdle that held in my stomach and held up my stockings was tight and protected me from feeling the hand that gripped me on my waist. There were rules to the dance, your feet went in boxes back and forth.

There were rules to the evening. He brought you a flower. You must give one kiss on the mouth, but you don't have to open your mouth. If you do, he might talk. If you don't, he might not invite you out again. I was frightened inside those boxes. I was hang gliding, I was free falling, but I had to be home by ten o'clock and you couldn't get-pregnant from a goodnight kiss. The consequences of certain feelings that fluttered and died were not invasive and my womanhood was suffocated and insulted but it did not bloom before its time. The dancing teacher wore a long violet evening gown with white gloves up to her elbow. The pianist was in a tuxedo, the walls had mirrors that took the simplest defect, a hunched shoulder, a pimple on the chin, a bit of lipstick on one's fingers, and multiplied it many times. Once in the coatroom Bobby Newhouse, whose father was in real estate, said he loved me. He put his hand on my breast and the pin of the corsage I was wearing pierced through to my skin. A drop of blood oozed out on my dress. I went to the ladies' room and cried with shame. What was the shame?

THE OTHER night I had a dream in which Rabbi Nachman from Bratslav appeared. This is because of Andrea and her stay at the yeshiva. I am walking by a river on a well-kept promenade and I am wearing a long white dress and carrying flowers, lilacs, in my arms. The day is hot and the sun hits the leaves in the trees like slivers of ice and the colors of everything are splintered and fragmented. Suddenly out from behind a chestnut tree appears a little man in black coat and hat and payess that curl down the side of his cheeks. He pulls at my skirt. I am startled and move back. I look at his eyes, which appear too far apart on his face, thin and slitlike, and I am repelled.

"Don't be afraid, Madam," he says in a language that is

not my language but I understand anyway. "I am a holy man, a man who has discovered new paths to redemption."

I pull farther away. He steps quickly after me. "Madam, I want to tell you a story, stories are the way to Hashem. Hashem is inside the story, right at the center you find Hashem."

I look around for help. The promenade is empty. The little man is sweating in the heat and his hands are twisting the fringes of the tallis that hangs beneath his jacket. He appears very old, but as I look closer I see his beard is that of a young boy. His skin is almost translucent, blue and veined. Is he a boy or a man?

"I will tell you a story." He follows me. I want to run but my dress is very long and my shoes are clearly unsuitable for flight.

"All right," I say, "I will listen, and when you have finished the story will you leave me alone?"

"For now," he says, and I accept this.

We sit down together on a bench. On the river a sculling boat pulls into sight. Young boys with striped round hats with the name of their college written on it are rowing furiously as if in a race. I want to call out to them for help but I hear a siren, loud and long, the sound of an ambulance racing along the empty path. When the ambulance is gone and the sound of the siren fades the boat is also gone and the boys are gone and the river is empty of all but blue water. There is silence except for the occasional slap of a fish who has extended himself briefly out of his element and gracelessly returns. I face Rabbi Nachman, who tells me this story.

"Once there lived a Queen who ruled in a kingdom so far away from all the other kingdoms that no one came to visit, no traders ever crossed the mountain paths and no letters were sent in or out. The Queen had five sons. She gathered them together and said to each, 'Go out into the world and bring me back a treasure of immense value. I wish to know what is in the world though I am enclosed by these high mountains. When I grow old I will hold these treasures and imagine the world outside.'

" 'If you want to know the world outside,' said the children, 'then come with us, we will take care of you, we will carry you on our backs so that you can travel far.' The Queen could not leave her kingdom.

"The first son left the palace and got as far as the bottom of the second mountain when he met a lion. 'I will bring back a lion's skin for my mother,' he said, and picked up his bow and prepared to shoot. The lion's mate sat on a rock above and in a leap she was down upon the boy and ripped him to shreds and ate his flesh and let his bones bake in the sun.

"The second son followed his brother on the path and traveled to the distant horizon. He traveled so far that when he looked back he could no longer distinguish the range of mountains behind which his home lay. He came to the water's edge. There he met a group of men with no clothes on, who spoke in strange grunts and groans. He offered them his hat with a grand green feather in it. They took it. Each tried it on, was admired by the others. When the sun lay on the water's edge they took large clamshells and smashed their visitor's skull. They went fishing with his brains placed on the end of long sticks. They caught large fish with this bait and feasted well."

"This is a terrible story," I tell Rabbi Nachman. He puts his small hand on my arm and moves his face closer to mine. He smells of sour milk and herring, and his sparse beard seems to be growing blacker and thicker as we talk.

"The third son," says the rabbi, "left the kingdom and walked into the desert. He went with the nomads to a distant town. He went to a bazaar to find a present to bring back to his mother. He had traveled five years and thought that now at last he would find the perfect gift and return to his home. He saw a big straw basket and asked the merchant to tell him what was inside. Look for yourself, said the merchant, and so the third son picked up the top of the straw basket and bent his head over to look into the dark insides. A cobra who made his home in this basket unwound himself and bit the neck of the third son, who fell over in a swoon and died there in the bazaar. The beggars stripped him of his clothing and the birds demolished the rest. The fourth son," begins Rabbi Nachman.

"This is a story without point," I complain. "Let me go on with my walk. I have had enough."

The rabbi has no intention of letting me go. He fixes his eyes on me and I feel as if I am chained to him. I feel my breath coming in short gasps. The water in the river seems lower and along the deep bank daisies and dandelions wilt in the heat. "The fourth son traveled for ten years. He found city after city filled with works of art, sculptures celebrating the deity of the land, colorful costumes and precious stones. He could not make up his mind which of the fine objects he had seen was worthy of his mother. He apprenticed himself to a weaver and learned to make clothes spun of the finest silks. At last he wove a wondrous coat for his mother. He married the master weaver's daughter and had three children of his own. He wanted to return to his country to bring his mother the present he had promised. On the way home his caravan was set upon by thieves. His wife was sold as a concubine and he was stripped of all he owned and buried in the sand up to his neck and left to die.

"The fifth son waited for the return of his brothers before setting out. He was patient, although eager to begin his own adventures. As the years passed and he became concerned that his brothers might not return after all, he retired to a small room at the top of his house in the kingdom so far away that no one came or went. He took a quill and began to think of the far-off journeys through deserts, fields and forests that his brothers had taken. He spoke to himself of what had befallen them there. He wrote of valleys and streams, of people with strange customs, with two heads and hooves, and he wrote of wheels that moved without being pulled or pushed. He wrote of a star that came down to the earth and showed men how to heal all their wounds. He wrote and wrote, and each day the pile of pages grew higher.

"One day he asked for an audience with his mother the Queen, who was weary with waiting for her sons to return. The fifth son brought to his mother the manuscript. 'Here, Mother,' he said, 'this is my treasure that I have found for you.'

"His mother began to read. It took several weeks before she had finished. She called the court together. She summoned her son. 'All that you have written, you have dreamed, none of it is true?' The son admitted this was so. 'In that case,' said the mother, 'you have disobeyed me. Your treasure does not come from the world outside this kingdom. Your punishment will be death.'

"The son's life was extinguished by the court executioner within a fortnight, and soon the old Queen died of congestion of the heart. Do you understand this tale?" Rabbi Nachman asks. He climbs up into my lap and suddenly is the size of a child; his black hat hits my chin. I try to push him off, but he hangs on. "Mama," he says. I wake up.

ANDREA WORE blue jeans to school and an army jacket that she had found in a surplus store. But she wore lipstick, dark red and deep purple. She wore nail polish, green and silver and shining orange. Her bathroom looked like my mother's. Shelves of glitter, bottles of color everywhere, spilled on the sink, some on the tiled floor. Just like my mother she wore dark mascara that sometimes slid onto her face. "Why, Andrea?" I asked. I wanted her to like her face, natural, clean and innocent.

"I have things to hide," she said, putting on her dark glasses. My mother wore dark glasses too. "I am mysterious," she said.

"You are," I agreed. "Brush your teeth," I said.

She smiled at me. "Only petty minds are afraid of tiny holes in their enamel," she said.

"But your teeth are gray," I begged, "they look dirty."

"Are you the toothpaste fairy?" she asked.

LETTER RECEIVED:

Dear Mother, Rabbi Cohen wants me to explain my new life to you. He wants you to share in my recovery and take part in my happiness. He is the most amazing man. He has blue eyes that seem to see right through to secret places. He wears glasses that keep slipping off his nose and his beard is black and unruly. He is always pulling at it with his fingers. Remember when you had that lover who was a psychologist at some medical school in the Bronx? His shirts were always too tight across his stomach and he had a funny laugh as if whatever was funny was also not funny. Remember he took me to the zoo one day and we went to the bird house and then we watched a film about flamingos? Rabbi Cohen reminds me a little of that man. Rabbi Cohen leans across the table when he is teaching and he stares at me until I listen carefully. When I give an answer he really likes he smiles at me gently as if I were a little girl. At first it made me feel silly but I think he does it to show me how much he cares. I have never before been so cared for. Everyone here seems to like me. One of the other girls in my class is from Woodmere, Long Island. One night I woke up with this strange feeling in my legs as if I were becoming paralyzed. Hadassah stayed up all night with me. We read from the Book of Psalms and she brought me hot tea. We are really good friends. Don't worry, in the morning my legs were fine. Mrs. Hanni Cohen, Rabbi Cohen's wife, says that unusual things do happen when people are in transition, traveling away from the false world toward the true world.

She says that one girl made slits all over her arms with a knife because she was trying to cut herself off from her past. Mrs. Cohen said that that girl had not learned that Gd forgives, accepts, welcomes us back and experiences our return as an offering as precious as any ever brought before Him in the first temple. Hadassah went to Smith College but she dropped out because she didn't care about anything she was learning. Her parents wanted her to be a doctor. She worked in a hospital as a volunteer when she was in high school. She played games with kids on chemotherapy. She said she never wanted to be a doctor. Being in the hospital, she says, made her want to talk directly to Gd and no one in Woodmere understood her. She went to a psychotherapist too. Hers was a woman who got divorced and moved somewhere else.

I don't want you to think that everything is easy here. Sometimes I just can't concentrate. I still get this buzz in my head that makes me feel weird. When that happened before, I would go find someone to do something with, some exciting stuff. Here I go to Mrs. Cohen. She's usually in the kitchen, and she puts something in my hands to do, to cut, to stir, or pound. We make this incredible bread. We put the dough in big white bowls on the stove and it rises, I mean really rises. She tells me that Gd respects me. Once my hands were shaking and she held them in hers and told me how brave the Jewish women were in the desert, after they had fled from Egypt, when they wouldn't give their jewels or their mirrors to the men who wanted to build an idol. Did you know that?

Rabbi Cohen knows everything about the Talmud. You can ask him any question and he knows the answer. He goes to his books and turns the page right to the words he wants. He has an enormous memory. He says we must remember everything because the world is always trying to erase our footprints and our covenant shows us how to sanctify life on earth. We can only do that, he says, if we remember everything. Women don't have to remember as much. We create the room in which the work takes place. We are the sun, the moon, the stars, the ocean, the forest and the field. We make the learning possible. There's enough studying here anyway. I would hate to be a male. They stay with their books all day long. Ugh!

Rabbi Cohen says that the temptations are many and the paths to righteousness covered in the vines of distraction. He does not think I am bad. He says I am sometimes weak and he forgives my weakness because he sees how strong I will be one day. Guess what! I can read Hebrew. I read slowly, of course. I still need the vowels. Hadassah can read without the vowels but she came to the yeshiva five months before I did. When Rabbi Cohen says that he is proud of me I feel as if I am in the presence of a king. He says he is only the messenger of the King and I must listen to the message carefully. I am trying.

Let me tell you about my day, perhaps that will help you to see why I am so determined to stay in Jerusalem for the rest of my entire life. At six in the morning we wake and we shower. I am in a room with three other women: Hadassah, Rivka and Namah. We go down to the kitchen and we set the tables and we pour the milk and we help the grandmothers who cook the cereal. Out the kichen window we can see the men coming from shul. In the courtyard there is a great stirring. We listen to the prayer each morning. My favorite part of the prayer: "Let all my being praise the Lord, who is clothed in magnificence, arrayed in majesty. He wraps Himself in light as in a garment. He unfolds the Heavens as a curtain. Praise are You, Lord Our Gd, King of the Universe, who sanctified our life with His commandments." I can say that in Hebrew. I used to wake up each morning as if I had been asleep for a hundred years, as if the light were trying to draw blood, as if I were being forced from dream; now I am alert right away. Of course it helps that I am not blitzed or stoned. I used to screw up everything I touched. I paid no attention to folding or washing or putting away. Here I try very hard to be neat. I am brushing my teeth twice a day. I have given up smoking. That was very hard but Rabbi Cohen said that I am beautiful now, my skin lets in the daylight and there are no puffs of smoke in my eyes. I still bite my fingernails and the edges are sore. Hanni says that in time, when I am more a woman, my fingers will heal too. Rabbi Cohen does not like disorder. He says that Jews make distinctions, mark things off cleanly and clearly. He says that tangles and piles are not for Gd's people. You would be very surprised at how many things my hands have learned to do. I am not as good as some of the others but everyone says I am getting better each day. You did not teach me at the right age. I know that you did not think it important to scrub the stove or make the curtains lie straight with the pleats in place. But it is very important to do those things and to wipe and dust and iron. After breakfast we take care of chores, taking turns at each. The time goes so fast because we are busy. I used to be waiting for something to happen, for someone to come, for something to rouse me. Now I am not waiting, I am doing. When I sponge the table and the crumbs are gone and the board is again honey-colored and the patches of light from the window shine on my part of the floor, the One Above is pleased with me. I take a deep breath and smell the pine and the ammonia and I feel good.

HERE WE HAVE IT—the way to serve God is on the kitchen floor, on your knees with the heavenly aroma of Ajax in your nostrils. It is beyond believing. A place for everything, a place for my daughter in the kitchen, scrubbing. A girl who had a tattoo of a rattlesnake needled in between her shoulder blades. A blue rattlesnake with a bright red eye whose scales slithered and curved with the muscles of the upper spine. What did Rabbi Cohen have to say about the tattoo, the one Andrea called her pet, trained to bite anyone who might get on her back? What had I said when casually she showed me that tattoo? I gave satisfaction. I called it a primitive act, a return to savagery, a form of vandalizing the self in hopes of appeasing evil eyes, wicked spirits, a stupid piece of unthinking graffiti on the human body. I told Andrea when she came sashaying into my office topless that writing on buildings or skin is a sign of helplessness. She had grinned, a smile that wasn't a smile.

I looked at her back and felt shivers of disgust. I had premonitions of black leather jackets and needle marks on all the crucial veins. I had a vision of girls in lace pants lying on silk cushions in Oriental ports while the smoke of hashish comforted the customers as girls with glazed eyes waited to be entered and paid. My goat was gotten, held over a high flame and roasted. "Couldn't you at least have chosen a rose?" I asked.

Andrea jangled her wrist chain at me. "A rose for Mother's Day?" she said. "Maybe I'll have them do one on my ass."

I kept thinking about the red blush on her body when they first put her in my arms and I saw the red strands at the top of her bald head and the beat of her pulse that throbbed through the thin skin at the frontal indentation of her skull. I thought about the first time she cut her knee and the jagged line scabbed over and I felt sad because the surface was no longer perfect. Was it hopelessly middle class of me to find a tattoo so repulsive? Where was my sense of proportion, of humor? Had I somehow made Andrea an outlaw? The tattoo bothered me even when I couldn't see it. (I had no antidote to snake bite.) I didn't like the fact that she smoked, either, that ashes dripped over her clothes and onto the floor and that she smelled of perspiration and nicotine and she never emptied an ashtray and I worried that at night she might set her bedclothes afire with the last cigarette of the day. But that did not disturb me as much as the tattoo. The rattlesnake placed her in the company of bikers and waitresses at desert truck stops and girls with venereal diseases.

LETTER CONTINUED:

After the morning chores are done we go into the rabbi's study. First we say a prayer. We stand together and face in the direction of the temple mount. The rabbi opens his curtains and the light comes in over his desk, on which so many books lie, even more than you have, older books, with leather bindings and gold writing on their spines. On the wall is a map of ancient Israel with the mountains outside of Gaza and the cities of old from Beersheba to Dan. In the morning the map shimmers and if there is a breeze it bangs gently against the wall while we say the words of thanks to the One Who has given us life. Are you beginning to see how good it is here? After that Rabbi Cohen talks to us about the holidays, or about Jewish history. You never told me anything about Jewish history. Hanni Cohen can trace her ancestors back to Spain, where they went to Morocco and from there to Dresden. Sometimes he talks about the daily portion of the Bible that the men have read in shul. Sometimes we give our opinions about why something happened a certain way. Rabbi Cohen tells us what famous rabbis have said. We talk a lot about keeping the Sabbath. That is particularly important for women because we light the candles. I have not yet had a chance to light our candles, but when my Hebrew is better I will surely be given a turn. After an hour or so with Rabbi Cohen we go to the main yeshiva. At this time the men are out in the yard. We can see them from the windows. They are talking and talking with each other, bending their bodies back and forth. They look like a flock of birds sitting on telephone wires. Some of them look up at us and then they look quickly away. Most of them wear the black coats and hats of our yeshiva, but some are still Americanized and wear blue jeans with the tzitzit under T-shirts. Some are even bareheaded. One plays the guitar in the yard. He plays "Puff the Magic Dragon" and "Yellow Submarine." He also plays Hebrew songs. He has a good voice. Hadassah and I try to stay by the window where we can hear him. But I do not think of men often. Rabbi Cohen has said that a man does not save a woman. A woman needs Gd. He has said that the feelings we have for the other sex are for the purpose of filling the universe with Jews, not for our idle pleasure. His words calm me and when I look into the courtyard of men I stay calm. Isn't that just amazing? We go into the study rooms and make everything clean. We wipe the covers of the precious books with cotton cloths. We kiss each book as we finish as a sign of respect for its contents. We do all this quickly because within a half hour the men will return and we must be gone. Do you understand that I am happy?

Then we go to Hebrew class. Mrs. Cohen teaches us. We work for three hours with a fifteen-minute break. There are twenty-four of us now and a new girl who is coming but hasn't felt well enough to join the class yet. I think she has some terrible chronic illness. Mrs. Cohen says that by the time the first cold air blows in off the hills of Judea I will be able to tell her my dreams, ask questions of street vendors, and learn to sew a dress, all in Hebrew. I hope she is right because Hebrew is the language of the Holy One and if I am thinking in Hebrew my thoughts will bring me nearer to Him. Mrs. Cohen says that women are always closer to Him than men and that's why we do not say so many prayers or fulfill so many commandments or learn so many pages of so many books. She says that a pure woman knows Him by just closing her eyes. We are His most important children because we bring forth and tend the next generation and it is our work to lead them in the path of righteousness. Mrs. Cohen says that men study and study to be clever, to please the Lord, but that without such study we are understanders and knowers of His way. She says it is just as important to know when a baby has a fever as it is to know the pages of Rashi. I know that you have many ideas on this subject and will not easily appreciate this point of view. I don't want to argue this with you because you always twist words, but I ask you to think about it. At the yeshiva we have the help of centuries' worth of wisdom and so we stand closer to the truth than most. Rabbi Cohen says that women like you have been misled not because you are evil but because a tide of confusion has carried you away from the true purposes. You drown but don't know you are drowning.

Anyway, the day passes so. We help prepare the supper for the entire yeshiva. We do the dishes for both the men and the women. By evening time I am very tired. We have another meeting with Rabbi Cohen after dinner to discuss any questions or difficulties that arose during the day. We say the evening prayer together. Mother, you don't have to pay the yeshiva for my keep. They want me here for free. They want me here because I am myself, Sarai, not because anyone is paying for me. If you want to send a donation to the Yeshiva Rachel, that would be terrific. I will understand and forgive if you don't. I am going to end this letter. I hope I have given you a good picture of my life here. I know you like words, so I tried. But Mrs. Cohen says that most often silence is better than words, it says more. I agree with that. Love, Sarai.

AH, THE BLESSEDNESS of silence—how deeply I have always distrusted all that cannot be formed into language. How I have spent my energy finding the right word, the better word, the sharper word. I am like a TV talk show host, the enemy is silence, the airwaves must be filled even at the risk of error, even at the risk of buffoonery. And now my daughter, she of the loud rock music, of the Who and Sting and the Talking Heads, she is scrubbing floors in silence. I am not only baffled, I am unraveled . . . a bag lady's sleeve, warp and woof separated.

If I had married again and provided a stable two-parent home for Andrea, would she now be in a postdoctoral program in biochemistry at Yale? If I had been a woman who was more domestic, more concerned with my appearance, with the condition of the furnishings of my house, would she now be a corporate lawyer in a Wall Street firm and would we meet for lunch whenever her busy schedule permitted and would she use her American Express card and could we confide in each other the exasperations and thrills of day-to-day life without interference from divine voices? What has happened that Andrea was sinking in the world of my creation and now finds herself walking on water in a universe of another century, in a faith that sustained another time? What is the purpose of having a child if that child grows up and cannot live within the tabernacle that the parent labored to build? I am confused.

On Rosh Hashanah my mother would wear her best suit, her black shiny heels, and over her shoulders she would throw her fox skin; the face, black button nose, little bead eyes, would rest over her chest, paws would hang down with small claws still attached. She wore a hat with a veil that would catch in her glasses. She wore her gold bracelets and her diamond ring and the gold earrings in the shape of scallop shells. Her lips and nails and toes were all magenta. By afternoon there was a run in her stocking. When the ark was opened and everyone was standing, she could not see because even in her heels she did not measure five feet two. She had not been taught Hebrew, but she followed along in English and rose and sat with the others. Sometimes I would see her lean over and whisper something to her sister and the two of them would nod together discreetly, but not so discreetly that I hadn't noticed they had secrets between them that were even more important than the words one might say to God on the high holidays. As on a ship where the distant shoreline appears deceivingly near, so as the last page in the prayer book approached there were repeats and additional repeats and then the rabbi and the cantor went back several pages to something they had overlooked before and the ark was opened and closed again and again and we stood and we sat and the September heat flowed through the synagogue and the silver crowns of the Torah, the gold threads of the rabbi's tallis, the gray stone, the Gothic ceiling, the aged walnut of the pews, the carvings on the balcony rail, seemed to melt together in an ooze of shining color. It was then that the fox and I would begin a gambol out in the meadow just below the mountain in which the fox had lived with her pups. I would feel the dirt underfoot, brush past the high weeds and follow the sound of wind against the cattails. I watched the fox low to the ground, faster than words running by on the printed page, hiding from the hunter behind rocks, dashing with heart pounding for the safety of the mountain, where on the uppermost cliff her babies were waiting in a cool cave, rolling on the stone, tickling and licking each other; all unaware, face under legs, paws tangled, they waited. I saw the body fall beside the honeysuckle and watched the few drops of blood stain the thistles that had bent to the ground. I saw the eyes of the fox narrow with fear and then turn empty as if in an instant the stars in the sky had been swept away to another, more deserving universe. I stroked the fox that my mother had placed on the seat next to her and fondled the soft brown fur. I held the small paw in my hand. Why had God placed the fox on that field on that exact day? I tried to be awed, but awe disappeared as I became sleepy, restless, anxious for a story with a plot.

My father did not enter the synagogue. He did not believe in prayer. He thanked no one for his existence. He was not the kind of man to appreciate the power of another, to suffer remorse, to consider himself accountable, to concern himself with the interstices of the soul. If, some morning as he walked down Park Avenue on his way to his office, he were to encounter a burning traffic light, he would reproach the voice within for not having made him a king with a kingdom that stretched from sea to shining sea. He was not interested in Zion or in redemption. He was interested only in his place in the New World, where it was hard enough to carry youself with your head high and keep the dirt off your shoes. I would walk fast to try to match his athletic strides. I would drop back. Wait, I would call, please wait for me. He was unafraid of the evil eye. He was unafraid of the writing in the book of judgment. He strode, a free man, across the streets of New York, serving no master, binding no one else's words across his forehead. He would catch his reflection in a window as he walked and he would smooth back his already perfect hair and put his shoulders down, and with the posture of a military man reviewing the troops, a landowner walking his acres, he would proceed. "Hear, O Israel''; he was not heard.

MY DEAREST ANDREA, Let us talk together a bit about your new religious experience. I am certainly delighted that you are among friends. I am grateful that you are not taking drugs, doing drugs? You have no idea how frightening it was to me to think of your mind reeling, bending, turning inside out for the momentary thrill. I judge nothing. I understand the temptation to destroy, it beckons each of us in different ways. I've wanted you clean for so long. I wanted to look you in the eye and see all the way through again. I am very glad to hear that your days are ordered and purposeful. But having said that, I am still worried about this choice of yours. It is a radical break with your upbringing and hard for me to understand. I am not certain that it can be accomplished without great risk to your sanity. I am not sure that human beings can turn themselves inside out and pick at random their spot in the universe. Are you comfortable or are you fooling yourself, hoping for a fit that is really cramping and crippling your spirit?

Consider with me some of my doubts. I am uncertain that you can maintain your center, your Andreaness, in a place that joins you not only to other Jews of like faith but to the entire history of the nation as it moved from Abraham's time on. In such a long line your particulars, your affection for the Talking Heads, for example, may be forgotten. I don't want you to be an anonymous part of a line of figures moving together toward the end of time. I want you to be a shape, to carry a destiny of your own, to be responsible for yourself. I want you to go on learning new things. I don't want you frozen in a time warp that experienced its grandeur in the backwoods of Poland several centuries ago.

I don't understand how you are tolerating the discipline of being part of a group that makes so many demands on your innermost thoughts and requests so much conformity of behavior. You might try to explain this to me. You might think about the consequences of abandoning so many of the pleasures of your former life that you so easily and perhaps too easily enjoyed before. You once reproached me because I said I had no desire to go to Tibet to see the monks praying in their own monastery. You said I had lost my appetite for life. Have you lost yours? Don't you still want to see and do and belong to as great a variety of human events as possible? If you close yourself off in this Jewish particular, this walled city of convictions, you must renounce the universal. You can no longer feel yourself kin to all the spinning colors of the globe. Can you possibly see progress for human beings as retribalization, where each of our little clans turns inward and becomes absorbed in the details of ritual and refines its own method of conning the sun into rising again each morning? Don't you think that soon trouble will break out on each neighboring hill, rapes and incursions will follow, sheep will be stolen and people will continue to die out of loyalty to one totem or another?

Don't you want to be part of the movement forward to a world without barriers, without hostile whisperings, mass exterminations and petty differences that can quickly meta-morphose into the Nuremberg laws? (Do you know what the Nuremberg laws were? Ask somebody over forty-five.)

Andrea, I have thought of a joke. In my grandmother's time if a child married a non-Jew the family would treat that child as if he or she had died. They would say the prayers for the dead. They would sit around on wooden boxes and receive relatives bearing pound cake. They would make a tear in their clothes and cover their mirrors. Today I am in mourning for you for having turned into the kind of Jew who might mourn if your child married out. . . . I feel a grief as great as if I were never going to see you again . . . as if I had lost you. Who are you? How can you be another person and still be my daughter: has the gulf between us grown so large that you are dead to me? Have I lost you? Please write, I need to be comforted. My love for you goes out but finds no Andrea—it returns to haunt. Love, M.

ANDREA HAD a father, of course, and at times, how many times in the last eight years, I had longed for this father, to take some of the blame, to take some of the responsibility, to visit the school, to keep the appointment with the therapist, to open his checkbook and pay for the typing classes Andrea never appeared at, to pay for the driving lessons Andrea intended to take but couldn't find time for, to pay for the clothes that lay in mounds about the floor and were discarded when dirty or exchanged with a friend for a chain or an earring. I longed for this father who would share my fear of the future and who would reassure me in the middle of the night, You exaggerate, you are letting your imagination run away with you, it will all work out, you will see. I longed for the father who could hold me and say, In every era children die, they don't all make it through, it used to be measles and scarlet fever and now it's the happy hour and the quick rush; you will not be the first woman to lose a child—steady there. I wanted him to say, Andrea is not the center of the universe. . . . But each of us is hypnotized by the dirt on our hands, and Andrea, uncontainable, unmanageable, at the edge of disaster, punishing me for crimes I could not possibly have committed (or had I?) was the one I loved, the one I watched, the one who made my scene, who was my climate, the one for whom I had intended my life.

Her real father was beyond making unexpected appearances. He was tall and redheaded just like Andrea. It was amazing how each day she grew more and more to be a replica of him, the same long neck, the same freckled skin, the same slate eyes, the look of a Yankee farmer in the nose and the forehead. It was that look that had brought me across the room to his side at the party for graduate students in English. I was in political science but had been invited by a small round man named Ben Tannenbaum.

I was wanting something exotic, something American, something that spoke of picket fences, white clapboard houses, Fourth of July parades in which children sold lemonade as the Lions and the Elks wearing fezzes walked past to the sound of the trumpet and the Veterans of Foreign Wars waved to their families as they marched in uniforms that stretched across stomachs greatly sucked in for the occasion. I wanted to bed with a man who had drunk in the Declaration of Independence with his mother's milk, who knew the purple mountain's majesty because he had inherited the vision from the kind of man who had made stone boulders into even fences. I wanted a man who was not a tourist in towns where the white steeples stung the sky and the houses clustered together by the rivers that meandered through the maples and the oaks and the pines. I wanted a man who couldn't tell a Yiddish joke, a man who didn't know that the enemy needed no excuse to move. I wanted a man whose nightmares were strictly personal and did not extend beyond his own experience. I wanted the kind of man who believed that the Second World War was a disaster but so was the Roman occupation of Tyre. I went over to Hilary Cabot Johnson and talked to him about Alice B. Toklas. In a little while we left the party. He was a poet and I was a political science major. Between us we understood everything. He quoted Gerard Manley Hopkins: "Glory be to God for dappled things. All things counter, original, spare, strange . . ." Those adjectives described me, or so he thought. He was the ride of Paul Revere through my sorry spirit. We were perfect for each other.

However, our graduate school life created some strains. Alcohol was his favorite muse and I believed that a person who wasn't working by eight o'clock was a wanton. I had a puritan streak that ran straight down the highway of my Jewish soul and he was a descendant of Puritans riding the highway in the other direction. I wanted to press fall leaves into scrapbooks and liked to go to restaurants with salad bars and wooden tables. He found the far side of town where the ethnics were apt to make remarks. He wrote poems about reabsorption into the earth, about coffins that were lifted on the back of sentences into the midnight sky. I wanted to have a child. I whispered about the importance of power for those without power and he spoke of absurdity and exhaustion. We admired each other without a doubt and we each made compromises. Perhaps he made more compromises than I did. Perhaps I dragged him into a pregnancy that promised him only dirty diapers and unholy responsibility. Perhaps I was pushy and used him badly. I saw a child of ours like a leap into a just world where the poet would be king and the philosopher would be queen and there would be equal rights and opportunities for all. He claimed I used him like a barnyard creature when the condition between us had changed from inflamed to inflammatory. By then I was teaching, without tenure, but teaching. I was six months pregnant, large and awkward. He claimed that when I moved toward him he felt as if all of Noah's ark was about to land and release its inhabitants over his body. This was an exaggeration. It was also not a compliment. His poems were rejected by several little magazines. This told us nothing of his future prospects. I believed that the child I was carrying had the genes of a true poet mingled with my more mundane sort. I knew enough of the literary world to expect the beginnings to be difficult. He wrote a ten-page letter to Rimbaud. He spoke regretfully of the passage of tuberculosis as a respectable disease. I made plans for us to move into a larger apartment and went shopping for a crib and baby blankets. I felt the baby kick and I did not believe that the Russians would drop the atomic bomb or that the world would end. Neither bang nor whimper scared me. I missed some important clues. Afterwards they were obvious. How had I curled my body against another's and suspected nothing? Had I stopped being Annie? Had I stopped my ears and eyes? Had I reduced myself to my womb? If that is the case, I paid the price.

One night we went to a party given by a professor in my department. He had married well and lived in a penthouse with a terrace. We sat on lawn chairs watching the lights of the Manhattan Bridge, tracking the flickers of planes arriving and departing. With the green shrubbery at our elbows, drinks in hand, we looked down at the streets where people and cars moved, shrunken, unimportant, as if we were gods and could enjoy the passing sport. We talked of Kennedy and Cuba, of Martin Luther King and the senility of our colleagues and the details of publishing and the fear of perishing. I sank into a chair and my weight kept me down in one spot and a woman friend came over to talk to me about the affair she was considering entering with a man forty years her senior, but a man with such a record of accomplishment that any woman would be tempted, flattered. I suppressed envy; after all, I was with child. I noticed that Hilary was on his fifth drink. I knew from the weave of his hands as he spoke, from the slope of his walk as he crossed

back and forth to the bar, that his liver was on overdrive.
There was no use suggesting that we go home. There was
no use asking him to stop. He would only make fun of me
and my Jewish ideas about propriety, about having a good
time. Her idea of fun, he would announce loudly, is to read
me her footnotes and have me guess where the commas are
supposed to go. I went on with my conversation, determined not to have the evening ruined; the Milky Way could
be identified up about the Chrysler Building, Orion's belt
was hanging over Central Park. There was every reason to
believe that my baby would be born healthy. I was living at
last, with a stake in the future, a faith in the world's
progress, its fundamental humanity, its capacity for surprising kindness and loving change. I felt radiant the way
pregnant women are rumored to be. I shone with the
mystery of reproduction.

I heard Hilary say loudly that not only does language float
on air, but the poet himself has so transformed his physical
being that he too can drift in the currents. I saw a graduate
student with stringy blond hair and the residue of acne on
her chin looking up at him with admiration. "See," he said,
and called out loud to everyone on the terrace, "poets are
made of finer stuff than the rest of you mere mortals." He
climbed on a chair, wobbled a second as we all watched
silently. We expected him to make a speech. He stepped
onto the terrace wall and walked off. Not like a man
jumping into a pool, but like a man who genuinely believes
that his foot will land in the next second on solid ground.
Was he surprised to find himself falling, or had he planned
it all along? Was it no more than a drunken gesture, to
impress the graduate student? Did he regret, did he have a
second to consider what was lost?

Andrea lost her father that night and I had to reconsider
my basic premises. His parents came down from Boston and
promised to send me something when the baby was born.
They looked at me and my belly sadly. His mother kept her
eyes on the ground. His father patted me on the shoulder.

"What did he want? What did he expect?" his father asked. Fame, perhaps, or immortality.

"He was always afraid of death," said his mother. "On the candles of his seventh birthday cake he wished he was a word that would get spoken in different mouths forever. He was also afraid of thunder and of heights." I had not known that he was afraid of heights. "He won't get old," said his mother comfortingly.

"Yes," said his father, "he won't have arthritis or prostate cancer, and his fear of death won't bother him anymore."

"I suppose," I said, "that was the point."

"It's my fault," said his mother. "I should never have sent him to boarding school."

"Nonsense," said his father, "you were a fine mother."

DEAR SARAI (there was no point in making a fuss about names), You remember, I hope, that you are only half Jewish. The other half of you is from good New England Yankee stock. I told you that your father's father was an internist in Boston. They were churchgoing high Episcopalians. Half of your genes are Christian, Yankee, American. I have always told you to be proud of your father, of the poetry he left, of the way he loved sailboats and seascapes, of the Oxford book of poetry he had carried with him since his first week at prep school. Your Yankee grandparents ignored you because they were ashamed of their son, because the thought of him gave them pain, not because you were not worthy or wanted by them. They had a need to forget me, to forget the event they couldn't change and concentrate on what lay at hand, what had not yet turned to dust. They did not reject you personally and you cannot blame them for rejecting me. In your blood are echoes of clapboard churches, Christmas mornings, Easter dinners, the Resurrection and the Birth. In your genes are maple syrup and the colors of the fall on the northern spread of the Appalachians. As you knit yourself together, use all of yourself.

BEFORE ANDREA dropped out of school she gave me a Mets sweatshirt, which I wear when I work, for luck, for warmth, for the thought of Andrea, who wrapped the package and put a ribbon on it for me. I have a box in my closet where I have kept the clay ashtray Andrea made me in second grade. I have the birthday card she gave me in which she cut out all the pictures of trucks she could find and pasted them on a poster board. This was a misunderstanding. I wanted her to be interested in vehicles if she wished, so I kept pointing out to her the different kinds of cement mixers, diesels, and vans we would see on the street. I did not want her mind limited to cradles and carriages. She thought I was particularly fond of trucks and that is why she made the card. I have the recipe book her third-grade class compiled with favorites of each child illustrated and mimeographed. Andrea's contribution was chocolate cupcakes, a recipe she had gotten from our housekeeper, who took care of her on the days my teaching schedule kept me out late. What am I saving this for? An anthropologist of the future will puzzle over the ticket stubs to a Broadway musical, Andrea's first composition, a drawing of her imaginary friend. I am not saving this for the anthropologist. This box of mine is a civilized way of writing one's name on the side of a subway car, or on a rock above the highway. As soon as I gather the courage I am going to throw it out. The Mets sweatshirt is going with the rest.

* * *

ONCE, my mother said to me, "Your aunt
        believes that a woman should make love in the
dark and keep her eyes closed. She says that it goes quicker
that way."

"And you?" I asked. I had not yet reached the age where
I had opinions of my own. I had just finished *Little Women*
and was about to begin *Treasure Island*. I was extremely
hazy on the details of how men and women did anything
together, including eating dinner. I did know, of course, that
sex was embarrassing. It was an act to be committed only
after marriage. I knew about virginity; to remain a virgin
was the major purpose of a nubile life. A girl with a broken
hymen could be handed back, unacceptable as a bride, a
leftover at the marketplace, a shame for her family. I was not
yet nubile but I was already dedicated. "And you?" I asked.

My mother said, "Dr. Levin says she's wrong. Dr. Levin
says that sex is a normal human drive and we should enjoy
it freely." Four times a week my mother went to see Dr.
Levin. I gathered he had shocking opinions. I could tell by
the way my mother said his name, sometimes with an
upwards lilt, sometimes extended as if she were rocking the
word to sleep, that Dr. Levin had gone too far in soliciting
my mother's affection.

I asked, "When Uncle Harold was in jail what did Aunt
Millie do?" I wanted to know if she lay in her bed with
other men with her eyes closed in the dark.

"Aunt Millie visited Harold once a week. She was very
brave. She dressed beautifully and had lunch at the Plaza
with me all the time. She ignored her friends who ignored
her. She suffered," said my mother. "We had to go to the
Plaza for lunch because all her clubs withdrew membership."

"Was he guilty?" I asked.

"Of course not," said my mother. "He just sent out an

annual report saying the insurance firm had more money than it did and when the firm went bankrupt and the doors were locked the lawyers claimed he had lied. They sent him to jail for such a little thing.''

I had heard the story often. I could see it: crowds of people leaning on the huge mahogany doors of the office, banging the gold knockers, pressing against the heavy chains the federal marshals had garlanded across the steps, pressing their faces against the windows, looking at the empty desks and the green-shaded brass lamps and the papers left in haste blowing across the floor. The desks empty as if a fatal illness had overcome everyone at once. Harold leaving hastily out the back. The chauffeur driving the Rolls through the streets for the last time. The insurance firm whose major asset had once been an immigrant tailor's wisdom and his willingness to work long hours in his tiny store on Hester Street had grown to be a real company, and Harold's father had left him a rich man before he was thirty years old. Before he was forty he was handcuffed and led away and his picture was on the front page of *The New York Times*. ''Handcuffed,'' my mother said, ''simply for wishful thinking.''

''But what did Aunt Millie do when Harold was behind bars? Did she fall in love with someone else?''

''No,'' said my mother. ''Aunt Millie doesn't need love the way I do,'' and she began to cry. When my mother cried her eyelids puffed up and she would have to put ice on them till they returned to normal. She would lie on her bed with ice in a table napkin and stroke her lids. Sitting there on the floor beside her bed I couldn't tell if she was still crying or if the wetness on her face was caused by the gradually melting ice.

Uncle Harold played the violin. With many repeats, with certain pauses as fingerings were considered, with the sound sometimes muffled or reminding me of chalk on slate, he practiced every day. I imagined him behind bars, playing to a moon that lit up the prison yard, his heart beneath his plump chest beating with complaint as he held his instrument tucked under his rounded chin, bow reaching across the strings as if music might wring pity out of God. "I was in Leavenworth when you were born, so I don't have to give you a birthday present," he said to me. But then he gave me a present anyway. My mother said he wasn't a real criminal. I wanted to meet a real criminal.

"Should I leave him?" asked my mother. "Dr. Levin thinks I am getting strong enough to reach out for a new life. Dr. Levin thinks that I should explore the world and find out who I am." She had crushed a package of Camel cigarettes and the tobacco crumbs spilled on her sheets. The blinds were drawn although it was eleven o'clock on a Saturday morning.

"Does Dr. Levin like me?" I asked.

"He would like you if he knew you," said my mother. "You are a mature little girl. You are the only comfort of my life, my one pleasure."

Leave him? My mother read mystery stories taken from the lending library in groups of threes. She played canasta with me and she did the crossword puzzles and she told me stories of drunken ladies, of women who cheated on their mates, of men who made fortunes on the stock market and lost it all on the horses. In all the tales of hypochrondriacs and kleptomaniacs and women whose children were feeble-minded or had run away with sailors who weren't even Jewish and got pregnant out of wedlock and who were shamed, there ran a theme. It was a question told in the form of gossip. It was something like "Why are we being punished?" or perhaps it was "What have I done to deserve my fate?" or perhaps it was a simple map reading, an attempt to find the way. This is how the world works or doesn't work. Shame lurks everywhere. The neighbors are talking. Weren't we talking? Shame was the name of the shape that waited under the bed or behind the unopened door.

"Maybe," said my mother, "all men are missing an essential soul. Maybe they are like golems put on earth to protect us but are incapable of real human feelings; quickly they go out of control and we have to put them back to sleep again."

"Leave him," I said. "It's all right with me."

I didn't believe she should. I believed that if she tried harder she could make him kind and gentle, considerate and loving, that rosebushes could grow in our living room and that birds could fly free in the dining room. I believed that if she worked at it he would stop leaving lipstick-stained shirts on his armchair and come home for dinner and put his arms around her and whisper in her ear and they could put on a record and dance together. Rum and Coca-Cola, Rum and Coca-Cola, sometimes she danced alone in the bedroom with only her stockings and garter belt on. I believed in miracles the way the near dead believe in resurrection.

"Millie says I should stay. That I take it all too seriously. 'Ignore him,' says Millie, 'just enjoy your life.' Millie says it would be a scandal if I left, another scandal. Millie says to think of my husband as a nuisance to be put up with because of the ways of the world."

I agreed with Millie. The known is better than the unknown. "My home for better or worse" could yet shelter a miracle.

WHEN ANDREA was four we went to Washington on a peace march. We left on the seven A.M. Metroliner from Pennsylvania Station. Andrea slept in the seat beside me most of the way down. I talked strategy with the women in the row behind me, gentle-eyed political experts who wore peasant blouses with embroidered flowers and sensible shoes for the day's outing. Andrea wore a T-shirt with a peace sign on the front and a dove on the back. I had joined a group called Mothers for Peace and we had a flag crayoned by an older child that said "War No More" and showed a flower being stamped under a boot.

Some teenagers were carrying our flag and in the Metroliner they jumped up and went from car to car unfurling their message.

I had to carry Andrea on my shoulders because the walk from the railroad station to the steps of the Senate was beyond her. She was heavy. The day was hot. I stopped to get her an ice cream, which then dripped down my neck. We lost my friends, who had moved ahead in what became a river of people descending from buses coming in from all the tributary side streets. Marshals with bands around their arms kept waving people forward. We stood next to an old black woman who was there with her church choir. The group sang as they marched. "Swing low, sweet chariot, coming for to carry me home . . ." Andrea sang with them and the old lady gave me a tissue to wipe the ice cream off Andrea's face. I looked back down the avenue and saw a million people swaying in the heat, their bodies floating slowly over the pavement.

"Judgment Day," I heard somebody say.

"No more war," shouted Andrea.

"You tell 'em, sweetheart," a voice answered.

I lifted Andrea down and held her in my arms with her legs wrapped around my waist. "Remember everything about today," I said to Andrea. "We are ending the war." I could feel her heart beating against my shirt.

Later, in front of the Capitol, we listened to the speeches. Andrea looked for four-leaf clovers beneath the knees and legs of all the seated, sprawled people, who were clapping, chanting, singing at various moments. I found the Mothers for Peace group. I found my friends sitting on a blanket in the hot sun. I sat down, my legs and arms tired, my face flushed and perspiration stains under my arms. We talked of napalm and body counts and massacres small and large, and we passed around a Thermos of apple juice. We inhaled deeply and breathed in the sweet smell of pot that rose from several yards away. Children were wrestling on the grass. Two little Chinese girls were dressing up their Barbie doll, who had on a ball gown. I looked for Andrea, who had been right behind me. I couldn't see her.

I stood up. The voice on the microphone set up on a platform right at the bottom of the Senate steps droned out a list of movie stars who had joined the peace movement. The crowd, now exhausted from the speeches, applauded each name politely, like a summer breeze in a field. "Andrea," I called out. "Andrea." I raised my voice, but the chatter, the speaker, an airplane overhead, dwarfed my voice. "Andrea!" I screamed.

My friends jumped to their feet. "Andrea," they called, as if a dog or cat or sacred cow had been lost, each moving off our blanket in another direction.

People were packed thick on the hill; below, one could see the crowds waving flags on Pennsylvania Avenue. The line of humanity, looking like a column of multicolored ants, stretched out into infinity. Litter baskets were overflowing with cartons of juice, soda cans, potato-chip wrappers. On the side of the slope the portable toilets stood with lines in front of them. Far off beyond vision the rows of buses stood like obedient behemoths, their drivers drinking beer in the shade.

"Andrea!" I saw a child with red hair and a T-shirt with a peace sign, but I knew instantly that the child was not Andrea. "God," I screamed, but it was a curse, not a prayer. I grew still and quiet as if I were a deer in a forest and the hunter had his sights trained at my flank. I waited in the eye of the storm, quiet, without feeling. Dread erased all pictures in my mind. It cut off all words and thoughts. I froze. There was Andrea sitting on someone else's blanket; a boy with a Magic Marker was drawing peace signs on her arm.

"No," she said when I pulled her toward me. "I want to stay here."

I slapped her on the face. Everyone around stared at me. "God," I said; it was still a curse.

On the Metroliner back to New York, I apologized to

Andrea. I explained I had been scared. She sat in my lap and put her head on my shoulder, and playing with a strand of her hair and fingering my stained and sweaty blouse, she fell asleep. I held her gently as the train swayed from side to side, as it passed through the tunnel, as it rattled past Baltimore row houses where laundry still hung from balconies, as it sped through the dairy farms of New Jersey and past the factories of Newark and the bridges that crossed the swamplands at the side of the Hudson River. I held her all the way home.

"We ain't gonna practice war no more," I sang into her ear.

"No," I said as we rode up the elevator, "you don't have to take a bath tonight."

"Did you go on peace marches with your mother?" she asked me.

"No," I said, "but I saved tin cans, and I knitted a square for a blanket my class sent overseas."

"What?" she asked, but fell asleep before I had to explain.

MY FRIEND Nancy, who had written a book called *The Gender Blues,* an exploration of depression in women, asked me to meet her for lunch. Before the waiter had brought the rolls she leaned across the table, her long arms reaching for the silver chain I wore around my neck. "You know why women are told to buy cosmetics, new cosmetics, better cosmetics, different-colored cosmetics, all the time? It's because of the oil industry. Don't be naive"—she noticed my incredulous expression—"do you know how much oil is used in every lipstick, every dab of blush, each swipe of eyeliner? The economic powers in this country want us to keep on buying. If we stopped—if for one moment each woman in America looked in the mirror and said, 'I like myself just the way I am. George doesn't put pancake on his nose every morning and he looks fine'—if *Vogue* put on its cover a model with a perfectly scrubbed face, do you know how many businesses would scream, how much behind-the-scenes pressure would be applied? Quickly, 'They' in the advertising industry would take *Vogue* off the newsstands and burn it in a great bonfire on Madison Avenue. Do you think, in your wildest dreams of a new golden age of equality, justice, and liberation for all, they wouldn't make ash out of a model whose face mocked their pocketbooks with her own natural skin?''

"Who is They?" I asked. My friend Nancy had lost her dear friend of five years to a younger woman and was not sounding altogether all right.

"They"—she waved her hand around the room in an inclusive gesture—"They are the ones who prevent women's books from being well reviewed. They are the ones who make sure that if a woman is elected to political office she's either too old or too ugly to inspire imitation."

"Are They the ones who also killed Karen Silkwood?" I smiled at her.

"You know what I mean"—she glared at me impatiently—"you agree, I'm sure that They allowed women into the job market when the economy was booming and there was a need for more workers especially at the lower levels; when the first whiff of recession comes along out will go the women, back to the kitchens, where, the press will suddenly be saying, they wanted to be all the time, poor things, driven from their hearth by unfeeling feminists who slipped value confusion into their morning cereal. You know that's the way it's going to be. As soon as They need us at home buying things in the supermarket, making an audience for the daytime soaps so we can listen to the ads and run out and buy some more, as soon as that happens, off with our measly jobs, back to the washing machine, that shining white altar of each home. Every women's magazine is going to discover the virtue of the large family that buys many boxes of Pampers and thousands of shoes that are outgrown in three weeks.''

"But Nancy," I said, "I don't believe in your They. They are us, all of us together, and that includes you and me." I was feeling foolish about the antiwrinkle cream I had just purchased for twenty-five dollars, even though I suspected it would work only on deposed Rumanian princesses who had affairs with well-known Hollywood actors and would prove ineffective on the skin of New York City feminists who had bad dreams about rabbis who lived in the eighteenth century and were best known for their interest in things divine, not those of the flesh. Before the coffee arrived, Nancy told me that her son had taken a job as a nurse's aide. I remembered when she wanted him to be a district attorney and put rapists behind bars.

"If you don't believe they are undermining us," said Nancy, "then why are you so undermined?"

I shrugged.

LETTER RECEIVED: Dear Mrs. Annie Johnson,

Your daughter, Andrea Johnson, has joined us at the Yeshiva Rachel. She has asked me to write to you so that you can take your rightful share in her new life. Several months ago I found your daughter in the Plaza outside the Hilton Hotel. She was sitting on the grass with her backpack beside her. She looked disheveled and confused. There was an odor in her clothes and no doubt she had not found the opportunity to cleanse herself for a considerable time. I struck up a conversation with her and encouraged her to return with me to our yeshiva, where she has remained ever since. Surely the One Above must have been looking out for your daughter and arranged this meeting. She told us of her very sad experiences at home, the early death of her non-Jewish father and your struggles to bring her up. She speaks of you with respect and affection. We believe that she is not a bad girl but one who has responded with understandable sensitivity and pain to the conditions of life outside the covenant. We have enabled her to understand that the world of the modern machine, the world of the jumping pictures on the television screen, the newest fashions and the latest sound, has not and cannot bring peace to her troubled soul. This is because your daughter is a very special person with a deep spiritual thirst. She has been reaching for the path, longing for the path, her entire life. Her inability to conform to your expectations was a sign of her real nature struggling to assert itself, searching in vain among the cleverness of the world for the truth that would nurture and cherish her, the place for her to dwell in righteousness and holiness. It is here among us. Each day she changes into an increasingly contented, useful and virtuous woman. Her progress has been remarkable. Her eyes are clear, her thoughts are ordered. She has demonstrated good learning skills and a true compassion and understanding of others. Under the direction of my wife she has adopted some important personal hygienic habits as well as our rudimentary expectations of a Jewish woman. We have taken care of some necessary dental matters and are instructing her by example in matters of modesty and devotion. Each day she settles into her self and we see her grow and become ready to take on increasingly complicated chores and responsibilities. She is truly a jewel in the treasure house of the Jewish people.

We know that her father was not Jewish. In America we know many women such as yourself became undone, mistook the stranger for the liberator and became blinded to the truth within. We are completely unconcerned about the religious affiliation of her father, for us he was no more than the physical convenience that enabled this precious soul to find breath. We count her as one of ours because her mother is Jewish. However, we would appreciate some proof of your original status. It would save your daughter from the additional effort, which she is quite willing to make, of a formal conversion. Perhaps you have a birth certificate with your maiden name on it? A letter from your rabbi will do. If you are at present unaffiliated, and I understand from Sarai that this is so, a letter from the rabbi of your parents would be acceptable. Perhaps you have some older living relatives who could vouch for you. They must be male and we need at least three of them. I hope that you will want to support your daughter in her return to a life within the people, a life dedicated to the will of the One Above. Your daughter is now living with the Halacha, the holy laws that give shape and purpose to human life. Your daughter is no longer cut off, a dangling spit of flesh and bone; now she is engaged with us in the effort to bring together the king and the queen, the spirit and the power, so that the Messiah can walk on the streets of Jerusalem and the Garden of the Lord one day open its gate and welcome us all.

Your daughter, Sarai, is a valued recruit in the army of Hashem. We extend our congratulations to you. K'lal Israel, all of Israel, rejoices when a daughter has opened her eyes and seen that the frivolity, the carnal delights of the world, have nothing more to offer her. K'lal Israel rejoices when she opens her heart to Him Who will hear her and bring her true sight as she repents and returns to righteousness. Holy is His name.

Your daughter has taken a Hebrew name, as befits a child of this place. She has chosen the name Sarai, the mother of us all. Sarah, who like your daughter waited a long time for the visit of the angel and whose goodness and piety has inspired generations of women to gentle acts of service in the pursuit of a pure body and soul, to keep the laws of the food, to keep the laws of physical separation, of immersion, of cleanliness. We felt that Sarai would be an especially appropriate name for your child because she seemed so in need of mothering and Sarah was the mother of the entire Jewish people. We have found in your daughter the capaci-

ties (stillborn in the secular world) to one day be a mother to
herself and then in time to be a mother to her children,
guiding them in the ways of Torah. It will give you joy, I am
certain, to learn that Sarai now laughs with her friends,
learns to cook and to pray, and when she is ready we will
help her find a husband so that she can increase the numbers
of the House of Israel and live with honor among us for the
rest of her days.

I have written many of these letters and have been visited
by many parents and so I am aware that this is difficult for
you. In your cities our light has dimmed, been replaced by
the incessant whine of the new. We must seem alien and
frightening to someone who has not heard His voice. Our
ways are the old ways that have accompanied us throughout
this pause between creation and redemption. We ask you to
trust us, do not fear for your daughter, do not pressure her
to return to a world where she wandered without place, like
a seed that cannot find the earth and remains in the belly of
the wind, sterile and hard. Such a child as yours needs time
for healing, for rising up, for returning. In coming to
Jerusalem, in sitting in the park outside the Hilton Hotel,
she put herself in the way of the One Who will continue to
embrace her as the days spin out, lengthening the distance
from her error-filled past as she forgets what must be
forgotten.

We would be most happy to have you visit us in Jerusalem
and see for yourself the peace and sanctity that reside here
with us. Our ways will seem less strange to you if you
spend some time among our people. We will house you with
one of our English-speaking families, who will welcome
you as a lost relative and show you every consideration. As
you consider all this, remember your daughter whirling
about this globe, afraid of the night, clutching at men as if
they could save her from the daily bruising she endured.
This was not her fault. She is not a failure. She is a spiritual
child who was destined to ascend to higher levels, whose
soul was uncomfortable in the fleshpots, in the marketplaces

of Sodom. We value her and she has come to value herself. As Gd will call all of His creatures to Him at the end of time, so He has called your child now and she has heeded the voice. We thank you for the gift of your daughter and hope to have the necessary documents in our hands promptly. Sincerely, Rabbi Joshua Cohen.

GIFT OF my daughter! A grown child is not a birthday present, is not a little package, a bundle of unwanted old clothes to be passed on. I had given Rabbi Joshua Cohen no gift. I had plans of my own for Andrea. They began when she was just learning the words for shoe and nose, table and dog. I thought I saw in her eyes the spark of intelligence, the speed of thought that would have made her a fine lawyer, a civil rights lawyer, who argued for justice, to uphold the Constitution, the amendments, who worked in dark places with poor clients to see that the country moved forward toward equality of opportunity, a better life, a better land. I saw her working into the early hours of the morning writing briefs on school integration and voter rights. I saw my daughter in a suit carrying an attaché case, prepared, a faint blush of excitement on her cheeks, but a simple, determined, realistic set to her lips, ready to argue for what can be reasoned, what can be used to improve the landscape and make more comfortable the social domain.

As her breasts grew, as she developed orange hair under her arms, as her interests turned away from the stuffed animals I had bought in such profusion, it became clear that she might in fact not even graduate from high school. Her gifts were not so much analytical as they were spontaneous, responsive, sensitive. It occurred to me that perhaps she was an artist, a painter who would astonish with a new vision of politics and form combined to awaken the senses and the

conscience. I anticipated critics and arguments that would
come from the reactionary press. Andrea drew all the time.
She filled sketchbook after sketchbook with pencil and
crayon. But she wouldn't talk about art. She wouldn't go to
a museum with me. She didn't want to be anything. She
drew but she stopped showing me her drawings. I understood. I knew perfectly well that mothers have no right to
determine their children's future and that Andrea should and
could find for herself a direction, a place. All I retained
from my original yearnings was the insistence—unspoken,
of course—that Andrea use her mind, use her soul, not
simply to consume meals, not simply to receive the forms
that melded and separated on the tube, not simply to rock
her body about as if she were trying to shake her clitoris up
into her mouth, but to do and be something, to try and
change something. That was a plan I have never relinquished.

But I could not help Andrea. I could see she was in pain.
I could see it in her eyes. I could hear her playing her music
in the early hours of the morning. I could see that she
couldn't concentrate on books or movies. Only the TV
would soothe her and then she would sit before it, pale and
still, sometimes sweating or shivering with eyes that seemed
not to be seeing. She seemed to respond best to the
commercials, which she would hum from time to time.

"Be firm," said the school psychologist. I tried to en-
force a curfew. She laughed at me. I insisted she do
homework each night. She drew pictures on the pages of her
textbooks and slept at her desk. She watched the late late
show, and often I would find her in the morning, naked in
front of the TV with a bottle of beer in her hand. She stayed
out of the house. She wouldn't tell me where she was going.
She missed appointments with her therapist. "It's hard," he
said, "at this age to engage their attention."

"What is wrong?" I asked.

"She hasn't told me yet," he answered.

Is it just possible that across the globe, in a country that
didn't exist when I learned geography, my daughter could

have found valid shelter? I accept, not easily, but I accept the fact that she obviously needs more than I can provide. This admission of failure is a negation of all I imagined, invented, aspired; it is as if I were an architect who had built a city that no one could inhabit. I hear the loosening of bolts, the falling of beams, the breaking of glass as the city rots.

DEAR RABBI Joshua Cohen, Thank you for your letter about my daughter, Andrea. The world is without doubt wicked and cruel. The advances of science are disappointing. It is true enough that in this war-torn world the leper of modernity should be shunned. It should now be forced to walk about wearing a bell so that decent folk can be warned. Rabbi Cohen, I admit that I did not bring my daughter to a state of peace, of resolution, of competence and contribution. I admit that on the back streets of New York she was offered and she accepted quick releases, instant solutions that brought her near death. I admit that she wandered through the early hours of the morning, in leather skirts, in red lipstick, in long earrings, looking for muggers, winos and beggars who might explain to her what she wanted and how to get it. I admit all that without admitting that you and your friends at the Yeshiva Rachel are any more than muggers in black coats; in ancient language, with soothing words, with rules and promises, you have bruised my daughter, brainwashed my daughter, so that she considers giving up what she had not yet given up, her mind, her independence, her knowledge of the multiple realities, the multiple choices, her willingness to be accountable to herself, for herself, under the sky, to be human without wailing to the clouds, to be human and know that when we cry, we cry only in each other's arms or we cry alone.

So much is my world view opposed to yours; you crawl
where I want to stand, you implore, follow orders, go to the
right or the left as it was written, as it has been said by
others to have been written. I invent, I judge for myself, I
do not accept the goodwill of a force that has been proven
ineffective, could not even save a small child from the arms
of the Einsatzgruppen. You are the followers of a deity that
chooses only to forsake you or perhaps was always your
own invention. I am a Jew, but one who does not beg
forgiveness for sins of omission or commission before a
Holy One that can only be known as cruel, indifferent,
lethargic, apathetic. Your deity, whose words have been
muffled in windstorms, appears to have no recent action to
his credit. Atonement! At One ment, why? I do not plead or
placate the forces that frighten me. I am At Lone ment:
more At Lone ment now that you have my daughter. Your
morality has led you comfortably into kidnapping, brainwashing, seizing children and secreting them away. Your
God asked Abraham to sacrifice his only son. Your God is
always testing and teasing and placing apples in Gardens
where they need not have been. He draws lines that should
not be crossed and then punishes when we cross them. His
tricks with waters that close over the heads of enemies are
as often as not earthquakes and storms that destroy us as
well or they come too late or too early. Your Conjurer has
used up his credibility. His silence is not acceptable. We
have a better moral sense than he does. Your God uses us
like playthings in his Cosmos or he has forgotten us like
playthings outgrown and lying in disorder on the closet
floor. King of Kings: I am a democrat.

You have my daughter captive. I believe that in time I
will give her a full life in which she will not need to cower
under the tent of nomads who could not convince their God
to let them stay unmolested in or out of the Promised Land.
I am Jewish, both my parents were Jewish, but I am not
sending any documentation that would make it easier for
Andrea to go down this latest of her blind alleys. Are we

clear, Rabbi Cohen? I am not charmed by old stories of rabbis who meet on the streets of Vilna and tell tales of other rabbis who are so wise that they have found all but the last letter of the name of God and can show you multiples of seven that will foretell your future. The last years of our history have revealed that all the wisdom of the Talmud, all the pages of the Zohar, all the oral tradition, all the wit of Maimonides, all the scrawls of Rashi, will only bring us to the ovens with our eyesight already damaged by the fine print and the dim light. Dear Rabbi Joshua Cohen, I am not giving you my daughter on a kosher plate. No use telling me that the choice was hers. I know that choices can be influenced. We live in a world in which the toothpaste you select can be determined by the cleverness of imagery, the right background music and a thirty-second voice-over. You have interfered with Andrea and I do not accept your programming. It is no more than blatant manipulation. Yours, Annie Johnson.

I LOOKED the letter over. Ridiculous! How could I hope to explain myself to Rabbi Cohen? How could he understand my words? It was as if on one of our visits to the zoo, where I would take Andrea each Sunday morning, she slipped from her stroller and squeezed inside the bear cage. Here I was talking to the bear: Dear Bear, don't bother my little girl, I have other plans for her. I didn't intend her to be your lunch. Let's talk about this, Bear. Only a fool would talk to the beast while coaxing a child to come back through the bars the way she had gone. Impossible. I tore up my letter. I could think of nothing else to do. Not fair to compare Rabbi Cohen to a bear and the Yeshiva Rachel to a cage. They want to give Andrea a new life and the bear would only have regarded her as a protein source. But this new life the rabbi offers, the one that changes

Andrea to Sarai, does it not also digest her? They would
turn inside out the fabric of her mind and consume the soul
as it was in order to replace it with another, more docile,
obedient and orderly. To look on a lovely young girl as a
servant of the Jewish people, as a private in the army of
Hashem, as a dayworker piecing the goods of the Shekhinah
back together again, is this so very different from regarding
her as a protein source, a matter to be ingested for the good
of something larger than herself? Body snatchers, invasion
of the aliens; how little fiction there is in science fiction.

I wonder if I should not once again try to find a mate for
myself, lose some weight, go to parties, faculty dinners, tell
my friends to find me a soul for the down slide of my life. I
need a body in bed with me so that I can stop thinking of
Andrea, of the broken promise she is to me, of the promises
I must have broken to her that she has run so far away, must
disguise herself as someone else, in order to feel safe. Safe
from me?

Once, I came home from a meeting and Andrea had
washed her hair. It was still long and full and she had not
yet pulled her shoulders together to hide the new body that
had just come to her. She had taken a shower and was lying
with a small towel on our couch watching television. Her
new breasts sloped outwards in a curve so gentle that a
strange taste rose in my mouth, the taste perhaps of happiness. She did not move when I came in, and discreetly I
watched her with the sunlight from the window over her
white shoulders, her long legs stretched out across the
pillow; she looked like a bird one catches sight of at the
edge of the swamp, elegant, still, ready for flight, poised as
if the body were a breath held for a second, the center of a
landscape in which the chirpings and splashings and the
sound of leaves turning against themselves, of reeds pulling
through the eddies, were all in readiness for eternity.

Years before I had consulted with Dr. Wolfert, recommended
by my friend Elaine's current companion, who was a psy-
choanalyst of a school that had no more than the ordinary

amount of quarrels with the other schools. Dr. Wolfert sat in his leather chair and put his feet up.

"What can you do for Andrea?" I asked.

"Watch her," he said.

I indulged him. A woman of my age knows how to indulge any man in his need to tease, beg, show off, dominate or whisper baby talk. "What do you mean?" I asked.

"The way you watch a hurricane, a typhoon, a mistral, the way you watch a car accident, a bridge rising, a train crash, the way you watch the nightly news or the report on drug trafficking on the Afghan border, that's how I'll watch Andrea; respectfully."

"She needs more than watching," I pointed out.

"True," he said, "but all I can do is watch and wait for age, or luck or both, to wash the storm out to sea."

"What will be left after the devastation?" I asked.

"Something battered, misshapen, bruised, but getting along. Something like you and me." He smiled.

"It is my fault?" I asked, reaching for the Kleenex in the box.

"I'm not a priest," he said. "Guilt is not my interest, never has been."

"Then you don't think it's my fault?" I said.

"How should I know?" he said. "Was I there?"

"In general, I mean, are mothers in situations like this usually at fault?"

"Nothing is in general," he said, "everything happens in the specific. I don't know if you are to blame, but if it would make you happy I'll be glad to blame you. I can call you a 'bad mommy.' I can open the window and shout it out into the street." He moved toward his window.

"Never mind," I said. "I think Andrea may take drugs," I added.

"Really." He leaned back in his chair and I noticed that his shirt pocket was bulging.

"You smoke?" I asked.

"Never in front of patients," he said. "They might think I was crazy."

"I don't know how regularly Andrea will keep her appointments," I said.

"You pay for them anyway," he announced. "But don't take it personally, a lot of my hours are filled waiting for patients who have forgotten, who have better things to do, whose parents are paying anyway. It gives me time to chain smoke."

"Andrea will come," I decided.

"Another adolescent," he said. "I'm going to have to batten down the hatches, get my spyglasses out, great weather ahead."

"But for Andrea, but for me, what will happen?"

"Don't think I'm not sorry for you," he said. "I am."

"Will you help her?" I asked.

"What do you think?" he said.

"I don't know," I answered.

"Neither do I," he said, and he wasn't teasing.

DEAR RABBI COHEN, I write, I received your letter and need some time to consider. It is true that Andrea was not surviving well in the secular world, and I have been deeply worried. It may be that your way of life can offer Andrea exactly those protections, inducements, nurturing, that were missing in mine. But you must accept that my beliefs still have value for me. I do not have a well-organized religious system with ritual and prayer but I have nevertheless found a way of holding my head up under the stars without excessive cruelty to others; my work is to ask questions, to learn, to be concerned about all on the globe. I have lived with my own kind of religious expectations and I cannot easily accept yours. I have placed a high value on the intellectual accomplishments of women. I have supported the changes in America that have brought women more power, more economic equity, and have enabled them to see for themselves a wider variety of futures. This opening is a triumph of justice. I fear you will deprive my daughter of equality, respect and choice. On the other hand, I see that choice, too much choice, a world without boundaries, has pushed Andrea overboard, and I, I am not sure I can save her. I must consider Andrea's welfare and happiness. I must not be hasty. She has gone through phases before. She may not wish to stay with you. It may in fact be as you say the right path for her. Let us wait, watch and consider. In the meanwhile I will try to confirm for you my Jewish parentage. My word alone, I gather, is not sufficient. Please write again and let me know how you find Andrea/Sarai. If she is still with you in the spring I will come and visit. Be kind to my child. In the meanwhile I will listen to you. Who knows, the doctor of religion may succeed where the doctor of medicine failed. I will be patient. I will hope that Andrea will learn to take care of herself. Annie Johnson.

This letter I reread several times and then decided to mail. It seemed tactically wise. It said only the truth. It reflected part of what I believed. It permitted me to hope that Andrea was safe and well. It did not prevent me from viewing myself as a fraud, a pretender, an imposter: a person who had ideas on politics and social systems, but who knew that nothing she believed had saved her own. My comfort: there were other frauds walking about.

             I HAVE a photograph of my grandfather standing by the open earth with a shovel in his hand. He is dedicating the first stone of the Beth Jesureth Hospital on the Lower East Side. My grandfather is a heavy-set man, bald with a full nose and deep-set eyes with dark circles under them. He is wearing a black coat and a black hat and black shoes. He is not smiling at the camera. He does not smile for his children or grandchildren. The other men in the photograph are all wearing black too. Time has erased the gloss on the picture and a cloud of ash seems to have swept over the scene. The men's shoes still shine but the circles under their eyes have deepened. It is a civic photograph of a man, of a community, going about serious work, work made possible by prosperity, and yet if one looks at the turned-over dirt, the pile of stones, the set of the jaw, the bend of the shoulders, the photograph appears to be taken at a funeral, perhaps a funeral of someone disliked but powerful. The ceremony is not a celebration. It is not the sort of occasion to be violated by a baby's cry or the rustle of a woman's skirt or the scent of her soap.

In those years there was no hospital in New York where the sons of Russian immigrants could practice medicine. There was no hospital in New York where the newest of arrivals could be sure they would be served kosher food. There was a need for a new hospital and a man like my grandfather, who had put his name on millions of pants, was a man to put on the first board of trustees. I look at the picture. My grandfather stares into the camera lens now looking like the generic Jew, the one who knows that whatever has happened is only the beginning of the trouble and whatever the trouble will be he will stand fast by the customs of his fathers and his covenant to God and he will not crumble ahead of his time, nor will he indulge in play. Play he believes is for those whose history weighs on them like the feathers of a sparrow. He is sad or tired, my grandfather. His loyalties have exhausted him, or has he imagined the future? Maybe he is only worried about his angina or his youngest daughter's marriage to a handsome fortune hunter, or is he glaring at his sons, who may have been there beyond the camera's eye, bareheaded, whispering to each other? I try to place Andrea next to my grandfather. Andrea at her seventeenth birthday in a photograph taken by her friend Josh, who believed that motorcycles could cross the river Styx in both directions. In that photograph Andrea leans against Josh's newest machine. She holds the helmet she never wears in one hand and with the other she makes the international sign of contempt. She wears a leather skirt, her hair is cropped and shaved two inches above the ears, dyed blue and yellow, its natural red color peering through the roots. But you can see in the slope of her nose, in her eyes, an unmistakable Yankee reserve. She smiles, a huge wide smile, but only her mouth smiles, the rest of her face waits for more information.

I place the photograph of my grandfather on a table. Next to it I put the snapshot of Andrea. It is hard to believe that only fifty years separate the pictures. The hospital now has five buildings, a nursing school, a reputation in nuclear medicine and serves a primarily Hispanic population, so the numbers of kosher meals have been greatly reduced.

RABBI NACHMAN from Bratslav appeared in my dream again last night. I was wearing a summer dress, all white with a lace collar. I was working in the library in a corner by myself with a pile of books in front of me. I was looking for my copy of Hobbes's *Leviathan*. Around the corner of the stacks Rabbi Nachman comes running. He sits down next to me, breathless. He smells of pickles and onions and sourdough bread. "I have a story to tell you," he says. "He who knows one story knows the word of the Lord."

"Don't tell me your story," I say, "I'm working."

"No," says Rabbi Nachman, "look, your page is blank."

I look down and it is true that the page I had been writing on is now empty. "I am thinking about my work," I say.

"No," says Rabbi Nachman. "You are waiting to hear my story."

I stand up, ready to leave, but then it seem too much

trouble to gather all my books together, to put away my
blank pages. I wait. This is the story he tells me.

"Once in the kingdom of Ur there was a Prince who had
a falcon who would do his exact bidding. It was a remarkable falcon, who could fetch a quill from a distant castle and
return it. He could pluck a jewel from a bracelet that clung
to a lady's wrist. He could find a coin that had been hidden
in the branches of a lilac bush. He was a fine hunter and a
perfect companion for the Prince. He rode on the shoulders
of the Prince. At night he slept on the gold bedpost at the
Prince's head. He was quick to raise his claws as anyone
approached. He was more than an ordinary falcon, he was
the Prince's bodyguard. It was said by the courtiers that the
soul of a master warrior had been placed inside the body of
the bird.

"A time came when the Prince was asked by his father, the
King, to take a bride for the sake of the realm, for its power
and security and longevity. The matter was swiftly arranged
by the ministers of state. The bride was to be brought from
many miles away with her servants. The Prince was not
happy about this change in his arrangements. He wanted
only to stay in the forests with his bird, to hunt and do as he
pleased without the demands of domestic duty, without the
responsibilities of dynasty.

"The bride arrived. No more than fourteen years of age,
she had sores on her face, and her body had not yet gained
its womanly shape. She held to the hand of her lady-in-
waiting, not like the future Queen but rather like the
humblest of kitchen servants.

"The King ordered the Prince to take the young lady out
for a walk in the palace gardens. The falcon sat on the
Prince's shoulder and stared at a point on the horizon where
the forests began. The Prince, too, wanted to go hunting
and not strolling through the garden path. The bride also
wanted to be at home playing card games with her little
sisters. The two young people walked in silence, each
certain that there was something that should be said and

neither knowing what it was. Finally, sighing as if he had dropped a rock down a canyon, the Prince picked a rose and handed it to his lady. She blushed and accepted it, and a certain light came into her eyes that promised the beauty she would soon achieve.

"The Prince wasn't sure what he was supposed to do next. The bride's mother had informed her that at the right moment she was to use her lips to brush against the mouth of her intended as a sign of her willingness, of her favors to come. The bride's mother had been imprecise as to how to identify the moment for this gesture. Perhaps it was now, the Princess thought, in response to the gift of the rose. She moved awkwardly. Her heavy brocade dress weighed her down. She approached the Prince and on tiptoe reached up to his face, and her lips touched his skin. The falcon sitting on the Prince's shoulder felt the sudden tension in his master's body; he smelled fear. He was only a bird and had received no instruction. He flew into the bride's face and pecked furiously at her eyes. She screamed. The Prince called out to his bird, who had settled back down, but it was too late. In a moment the bride was blind and bleeding.

"After several days she developed a fever and died of her wounds. The King wanted to punish the falcon but the Prince would not hear of it, a poor bird who had misunderstood, who was only trying to protect his master, he said to his father.

"War broke out between the two kingdoms as the father of the bride sought vengeance. The Prince was killed by an arrow on the battlefield."

Rabbi Nachman grabs my hand. "A good story." Then he turns on me with disapproval. "Why aren't you writing down the tale, my disciples always write down my stories." Now he is sitting on the table. He is quite small, the size of a child. He reaches up and pulls a handful of my hair. He draws his face right up to mine. "Mama," he says, and I wake.

* * *

"ANDREA has promise, yes," said the principal
of the high school, "but she lacks discipline."
I sighed. I knew the sentences that would follow. "She
loses all her homework papers if she does them at all. She
sings out loud in class even if the teacher is speaking.
She distracts the others with jokes and obscene words. She
draws all over everything, scribbles on tabletops. She is not
stupid, certainly she is not stupid, but we have failed,
perhaps it is our failing," he said in the voice of one who
knows such a thing is impossible, "but we have not been
able to reach Andrea and we ask that you immediately find
another place for her."

I thought of pleading for one more chance, but what
would that accomplish? My face was flushed.

"One would have thought that the daughter of such a firm
advocate of women's rights would have been more of an
achiever but these days we see many children from single-
parent homes who have lost their moorings. You are not the
only mother faced with this sort of problem." He smiled at
me as if I were a small child who had not reached the
bathroom in time. His secretary was now offering a folder of
Andrea's transcript for me to take to another school. "Perhaps
a school for children with exceptional natures," he added in
an attempt to be professional, helpful. "Perhaps a boarding
school for the disturbed. We do not want her back tomorrow. I have spoken to Andrea this morning," he said. "She
has been informed of our decision and the reasons have
carefully been explained to her. The shock may cause her to
collect herself and she can begin with a fresh start and new
determination." He was trying to be encouraging. He didn't
want me to cry in his office. I didn't want to cry.

"Your school," I said, "is perhaps too conventional for a
free spirit like Andrea. She does not mold easily."

"No," he agreed with me. "She is not a molder."

Enough, I thought. I rose to my feet and sailed, a leaky ship, out the door.

DEAR MOTHER (a letter arrived), I thought of you this morning as I walked through the Arab market, the oranges and melons made such a smell and I remembered how you prowl through the Korean markets squeezing everything in sight. This morning they had a goat sale at the corner of the old city near the Rockefeller Museum. Small Arab boys took their goats and walked them up and down for buyers to inspect. A new friend of mine and I went over and the little goats licked our fingers. Their fur was soft. It made me wish I was an Arab boy who lies down in the evening with his goat next to him. Imagine, goats in the middle of a city, in front of a museum. Here everything seems to bloom and spoil and smell at once. The Armenian priests walk through their quarter waving incense about. They are so large and black-robed and heavy-bearded that they seem like evil spirits themselves instead of priests warding off evil spirits. Before I met Rabbi Cohen I would have been frightened of them. Now I just ignore them. They are not of us. I walk about our courtyard with my friends on Shabbat. You can breathe the calm. No cars dare come here. You can hear the swallows and the sound of feet on the cobblestones and the murmur of voices out the windows. It is as if everyone were swinging in the same hammock, gently back and forth under the tree of life. That is Rabbi Cohen's image and it is just right.

Sometimes I think of you left in New York with all the voices talking at once and wish you would come here and see my yeshiva. I believe now that Gd is good, that when He created this earth He intended man to be good, He intended His creation to be good, and He intended me to play my part. Can you, will you try to understand? You must understand because you are my mother. Gd is a Gd of Lovingkindness. He is the Master of Life and Death. He is the Redeemer. He brings flowers to the field and sweetness to the fruit. Rabbi Cohen says I am a good student. This is the first time you have heard that. Are you surprised? Mrs. Cohen is teaching us about the Mikvah and the laws that married women follow. I am so amazed. I thought my body didn't matter to anyone but me. Mrs. Cohen says that even the crevices, even the parts that get stained, can be cleansed and made good and serve their rightful purpose. When I learn more I will write you about it. I know that you will think that purity laws are against women but that's because you don't understand. The truth is they bring us closer to Gd. You never believe me. You never listen to me. You have such strong opinions about everything. But now I am right. Love, Sarai.

Suddenly she sounded young. She who had been so tough, so independent, so willful and disguised, now seemed like an innocent, like a virgin who has not yet learned that lust is rarely tender and that the beast one makes with two backs slouches off to porn movies in its spare time.

What has Andrea done with her humor? What of honor, of choice? Is she going to get that same look in her eye that my grandfather had when he turned over the dirt for the first stone of the hospital? I am sad, all my friends know I am sad. I cannot tell them what is the matter. I cannot explain even to myself why I am so sad. Today when the girl at the supermarket counter told me I had to purchase two jars of applesauce in order to get the discount, tears came into my eyes. I am a household of one, not two persons.

LETTER RECEIVED: Dear Mrs. Annie Johnson,
Your daughter will be a true woman of valor. She remains steady in her work and her good humor, her

virtue, her smiling nature, bring us all pleasure. We can hardly remember the child who once turned her face away when asked a question, who could not sleep at night and who complained each day of stomach pains and headaches. She told us at first that she would never believe that the Holy One could love her. "I don't care," she said all the time. At first she could not set the table, her attention wandered. Her hands shook. We had to see to it that she changed her clothes. We had to do her laundry. The simplest task would distract her and end in disaster. The Lord has given her strength and purpose and cleared her mind of the unessential. Now she says yes and when and how. She learns and takes part with the others. She has almost completed the necessary sessions at the dentist. We feel that she is ready to take her place as a woman among her people.

We are arranging a marriage with a young man, also a Ba'altshuva, a returned, an American from Cleveland, who found his way to us just as Sarai did. He has been with us two years and we are extremely proud of his progress. He studies at our yeshiva. He works as a jeweler and is a very serious student of his trade. He is ready for the responsibility of marriage, of bringing the next generation forward. He is a boy of faith, commitment and diligence. He will make a good husband for your daughter. His name is Micah Rose. The young people's backgrounds are similar and this we have found from centuries of experience will tighten the bond between them. Assuming that the two young people like each other, as we feel quite certain they will, we plan to make the final arrangements as soon as possible. We will stay in touch with you on this matter and hope that at this important turning in your daughter's life you will consider a visit to Israel, perhaps a stay with us. We welcome you with open hearts and are willing to share with you all that we have. We will support Sarai and Micah in their new life together. They will live in an apartment house owned by our yeshiva and they will continue their studies and work with us. However, we have found that all children do best when their biological parents give their blessing to the union. Otherwise the amputation with the past can never heal properly and threatens infection at any time. We believe from what Sarai has told us of you that you will not want to cause her pain, or to be separated in spirit from the grandchildren you will soon have. Your choice is to join in our celebrations or to leave your child forever. I am certain that Gd will guide you in the right direction. May I remind you that we do need some simple proof of your Jewish parentage to ease matters. The community here is mindful of things that may not seem so important to you but will help considerably in assuring the legitimate status of your daughter and her children. Sincerely, Rabbi Joshua Cohen.

A MARRIAGE! A marriage to a pale-faced fuzzy-bearded boy with a long black coat and a round black hat and black shoes on his long skinny feet with ingrown toenails . . . a boy with shoulders rounded from studying the footnotes to the footnotes of forgotten decisions, a boy with glasses and unbrushed teeth and hair growing out of his ears, permanently rocking back and forth on his toes, afraid to make a decision for himself without consulting the rabbi or maybe five rabbis, a boy who would consider himself the superior of my daughter, a boy who would say each day, "Thank God I was not born a woman." Marriage may not be forever, but it changes the weather. It freezes the pond. It lures and seduces and bears down with its own murky climate. It becomes a thing in itself, a responsibility, a stone on one's back that turns into a flesh-and-blood hump, an umbrella that transforms itself into a room without a door; marriage for Andrea, who had proclaimed her freedom from leashes, who walked in the valley of the shadow of death without looking back, my

single sparrow, my dove, my pinion of the morning, band-
ed, coupled, enchained; my God.

Sheared. Will they cut off her hair and hide her under a
wig? Shaved again. Is all this an elaborate way of achieving
her favorite hairstyle? Why has she always wanted to hide
her hair? I remember when she dyed it green. She said,
"Carrot top turns to parsley top, next I'll be a cloud and dye
my hair gray." What color wig will she choose? Or will she
walk around with a scarf or a beret placed like a pot on her
skull? Whom am I loving and losing at this great distance?
Do I invent Andrea or do they?

After Andrea was born I considered marrying again. I
don't clearly remember the psychologist Andrea says took
her to the zoo, but then there were always possibilities.
George, who was the dean of students and whose passion
for the harpsichord was equaled only by his fondness for
Baroque music, almost convinced me. But after two years
of sharing friends and bed a certain boredom overcame me.
I felt I was losing my edge. I was no longer surprised by my
life. Perhaps I was frightened. I was not capable of loving
with abandon, and without such love who would take the
risk of marriage? Four or five other men drifted near and
then far. Once I thought I might be tempted, but the object
of my fantasy came out of the closet and that was that.
Marriage, I believed, was of another century, a yoke, an
economic division of labor that made sense as the Industrial
Revolution found its legs, but finally an institution that
shackled male and female in a long-term struggle that ended
either in repressing the normal drives or in dulling the brain.
Marriage became the symbol of the dominance-submission
seesaw that caused so much mischief, so much misery,
wherever one looked. I had without intention become an
independent woman and found myself appreciating the condition. It suited me. Of course I had Andrea to give my days
a human shape. It had never occurred to me that marriage
was the divine will revealed or that the function of sexual
contact was to serve the nation or the species. What if the

damn psychiatrists were right and Andrea needed a father? What if the two-parent home is the only route to sanity and all other arrangements mere bravura, gestures of the blind in a ballet class?

I made an appointment with Dr. Wolfert. He had seen Andrea for two years three times a week and as a result my cottage at the beach was sold. I was certainly willing to exchange weekends in the country for Andrea's well-being. I knew that there were no guarantees and therefore did not resent Dr. Wolfert except on certain summer nights when the streets steamed with the sound of salsa and I imagined him swaying in the hammock on the front porch of my former cottage listening to the evening crickets and watching the fireflies mating in the reeds at the side of the deck.

Dr. Wolfert registered no surprise as I settled into his leather armchair. His office was blanketed in gray wool and nubby tweeds and had that peculiar soundlessness that floats only in the rooms of psychiatrists as if the very air were holding its breath, bulging from the effort of carrying all those undertones, overtones. The stillness in the room was false, like the calm of a lake that covers the overturned canoe. Dr. Wolfert waited for me to explain.

"Marriage," I said. "They are planning a marriage. Can you imagine Andrea, in a yeshiva, married?"

"Why not?" said Dr. Wolfert. I reached for a tissue from the conveniently placed box at my elbow. "Sooner or later Andrea had to find a way to leave you," he added.

"Why?" I asked. "Why so abrupt and drastic a journey? Why couldn't she just grow up and ease into adulthood, a good job, a nice apartment, a romance, a bank account, a share in a house on Fire Island? Other people's children do that."

"I cannot," said Dr. Wolfert, "explain to you why Andrea behaves the way she does; to do so would be to break professional confidence, and besides, my nose might grow longer."

"Just tell me," I said, "was Andrea so sick that this is the only way she can live without dying?"

"We're all dying," said Dr. Wolfert. "I don't know if this is a good choice for Andrea or not," he added. "I'm a psychiatrist. I don't do tea leaves."

"All psychiatrists are gypsies," I said. "They steal little children from their cradles and carry them off with the traveling caravan."

"You understand us perfectly," said Dr. Wolfert.

Why do psychiatrists believe so firmly in separation? Why do they insist that each of us must stand free of the background, never cleaving or clinging or God forbid merging with another? Is it not excessive puritanism, this hellfire and brimstone preaching, this vision of the moral life as one in which one works through memories, parents, childhood, fantasies, and emerges from the past, single and singular? This is a cruel vision that goes against the grain of human effort. Is it some ill wind of Freud's that has broken across our time and causes this absence of love we call maturity?

That night I had a dream. It is summertime and the heat causes vapor to rise from the cement. My feet have swollen in my sandals and I feel the haze and sweat mingling on my face, leaving smudge marks around my neck. The air tastes like spoiled milk. I am walking downtown. There are tall buildings on both sides and trucks and taxis are stuck in the congested street. Horns are blowing. I can hear the siren of an ambulance a few blocks away. I see a pack of Hasidic Jews in black coats, hats and payess. Most of them also have beards and glasses. They are waving pedestrians around an area in front of a residential building. Several of them are bending over and unrolling what appears to be an enormous fish net. I stop and stare.

"Move on," says one.

"What are you doing?" I ask.

"We are the Safety Mitzvot patrol," he answers.

"Well, what are you doing with that net?" I ask.

"Are you Jewish?" He turns on me.

"Yes, but why are you spreading that net?"

He ignores me. I see Rabbi Nachman supervising the work. He rushes over. "You may watch," he says, "but it is not allowed for you to help."

"Help what?" I ask, offended and curious at the same time.

"We have had word that we are needed." He points up to the sky. He jumps up and down screaming out orders. All the Hasidim form a square at the edges of their net and suddenly lift it up at once. The net is suspended from their raised arms and sags in the center loosely. At the top of the building I see a figure, high up, very small, in shadow, I cannot tell if it is male or female, adult or child, floating, falling downward. A crowd has gathered and someone sobs. The net is spread. Everything will be all right. I am relieved. I no longer feel the heat. The figure comes closer. A Hasid appears from around the corner and whispers in Rabbi Nachman's ear. He shouts a command and all the men drop the net and begin to roll it up. The figure is falling.

"What is it?" I say. "Why are you removing the net?"

Rabbi Nachman stares at me sternly. Then he says, "I am what I am."

"But the man is falling, he will die," I scream at Rabbi Nachman. "To save one life is to save the whole world," I shout.

"Are you certain," says Rabbi Nachman, "that you believe that? Your heart beats only in your imagination."

The Hasidim are getting into a green bus that had pulled up on the sidewalk. The man is falling.

I wake up. My heart is pounding. My throat is dry. Am I having a heart attack? I listen to the sound of heavy footsteps in my chest. I should go to the emergency room. I should have a cardiogram.

I take a bath. I turn on the television and watch a World War II movie in which all the ethnics are killed before the final reel. My heart disappears back into my chest. No one dies from a bad dream.

WHY IS my grandfather's Rabbi Nachman following me into sleep? In graduate school I bought a translation of his work or at least part of it that his followers had written down, from an old woman who sold books on upper Broadway from a blanket she spread over the street. She had hair on her chin and her stockings were rolled at the ankles and this was years before every corner had a woman wrapped in stained woolens looking at you with suspicion or derision or the sincere conviction that you were the bearer of a sinister message from the poltergeists or the Martians or the CIA. My bookseller was ahead of her time. I bought a book from her out of obligation, to make up to her for the inequity of our places. Look how my act of charity has come back to haunt. Rabbi Nachman was simply a pathological religious who had visions, fasted continually, believing he was at all times guilty of violation, of impurity. He did not make his wife happy but did not consider that fact one of his violations. I banish you, Rabbi Nachman, from my brain. I am not interested in ultimate reconciliations, in divine unity. The world is in fragments, but I do not think either of us can put it back together again. Leave me alone, Rabbi Nachman.

ONE MORNING before Andrea left for Europe I woke up to find her in the living room shivering under a blanket. It was a spring day and on the street below the young lawyers were leaving for work without their raincoats, with jackets open. There were dark circles under her eyes.

"Are you sick?" I asked.

"I'm fine, just fine, why do you always think something is the matter with me?"

"You don't look well," I said.

"You never think I look well; you have in mind someone who is majoring in economics and minoring in seventeenth-century poetry and I never look like that. Why do you always tell me I don't look well? You know that makes me feel awful. How can I be a confident person if you're always telling me I don't look well?"

"I think you're beautiful, I always think you're beautiful," I said. She was very thin and her skin appeared greenish. Her hair was in spikes. She looked like a rooster who had lost a fight. There was a huge burn blister on her forearm.

"How did you get burned?" I asked.

"Say something friendly to me," she said. "I didn't come here to be inspected like a piece of meat."

"Did someone burn you?"

She shivered and pulled the blanket over her shoulders. "Things happen," she said.

I was sorry I asked. I didn't want to know. "I have some muffins if you want one," I offered.

"I'm not into muffins," she said.

I turned into the kitchen to fix myself some coffee. She followed me, dragging the blanket over her shoulders. "I burned myself," she said.

"Why?" I asked.

"The music was loud, no one was paying any attention to me, I felt weird like I wasn't really there and I had just taken something that wasn't helping and so I burned myself."

"Maybe we should call Dr. Wolfert?" I suggested.

"That asshole!" she shouted. "You can call him but it won't help."

I put my hand out to touch her damp forehead. She

backed away. She went to the couch to watch TV. I sat down
next to her and watched with her a rerun of *Bewitched*. She
let me pull the blanket up over her arms and tuck it in
around her knees. I brought her a Coke and a muffin with
jam. I went into the bedroom to call Dr. Wolfert. Later,
when I dressed to go to class, leaving Andrea asleep in front
of the TV, I looked in the mirror several times, readjusting,
reapplying, restudying the lines. I put on dark glasses. I was
concerned that if anyone looked in my eyes they would see
my brain flattened as if it had run into a cartoon steamroller.

Several weeks later I came home from a meeting and
found her in the kitchen drinking coffee. With her was a
large, tall young man with paint-splattered jeans, eyeglasses
that were bent, hair so blond it was nearly white and a
stunned expression on a face that was meant to be corn fed,
middle American, trustworthy, but was oddly blank.

"This is David, Mother," said Andrea. "He is a painter.
He is going to Europe and I think I'll go with him." She
smiled at the lumbering form whose legs hardly fit under
my table.

Later she came into the bedroom and said to me, "Be
very kind to David, he has a daughter named May whom he
left on a commune in Georgia and he misses her so much.
It's so sad. Would you like to see a picture of May? David
carries one around wherever he goes."

In the living room we found David lying on the couch,
his paratrooper boots propped up on a pillow. I looked at the
picture of May, a child about five, with long blond hair and
a daisy pattern on her coveralls.

"Why did you leave?" I ask.

"I paint," said David.

"The painting scene is in New York," said Andrea as if I
were a little deaf.

I consulted with Dr. Wolfert about giving Andrea some
money to go to Europe. He wanted her to continue in
treatment. She wanted to find herself in exile. I thought of
Gertrude Stein and Ernest Hemingway, of the Murphys and

the Fitzgeralds and the cleansing effects of another culture. I
told her to stay in New York and get a job. David's father,
an insurance salesman from Princeton, New Jersey, had
died. David bought Andrea a ticket. I went to the airport to
see them off. I put my arms around my child, who said,
"Don't worry, Mother, David and I'll be just fine. I'll send
you postcards from everywhere."

David was carrying a knapsack. He didn't believe in
possessions. Andrea had a canvas bag. When they announced
the boarding of the plane to Zurich, I watched the two move
forward toward the line at the door. Andrea bent over and
began pulling clothes out of her bag.

"What is it?" I came over.

"Damn, shit," said David, "I forgot to pack my paints
and brushes. I thought Andrea had them."

"You were supposed to pack them," said Andrea, now in
tears. She saw me watching her and she turned toward me.
"I'll never forgive you," she said.

"Good-bye, have a good trip," I called after them.

When I was at college the boys were not permitted up the
stairs. If you were found with one in your room, you were
immediately expelled. On Saturday afternoons we would sit
in the dormitory foyer and boys from all-male colleges
would come walking through. Some had driven hours across
New England to gawk at us. A few girls were asked out. We
had to be back before they closed the doors at midnight. We
survivors of the lineup would arrive at the local tavern,
where the boys would slug beer and whiskey and we would
try to look as if we were having a wonderful time. Some
girls got pinned. They wore on the left breast of their
cashmere sweaters the fraternity insignia of their future
spouse. If you weren't pinned by senior year you had good
reason to worry. I was already objecting but my objections
had no words. It was too soon for that. I figured that just a
little song and dance would take me away from the expected,
the predictable, the inevitable, from PTAs, from country
clubs and into the real world where one could knock down

the foundations of society and build a new edifice out of the ruins of the old. In those days I was always afraid. I was also overconfident. Years later I believed that if men were allowed in the dorms, women would go to the Senate: a miscalculation that seems to have led Andrea to Europe with a man named David who left his daughter May in a commune in Georgia.

DEAR MOTHER, Today was Shabbat. I spent the afternoon with Avram Berg. He came over to our yeshiva just to meet me. He is a very famous man here. Ten years ago he was a well-known painter. His paintings are hung in the museum at Haifa and the University at Tel Aviv, and in Jerusalem at the arts center. He made a lot of money and some of his paintings were collected by people who lived in Paris, London and New York. He told me that he went to parties with artists and took coke and drank. He had girlfriends who were models and film stars. He was always being interviewed on television. One day he went to Jerusalem because a friend's brother had told him that a rabbi there had interesting things to say. The trip, he said, was just a joke, he was bored and restless. He had always laughed at the black coats of Jerusalem so he had a desire—a whim, he said—to hear one for himself. The trip was meant to be a tasting, the way you always wanted me to try calamari. He met Rabbi Goldstein and that night he moved into the yeshiva and began to learn, to relearn, the meaning of life. Now he says he only paints when melancholy overcomes him, and that isn't too often. His days are devoted to the study of Torah and to the guiding of those fine men who have come to Israel to begin again at the base of Mt. Sinai. He says he has been healed of the need to paint. Isn't that a dramatic and beautiful story? He gave up fame and fortune in the material world for the hard, risky climb to the heavens. Gd must love him especially. He is married now and has three children already and one more is coming in August. He says that by keeping strictly to the Halacha, the laws, he has compressed the *holy* until it covers the pigment of his soul, night and day. He is never without Gd. He says I have a spirit that soars toward the righteous. He says that red-headed Jews are special, they suffer a lot, but they give to others in generosity and Lovingkindness. He says red-headed Jews are the Holy One's favorites. He gave us red hair so that he could spot us in any crowd. We are like the signposts among His people. He says he will invite me to a Shabbat dinner at his house so I can meet his wife and babies. I remember in New York when I was riding the subway and I was always invisible. I could vomit on the floor and everyone would look away. I could weep and they would pretend I wasn't there. In New York I knew even if I drooled and bit my own fingers off no one would pay attention. Here it is not like that.

Avram Berg came to see me because there is some talk that I might be betrothed to a young man in his yeshiva. Mother—don't freak out. Rabbi Cohen has not told me his name yet or what he looks like so I cannot identify him in the courtyard among the others. Sometimes I imagine that it is his desk I am dusting and his books I am straightening. We do the laundry all together but sometimes I pick up a shirt and I feel an electricity in my fingers and I am almost certain it must be his shirt I am holding. Rabbi Cohen says he does not want to rush. He waits to see if I am truly ready for so large a step. Avram wanted to meet with me to see if the proposed marriage seemed right to him. He is in charge of the American families in our section. I think he liked me, I really do. I think I was fine. I told him the truth about me, everything! He too was in the secular world so I did not shock him. He saw how I have changed. I think he will soon allow me to meet the one that they think is meant for me. Imagine how eager I am. It means a great deal to me that Rabbi Cohen and Mrs. Cohen think I am nearly ready to be a Jewish woman with my own family. I try not to think about the men at the yeshiva in the ways that I used to think about men, part enemy, part pleasure machine, part cloud that would change shape and disappear, partners 'til the road forked, dumb about the things that mattered. In the beginning when the friendship started I would also plan the escape, the final words, the end, so that I would not be surprised. Now I am thinking of myself walking with my husband across the cobblestones of the old city. It seems like a wonderful dream. Of course I still have a lot to learn but Mrs. Cohen says I can always ask her questions, especially about the holiday preparations. They are very complicated and must be done the right way. There are so many Jewish holidays, we hardly finish one and it's time to begin learning about the next. It's not like Christmas where you get presents and you always feel empty because you never get quite enough. It's more like a light has broken through on a stage and there is a freeze of the action and you see the particles of dust in the spotlight. We are at Succoth now and we built a tabernacle on the roof and we ate in it and we prayed and the stars came out and I sat with my friends and we sang together. I think I caught my cold up there because the wind came up suddenly and I knew I should go down and get a sweater but I didn't want to miss anything. Mrs. Cohen is making me honey and tea for my cough and I will be better soon. I just wanted you to know what was happening with me. I hope you are writing well and will come and visit. Mrs. Cohen says she wants to explain to you how women who believe are not victims of oppression but instead the benefactors of the ever-streaming light of Gd. I warned her that you are very hard to argue with but she laughed and said she is ready. I have gained five pounds and everyone says it becomes me. I looked in the mirror the other day and I saw that my hair is long enough for a clip. Hadassah gave me one of hers that is silver and has the Hebrew word for female on it. Isn't that a terrific present? Love, Sarai.

* * *

DEAR MRS. JOHNSON, I am taking the liberty
of writing to you for the sake of our children. I
have received a letter from a Rabbi Israel Goldstein from the
Yeshiva Heiram in Jerusalem that my son may marry your
daughter. As of now the young people have not met. My
wife and I are convinced that this marriage, arranged by the
people I consider the captors of my son, will be a further
entanglement, will make escape so much more difficult and
will aid the entire brainwashing process that my son is
undergoing, which has changed him from an average American boy into a religious fanatic who has sworn an oath of
citizenship to a nonexistent ancient Israel whose traditions
seem (like the tentacles of an octopus) to have wrapped
themselves firmly around his throat. Do you share my
sentiments? Can we collaborate on a plan to redeem or
reclaim our own flesh and blood from the zealots who have
imprisoned them?

My wife and I are professional people without vast
resources in the bank, but we are prepared to go to any
expense to reach Michael and bring him home. Michael
played the flute in his high school chamber music group. He
loved the Tigers and the Indians and he liked cars and had
the usual nasty magazines hidden under his bed. His mother
and I can't imagine why he has turned against us. We have
always had a good marriage, no more arguing than most.
We wanted the best for our boys. My parents were religious
people, but Michael hardly knew them, as we moved away
from Montreal before Michael was born. We belong to a
country club in our suburb, but we are not boring consumers
of the latest high-tech products. (Michael's letters are so full
of such accusations that I've taken to defending myself in
my sleep.) I am a pediatrician at Jewish Memorial Hospital.
I have a private practice near our home and have spent two

days a week for the last fifteen years in a clinic for diabetic children in downtown Cleveland. I once had ambitions of doing research on the side, but as it turned out I wasn't meant to be an Arrowsmith. It was in my mind, I admit, that one of my boys should go into the laboratory and find a new gene, a new splice, that might open the way for others. But I never forced them into medical school. I never made them feel that I wouldn't be behind them if they chose other careers. I knew it wouldn't work unless they loved it, wanted it themselves. I did not push them beyond telling them that I always wanted them to do their best, that being second or third in your class was all right if you couldn't do better. I wanted them to be competitors. It's not easy to get into medical school and I didn't want them to be disappointed, to start out life failing. I didn't want to be disappointed myself. My wife, whose younger sister was deaf, is a teacher of the deaf. She has worked with kindergarten-age children at the Cleveland Institute for the Deaf ever since our boys entered grade school. Yes, I have been very busy and spent less time with the boys as they were growing up than I would have wanted. Sometimes I had to leave in the middle of a birthday party, a soccer game, and there were one or two school plays I never got to at all, but I was aware of my sons all the time. I wanted them to have an easier time than I had, more fun, less fear. Now Michael has no fun and wastes his time in chasing the words of rabbis around the margins of the page. Michael writes that we never taught him right from wrong, that we never gave him a reason for caring about others, a reason to care for himself. My wife and I have spent long nights going over everything, everything we can remember. We think Michael is talking about stereotypes, a cardboard mommy and a cardboard daddy that they have forced on him at the yeshiva, not about us, his flesh-and-blood parents. We know that our boys learned decent democratic caring attitudes at our table. We taught them to care for minorities. We always spoke of the need to make this country better, to increase

opportunities for the disadvantaged. On several occasions I
took Michael and his brother with me to the clinic, where
they saw me holding black babies and explaining things to
mothers who hadn't graduated junior high. My wife talked
about the children she worked with and how they struggled
for every small academic achievement and how proud she
was when they moved forward and when she could see the
results of her work. My wife took several courses at the
museum in art history and we went, when Michael was
between his junior and senior years, to Florence and Rome
and my wife was able to tell us about all the paintings and
sculpture. She is not, as Michael has said, a frivolous
woman whose days are like a shadow and who will return to
dust. Michael was cherished, nurtured. We do not understand his revulsion at what he calls our "secular sickness."
He thinks we are very ill and in need of spiritual therapy.
We think he must be rescued from this folly. When a son
says to a father, "Everything you are and have done means
nothing to me, I want none of it; I choose to live 4,000
miles away from you, obeying the laws of a land so arcane
that most all of its descendants have broken away," such a
father cannot help but feel stabbed in the back by his own. It
has given me high blood pressure. My wife cries at every
commercial on TV that shows a baby or a puppy. We feel
mocked and helpless. I write this to you because I am
hoping that you too are in this state and that we can
collaborate on a plan. I am aware that it is a strange thing
for me to speak so openly to a stranger in another city who
has never met my family, but we are suffering and my
friends look away when we speak of it. Gloria says even her
best girlfriend, the one who took the art history courses with
her, doesn't want to hear any more about it, and I am taking
care of new mothers nursing their new babies every day. I
weigh them and give them their shots and tell the mothers
how to nurse and when not to worry, and all the time I am
ashamed because I know nothing about children . . . being a

pediatrician all these years has taught me little. Hope to hear from you soon, Arnold Rose.

A FRIEND, a fellow sufferer, a victim of a child's caprice—at first reading I felt pleased. These parents sounded so normal, so apple pie, mainstream, middle class nice that I felt in good company. It was a childish relief, as if I were standing on the deck of the *Titanic*, pleased to be going down with the likes of the Strausses. I felt like a syphilis patient who blushes with pleasure on catching a glimpse of the local viscount leaving the clinic by the side door.

But on second reading I grew suspicious. This boy could not have turned from all-American stars and stripes into a frum, davening, bearded, cloaked young man who was studying Talmud and Jewish history in the old city of Jerusalem without some reason, some discontent that had driven him, some demon he was fleeing, some incident that sent him out upon his quest. It was possible that these parents were not being altogether honest with me. The plan to kidnap, to reclaim, to debrainwash seemed like a General Motors scheme to keep the Toyotas from coming ashore; a plan that would not only fall on deaf ears, but would deafen ears. I wrote back a cautious letter; after all, the children had not even met yet and marriage plans might be discarded. This could just be talk to alarm the folks at home. Wait, I said, and in the meantime please write me and tell me more about your son and why you think he may have wandered into this historical cul-de-sac. At night I pictured the faces of Dr. and Mrs. Arnold Rose. I pictured their living room with a Matisse above the fireplace and the Book of the Month Club selection on the coffee table. I saw Dr. Rose at his clinic, bending over a black baby with scabs on his body, and I liked his eyes; the way I imagined him, his son had no right to spurn him.

It is hard to believe, I wrote to the Roses, that our children have been brainwashed. The yeshiva is in the middle of Jerusalem. The children are free to go and come. They see the secular normal life of the city around them. Rabbi Cohen has invited me to visit and to talk with Andrea. There is no element of coercion that I can detect. The truth, harder for us to accept, is that our children are at this moment satisfied to stay in a place that asks voluntary restraint in so many areas of life. My daughter, I must admit, has found a refuge, a shelter from the streets. She is not being held a prisoner. She is willingly shrinking herself to fit into someone else's box. But that is another matter. I too am deeply upset. Let us write to each other. Your letter brought me comfort. Annie Johnson.

I called my friend Louise, an expert in Asian art, the only one of my friends who could read Sanskrit and had spent several months in Tibet looking for both scholarly illumination and eternal truth. She had divorced her husband, a portly man with an interest in acid rain and dioxin-soaked soil, when our children were still in nursery school together. "Louise," I said, "I have something to tell you that I don't want shared. Andrea is now in a yeshiva in Jerusalem and thinking of marrying a fellow student and living forever under a shawl, arms covered, eyes down, pious and pregnant."

"Oh, God," said Louise, "how did that happen?"

"I'm not sure what to do," I said. "I feel like someone has handed me a ransom note and I don't have the money to redeem even the cold body."

"What does she say?" said Louise.

"She says she's happy. She says she feels peaceful, no drugs, only scrubbing the floors."

"Doesn't sound so bad," Louise said.

"She's changed her name to Sarai. She does all that nonsense with the kosher and superkosher and she prays three times a day and she learns a little Talmud and some holiday preparations and she peeks at boys in the courtyard.''

"It doesn't sound evil," said Louise.

"Is that all we wanted?" I asked. "That they shouldn't be evil?"

Long ago Louise and I had sat next to each other in the shoe store, and in the long wait for a salesperson, while the children tore through the aisles, climbing over the seats, we talked of our plans for their adulthood—education, of course, but dedication to a cause also, beauty and comfort, but concern for others and love of music and books, and Louise wanted her son to have a working acquaintance with the Orient and a love of travel and the capacity for sexual pleasure and decent affection, and then we confessed to each other that we wanted our children to cast a small shadow over the planet, maybe build houses or design new methods of production or improve our health-care delivery system. We wanted them to change the order of things, to fight it and improve it. By the time the shoe salesman arrived to wait on us we had tagged the future and felt confident we knew its contents. We wanted children who would take up our work and carry it further. It seemed a simple, modest ambition.

"And Jackie?" I asked.

"Jack," sighed Louise, "is at Goldman Sachs selling tax shelters to corporate entities."

"I don't believe it," I said. "He was such a sensitive child. He wrote poetry on his pajamas in ink and wept for three days when you threw his goldfish down the toilet bowl. Remember when we took the kids to Chinatown and we passed all those winos sleeping in the alleys and he wanted us to call a doctor for each one?"

"I remember," said Louise, "but it just didn't work out that way. The zombies got him. He has an insurance plan now."

"Louise," I asked, "did we do everything wrong?"

"I don't know," she said. "I think it's more as if we were sitting on the beach having a picnic, opening peanut-butter-and-jelly sandwiches and pouring iced tea from a Thermos when a tidal wave came and washed our children out to sea.''

"If that is so," I asked, "how come we weren't swept away too?''

"We probably were," she answered.

Perhaps the Roses are right and the children have been kidnapped by bandits and pirates as in the old tales, and perhaps we can go and find them and bring them home and start again. I felt hopeful. It should be possible to rescue a child who had slipped under bad influences. Andrea was young and she had strength and unexpected vitality. It wasn't over yet.

ONE AFTERNOON my mother was playing canasta at her usual weekly game when her cigarette burned down right through her fingertips. She was concentrating on her cards and might have ignored the cigarette, whose ashes were wantonly spilling on the green cloth that covered the table. But when the burning tip reached her skin and she didn't flinch, her partner screamed out. They finished the game, the four ladies in pearl earrings, gold chains and stockings with seams that ran straight up the back of their legs, but then as they counted out the money they fell silent, each thinking about the shortness of time, the taste and smell of future autumns, their desires and ambitions that were yet unsatisfied. They left without comment but with the conviction that no canasta game lasts forever.

My mother lay in bed in those last days with her gray hair showing at the roots, with the paint on her fingernails redone each day by a nurse who told charming stories of Irish children looking for seashells along the rocky northern coast. Soon my mother had a convulsion, signaling the robust health of the tumor in her brain, and she lost the ability to speak. Her left arm hung from her shoulder like a dream that chases you into the day. I sat by her side, not loving but dreading—not so much the ordeal of loss, but the nasty details, the humiliations of incapacity and the proof before me that mind was nothing without body and body had the capacity to kill the resident soul. Everyone knows this, of course, but to see it is to realize that death, unlike its poet advocates, is not concerned with beauty, form, rhyme or reason.

My mother had been afraid to leap into the large world on her own. She read mystery stories and did crossword puzzles and waited for someone to love her. She dreamed of her psychiatrist, Dr. Levin, but her dreams were interpreted, not fulfilled. Those last weeks when she lay on her embroidered pillow in her pale blue silk nightgown with lace sleeves I thought of her as a chameleon, taking on the colors of death because it was safer than living.

I had no idea how many times in the following years I would miss her, how her stained, smudged face would grow so dear to me that I could hardly hold it in my memory. I intended my fate to be quite different from hers. I would not be a pigeon in a coop. The entire universe was to be mine and I would wait for no one to give me permission. As she lay on her bed she looked in my face with such cold eyes. Go on, live, they seemed to be saying, but you're running in place, you're spending yourself in useless effort, nothing is worth it, you won't succeed in leaving me behind. A lifetime of sour tastes rose in her mouth as she looked at me. She was not sentimental about the next generation. She did not feel she had to curse me. "I'm here with you, Mother," I said, but she turned away from me. She did not think I had a chance or she begrudged me whatever chance I had, I wasn't sure which.

* * *

DEAR MOTHER, I have copied out a psalm of David's for you. "The Lord is my light and my help. Whom shall I fear? The Lord is the strength of my life. Whom shall I dread? When evildoers draw near to devour me, when foes threaten, they stumble and fall. Though armies be arrayed against me, I have no fear. Though wars threaten, I remain steadfast in my faith."

Isn't that beautiful? We studied that psalm last night and Rabbi Cohen says it means that our souls are safe for the world to come even if harm should befall our bodies in this time. I know you have never prayed because you don't think that Gd will answer or that He hears or that He cares, but it is your ears that are stopped up, your heart that has turned to stone and your voice that is mute. He is waiting.

Sometimes in the early morning when the cypress trees on the Mount of Olives are just silhouettes in the haze of dawn I think of you and I want you to be here with me, in my room. I have so many things to apologize to you for; not only the rude words, but so often I must have frightened you. I know how much you wanted me to go to college but I just couldn't see the why of it or of anything. Dr. Wolfert said that I was angry all the time but mostly I felt scared and confused and I didn't want anyone to know I felt scared. Here the fright has dwindled. Now it only comes occasionally; if I am left alone too long or I see an American girl like I used to be in the street holding on to a boy, I get a wave of remembering and mostly I remember you. Are you still angry with me? Have I disappointed you or will you come and see me and be proud of all I have accomplished? Love, Sarai.

* * *

OUR MYTHOLOGY tells us so much about fathers and sons. We know that Chronus nearly devoured Zeus and Zeus in turn beheaded his father. We know that Abraham nearly sacrificed Isaac for his Lord but the ram appeared in the thicket just in time to allow civilization to continue. We know that God placed His only son on a wooden cross on a high hill and watched him suffer. We know that Aeneas carried his father on his back out of the burning ashes of Troy and Henry V snatched up his father's crown prematurely and Hamlet sought vengeance in his father's name. We know that struggles between fathers and sons involve sacrifice, hidden and open jealousy, revenge, punishment, the grasp of power, the fear of the waning generation for its own meager future. We know that the kindness of son for father can disappear in a wave of trickery as birthrights are exchanged for a mess of pottage. We know that the fathers are not to be trusted, either, and if God is our father, His behavior to His sons is not unexpected. We know that a little child shall lead them, but he must pay for his father's favor. We know that the sons of Noah covered their father's nakedness, but one son laughed at him and was drummed out of the clan forever. We know that the temptation to mock the father exists. We know that elder statesmen are always sacrificing their young sons on battlefields, but often old soldiers fade away in ignominy and disgrace because their sons cannot be bothered to carry them on their backs. We know that Oedipus took what had belonged to his father and we know that every little boy covets what may not be his and out of that coveting rise strange fantasies: fears of vacuum cleaners and goblins who may seek revenge on behalf of the wronged father. It is a grand human drama but only half the tale.

What do we know about mothers and daughters? If there

is a recurring myth of matricide and usurped power, who tells that story? If mothers and daughters form a unit that crackles and splits and sends particles out into the universe, particles of hate, revenge and passion, where do we hear it? Mothers are not afraid of their daughters (except for the wicked queen in "Snow White"). Our power is so oblique, so hidden, so ethereal a matter, that we rarely struggle with our daughters over actual kingdoms or corporate shares. On the other hand, our attractiveness dries as theirs blooms, our journey shortens just as theirs begins. We too must be afraid and awed and amazed that we cannot live forever and that our replacements are eager for their turn, indifferent to our wishes, ready to leave us behind. For women too it must be a struggle to honor, to love, to respect, not to fear, not to be cruel, not to exercise too much power when you have it, to accept its loss with grace. To maintain affection while dying is as complicated for women as for men. The daughter cannot help having this urge to get on with it, to get away, to pull apart and fly off, leaving the decaying old lady on the ground where she is free to crawl after his disappearing child, dragging herself along with longing, hope, unsatisfied tenderness. Mother and daughter tales are not apt to have bloody sacrifices at apex. They will be about minor acts of treason, a tablecloth burned accidentally, a recipe given without its crucial ingredient, a desertion to another city, to another country, to another group, a sticking out of the tongue, a teasing good-bye poke; a daughter whose mother was the chairperson of the local chapter of Planned Parenthood has eight children, the daughter of an opera buff plays the drums, the daughter of a horsewoman in Connecticut raises miniature poodles in a penthouse apartment in Hong Kong. Between mother and daughter the affair is fraught with small needles, little pinpricks, an occasional bloodletting, a wrenching away from exactly the unity that was once so desired, so needed, so always imperfect. As the mother withers, her need for her daughter mounts. She pours herself into her child. Each triumph, each flash of beauty, each step in the wider world is enjoyed as if it were one's own. But exactly this stickiness, this glueing of completeness onto incompleteness, drives the daughter to secrecy, to abandonment, to a ferocious fight for her own skin, her own destiny. If she succeeds in shaking off her mother, she will remain a glorious self—but only briefly, just until the moment she forgets what she has learned and gives birth herself to a daughter who will call her in the night, press hot skin against hers and frighten her with myriad misfortunes, and as it started so it repeats with daughter racing toward freedom and mother running behind, "Wait, wait, tell me what is happening, speak to me, darling, don't you remember when I was the ocean and you were the fish, when I was the night and you were the moon?"

Persephone had to die in order to escape Ceres. She married the King of the Underworld and all the earth turned brown with Ceres' grief. But was Persephone sad or was she gloating in her palace on the dark side of the river? Is death or life a matter of point of view? Was Ceres the first grasping mother whose daughter was willing to leap even into oblivion to remove the annoyance of a parent who rejoiced too much in her presence?

If God had come to Sarah and asked her to take her daughter to the mountaintop and tie her to a rock and slit her throat because God commanded it, there would have been no chosen people. The Jews would have wandered, nomads in the desert without the law, dancing before golden calves, idling through the centuries indistinguishable from their neighbors. No mother would give back her daughter, which may be the explanation for patriarchy. But on the other hand, if God were a woman would She ever have considered giving Her children free will, would She not have created a more harmonious, closer, loving family in which one small bite of an apple could be forgiven and the gates of Eden be sealed so that exit was impossible?

Precisely because Sarah could not, even for the Deity, even for the welfare of all humanity, sacrifice her daughter (the daughter she didn't have because if a miracle is to be a real miracle it shouldn't produce a second-class baby), our mythology about mothers and daughters is thin and low on plot. There is a reason why the Ten Commandments have placed so prominently the words, "Honor thy father and thy mother." It is clear that no one, naturally, easily, without the force of law, wants to honor their father and mother. Dishonor to the elders is the natural human inclination.

I don't understand this clearly, but I am thinking about Andrea and missing the flush of her skin, the way her legs move across the room, the way her eyes glare at me, and sometimes she makes me laugh. I will have to see her, the new her, the one that I do not know. I will have to follow her since she will not come home to me.

DEAR MOTHER, Today has been a very difficult day for me. I went this morning after our prayers to buy some bolts of cloth that Mrs. Cohen is going to sew into skirts for us. Hadassah was with me and when we came to the corner we saw a group of Americans sitting on the grass on the hospital lawn. One was playing "As Tears Go By." I began humming with him and then I sat down on the grass and someone offered me a smoke and my hand reached out for it. Hadassah called to me and came and led me away. But I was sweating all over and I stained my white blouse through. The girls on the grass looked so carefree. Their bodies were flopped all over and one had her head in a boy's lap and the boy's fingers were playing with her nipples even though they were right out in plain daylight. I had such a longing to join them. I wanted to hear my old music and when we came back from the store carrying the heavy bags of material and the group was gone from the corner I looked for them up and down and made Hadassah take several detours just in case we might find them again. I felt so confused and frightened. Later in Hebrew class I wouldn't listen. I didn't want to learn another foreign word. I wanted to be by myself. I remembered so many things about before I came here. While we were fixing lunch and afterwards while we were saying prayers after the meal, my mind kept wandering back to certain things, mostly that happened in the early hours of the morning that you don't want to know about but made me feel good and I wanted to go out in the streets and go somewhere without rules and prayers and a right and wrong about every little thing. We were sitting around the table in the big kitchen and the windows were open but I still felt as if it were unbearably hot and I needed air. Hadassah came and sat next to me very quietly. She didn't say anything but she put her hand on mine. Mrs. Cohen sat down opposite me and asked me to tell her what I was feeling. She has a way of looking into your face that makes evasion impossible. I felt as if her eyes were holding my entire body together. I tried to tell her about the group on the grass and the Stones and the nights that I was remembering. I kept thinking, She won't understand this at all. It has nothing to do with her world. But she did. She said that all my feelings were natural and even healthy. She said that I was right to remember the things I had known before and to care about them. She said that people could not cut themselves off from their past in a sudden swoop without mutilating themselves. She said that the secular world with all its noise and variety, with all its color and movement, was a part of me forever. But that now I had learned that there was a better way, a way that belonged to our shared past, that stepped around the cruelties and emptiness of the new. She said that all the bright and shiny things in my former life had brought no happiness, no purpose, and each adventure had further torn me into little pieces because I had no sanctuary, no real home. In Jerusalem and the yeshiva I have a home, and the loss of the music is nothing compared to the finding of a path, a connection to my people and my Gd. As she spoke I felt so relieved, so happy, so cradled by her words and yet so strong myself. We went on to class, where we are studying the Ethics of the Fathers, which incidentally you would find very interesting. And then the most surprising event: that night after supper when I was putting away the prayer books Rabbi Cohen came into the room and he gave me a shopping bag and told me to open it. Inside was a tape of a Rolling Stones album. We have a cassette player in the yeshiva that we use for Hebrew language lessons. Rabbi Cohen said that I can listen to the music as often as I want although he expects it will grow increasingly meaningless, unnecessary, to me. He said that as long as I am hungry for old sounds I should allow myself to listen and remember. "Remember it all," he said. I think he is the wisest, kindest man in the world. He wants me to find my own truth. He says he is here to support and encourage, to show the way, not to punish or push. It frightens me to think that I might have run away and lost all I have found, undo all I have done and be again a piece of dust floating on whatever winds are blowing. If I am lucky, Mother, I will be able to stay here forever. However, there has been no further word on my marriage. I am afraid that everything that happened today will make the delay longer. They want me to be strong enough to take care of myself. Love, Sarai.

A FRIEND invites me to dinner with a second attaché at the Israeli consulate in New York. I ask him about the Bratslav Hasidum. Unlike other Hasidic groups, who have passed on the leadership of their community from father to son, from generation to generation, the followers of Rabbi Nachman have taken no other rabbi for their leader. They took his mahogany chair apart and carried it piece by piece to Jerusalem, where master craftsmen seamlessly placed it back together and where it sits today with empty presence. There the men sing on Shabbat with such fervor that many secular Israelis find their way through the back streets of the old city to a small courtyard where, leaning against the stones, seated on the curbs, they can listen to a sound that falls between a wail and a croon, a lullaby and a love song, wing-tipped with the erotic but never more than a half tone away from the grief that resides at the bottom of each Jewish Pandora's box. Their song is formed of melodies begun in long-ago Poland and transported across the Mediterranean in the throats of men who refused emancipation, refused the value of things that run by electricity, send pictures through the air and confuse the mind with alternatives to God, Who is waiting only for the pious to build ladders up to the rear entrance of the Garden of Eden so the rips and tears in the skein of the holy will be repaired and the earth and all its unruly, weird, despairing creatures be redeemed.

They are still singing in the Bratslav shul and even dancing with each other, eyes bright, cheeks rosy, sweat pouring from under their black hats. They did not replace Rabbi Nachman because they expected a shorter interval between his death and the coming of the Messiah. The longer they wait the more they insist, otherwise they might consider that they have been mistaken, foolish, betrayed by their prayers. Their voices grow more beautiful, their melodies reach higher each year. It is a question whether God has reached down into their larynxes or whether they have extended themselves beyond limit in their effort to avoid doubt.

The second attaché says that the Bratslav followers are fossils, antiques, good for the tourist trade but for nothing else. "The land," he says, "was won by soldiers and farmers, by socialists and carpenters, and men who could fly fighter planes. The ostriches who stick their heads in the eighteenth century and think they won't be seen are a blight on our cities, a drain on our economy. They would turn Israel into a museum and once again we would be like the temple kids, the two that were chosen each Yom Kippur, one for sacrifice for God and the other to be driven out into the wilderness. If it were up to those frummer-than-thous, we would be both goats once again."

The second attaché has a round-faced wife, who stares at me across the table. "Don't worry," I want to say to her, "I am not flirting with your husband. I am listening to him." After dinner the wife says she is not feeling well and they leave the party early.

Again I have dreamed about Rabbi Nachman. This time I dream I am sitting at my desk writing a book about Rabbi Nachman. I am explaining why his form of religious fanaticism depends on the repression of sexual feelings and as a consequence is rife with fear of the woman and her erotic power. This fear turns into dislike, and the rabbis who gather around Rabbi Nachman share his definition of piety as a turning away from the earthly, the sexual, the natural communion of man and women. Torah is everything and women, like donkeys and rabbits in the forest, cannot know Torah.

A hand appears on my typewriter. It lies across my keys. I stare at the hand, old and veined, blue and transparent. I look up at the man standing by my side. He is young and even handsome. He has a black hat on his head but he wears it tipped back at a rakish angle, like Humphrey Bogart playing Sam Spade. "Were you writing," he says, "when your child needed you?"

I ignore him. "Please remove your hand," I ask, "so I can continue to work."

"Do you submit to no law outside of your own making?" he asks.

"I share," I say, "the usual ethical beliefs of most decent people the globe over."

He laughs. He is extraordinarily like Humphrey Bogart when he laughs, a man who smiles but keeps on hurting, whose hurt you can't help but want to soothe. "You mean," he says, "that you have seen an ethical belief: you could actually prove to me on paper that one exists? Are you saying that the ethical beliefs of most people on this calamity of a land rose up into an army of beliefs that overran the Storm Troopers in their barracks as they slept and gave them bad dreams?"

"Go away," I say. He stands there. "I will take off my blouse and offend you with the forbidden sight of my breasts," I shout at him.

"I think you're too old to offend me or tempt me," he says without blushing, looking away, or changing his pedantic tone. "Now explain to me," he says, "how can there be ethics without Gd?"

"No," I answer. "You explain to me how God was able to sleep in the Warsaw ghetto."

There is a pause and I look down at my typewriter; when I look up again Rabbi Nachman has shrunk into a child. His face is that of a young boy of eight or nine. He leans his head down into my lap. His black hat falls off and his suit seems absurdly large for his frail body. "Take care of me," he whimpers.

I wake up. My bedsheets are rumpled and soaking wet. I can hear my own heart beating or, if not quite beating, fluttering as if it were a butterfly caught in the lepidopterist's net. I get up and look out over the Hudson River and see the lights of the new buildings in New Jersey, standing there glittering, like Broadway stars waiting for applause at the end of the show. The river is moving toward the harbor but I cannot find its motion. It seems still, like a pavement or an empty highway.

I wish that Andrea had heard the call of Mick Jagger and come home. I think about the Stones. I could never clearly understand their lyrics, a generational deafness or dumbness that couldn't be overcome by mere listening. The sound was angry and certainly something was wrong but I had not grasped what the specific complaints were. Were they mine as well? I wasn't sure.

DEAR SARAI, I have had word of your possible marriage and have received a concerned letter from the father of a boy at the yeshiva. I can't really defend the marriage habits of the modern world. I accept romantic love as a clumsy performer, prone to pratfalls and other accidents. My own marriage to your father was an example of miscues, misreadings, misfortune. I have never been a believer in marriage as the Happy Ending, the Ever After to crown all Ever Afters, the way out, the salvation of either man or woman. I demonstrated clearly that the spinster ladies of New England lived longer, healthier, happier lives than their more respectable and fertile sisters. But an arranged marriage strains credulity. I still believe in the possibility of love, of attraction, of choice, of free choice in a world of many options. I want you to be brave enough to attach yourself, if you must attach yourself, to someone who fascinates, absorbs, demands your attention. I don't want you to marry because others deem it, or others will accept you, or the world works that way. How is it possible that a daughter of mine could have become such a feudal maiden? The advantage of our century is that you matter and the inner linings of your mind, the peculiarities of your taste and desire, are all counted as important and worthy of attention. The present may offer divorce at the same rate it sells hamburgers, but the past? In the past happiness was a word reserved for fairy tales. Individual private happiness, sexual pleasure, affection, interest, were all beside the point. What a sad and dreary existence you are rushing toward. I caution you to consider that any marriage requires a spark, an eternal light, if you will, of its own. Real life makes such harsh demands, it bores, it wears, it frightens, it rubs against the soul in such an abrasive way that each of us would like a partner who may enfold us into secret places, into sheltered corners, into an oasis of affection. Without that nothing will work. I find it hard to believe that a group of people who hardly know you, the Andrea you, can select a mate and that that mate could provide more than a surface compatibility. What if you wake up several months after the wedding and discover that you two do not really like each other? What if he has weaknesses that were not at first apparent: a fear of the dark, a dislike of his body, a terrible temper, a nervous way of playing with his eyelashes that drives you crazy? What if he wets the bed or demands that his socks be perfectly matched? What if you find him boring or stupid or without charm?

When you were first placed in my arms I thought I didn't want you ever to marry. I wanted you to be free and independent. But then I changed my mind and I had hopes for your marriage, one that would improve on mine. I did not have images of long white gowns and little boys in velvet pants bearing rings. But I did want you to be braver, more equal, less fuzzy, wiser and more content than I. You are entitled to do as you please, but remember your life affects mine, is a reflection of mine, and you cannot forget me as if I were a best friend suddenly on the outs with the larger group in the playground. Please remember that I am still here demanding that you have the strength to be yourself, to make your own choices, to love or not love without the laws of the community sanctifying what I believe can only be sanctified by the day-in and day-out bruising of two people who have dared to risk something of themselves in creating a family. I don't think you are old enough or mature enough or independent enough to join with someone else. Wait. I feel you are in quicksand over there. Don't be in such a hurry to sink. Why don't you call me collect on the telephone and we can talk this over? Love, M.

I KNOW I haven't an argument that any child would respect. The variety and choice of mates dizzies and confuses, and every one of us is pulled toward a choice that repeats the patterns of the past, re-creating the pains of childhood, now with an adult face. I know that family life in America is a minefield, an economic trap for women, a study in disappointment for both sexes. But still, what are we if we give up the power of choice, the erotic pursuit of pleasure that is supposed to lead us home? Won't we diminish ourselves to the status of mere communal animals, like the ants whose endeavors do not require separate faces or histories, like schools of fish whose mating frenzies take place at appointed times at an instinctively agreed-upon depth of ocean above a particular coral reef whose election remains uncontested through the aeons? Is this problem we have with romantic love not the sign of our human aspiration, our badge of honor worn on our unique and distinctive bodies and sustained in our higher cortex as proof that we are not so many jellyfish pulsating in the outgoing tide?

I don't know anymore how families should be. In the early days of the movement we thought we could do without them. Then we created a model of equality that left the children waiting at the window for someone to come home. Then we floundered and demanded day care and deprived women who wanted to watch their two-year-olds pound pegs into holes of their earnest desire. We woke up to discover that our goal of equality had created a generation of gray flannel suits who played tennis to win and could tell you all about IRAs and CDs and nothing about Winken, Blinken and Nod. Now I am exhausted, a secret I am not yet willing to tell my friends and colleagues.

WHEN I WAS a child we had a maid named Bella who lived in the maid's room behind the kitchen. It was a room big enough for only a bed and a small chest of drawers. There was a sink in the room itself and its small window opened onto a brick wall. On the closet door someone had left a framed picture of Jesus hanging politely from his cross. Bella came one January afternoon to replace the maid named Ina, who had saved up enough money to go back to Ireland and marry her child-hood sweetheart. Bella wore high black shoes with laces and her long, thin, bony face was surrounded by wisps of brown hair that hung limply around her face.

Bella was not interested in my goodwill. "You are in the way," she said to me whenever I approached. "Get out of the kitchen," she said to me if I opened the door and looked in.

I missed Ina, who had taken me into her room and shown me the pictures of her mother and six brothers and sisters and the sweetheart who eventually took her away. On Saturday nights Ina would let me sit on the edge of her bed and listen to "Dr. Christian" with her on the radio.

Bella came from a coal-mining town in Pennsylvania and her father had died in a mine accident and that is why she looked so forlorn, said my mother, who told me that I was imagining that Bella was staring at me from behind doors kept slightly ajar. Bella cleaned very well. She wiped handles and all kinds of knobs several times before she would touch them and she would cross herself constantly while scrubbing a bathtub, and once I saw her on her knees praying by the window in our living room. Her skin looked as if it were covered with cobwebs and she was always scratching at her face with her hands. Sometimes she had bleeding sores on her cheeks and across her chin. At night when it was dark in my room I thought about the mine accident and how it would be if your father were caught in the tunnels and the gas was leaking out the cracks and up above the earth looked normal with bushes and flowers and little houses with white picket fences and underneath he was gasping and clutching at the crumbling walls.

Bella began to mutter things under her breath as she went about her work. She would clean the same spot on the floor over and over again. She began to wring out her hands as if they were wet towels. I would see her bringing my mother her breakfast tray and she would be biting her lips and looking over her shoulder as if someone were following her. One day she caught me looking at her and she screamed out, "It is not true. I am not pregnant. It is a lie they made up to get me fired."

Soon she told my mother she was not pregnant, that the back elevator man and the handyman and the front elevator man had been talking about it, but she was not pregnant. Then she said the night elevator operator who took down the garbage was spreading rumors about her through the building.

"What kind of rumors?" I asked my mother.

"Not nice things," said my mother, who did not believe in revealing her cards until forced.

Bella wore the black-and-white maid's uniform that all our maids had worn, but on her it took on a new quality. It sagged and sank almost to the top of her strange high black shoes. It seemed stained with sweat and smelled of ammonia. Bella served me breakfast before I went to school. The pantry door would open. She would swoop in with my cereal and her eyes would search each corner of the room.

"No one's here but me," I would say.

"You haven't paid for my opinions," she would say. "My opinions are my own business."

She made my mother put an extra bolted lock on the back door because she was certain the night elevator operator was planning an attack. "It is not as easy," said my mother, "to get good live-in help as it used to be."

Then one Thursday my mother had her usual canasta game and the den was filled with smoke and the click of long nails on new decks of cards echoed into the kitchen. The ladies had iced tea and cookies and then as the hour reached four o'clock they began to drink Scotch and sodas and their voices got louder and louder. My mother kept careful score of the winnings on a clipboard with a picture of a barking red-and-white-checked poodle at the top. They settled up and money exchanged hands. They kissed good-bye at the front door. My mother went into her bedroom to lie down after her long and exhausting afternoon and there in her bed was Bella. She had put on my mother's blue silk bed jacket over her uniform and on the floor by the dust ruffle the high black shoes were neatly placed.

"I think," said my mother, "perhaps this job is not the right one for you. Let me write out a check for two weeks' salary and of course I'll give you a fine letter of recommendation."

Bella sat up in the bed and stared as if she were looking all the way to the Rocky Mountains. "They said you'd say that, but I'm not leaving. You gotta prove this bed is yours, not mine."

My mother looked frightened. Her nose turned red and her eyes filled up with tears. "You are my maid," she said.

"I fire you," said Bella, "and your girl too. They declared you don't get anything anymore."

"Who are they?" I asked, standing a good distance across the threshold of the door.

Bella smiled a secret smile like a person who knows that a truck is turning the corner and is going to run you over in the next five minutes.

My mother closed the door to her bedroom. My father was away on a business trip. Her sister told her to call the police. The police told her to give the woman till the next morning to leave and if she hadn't packed and gone they would come. My mother said she wouldn't stay in the house with Bella lying in her bed with the pink satin coverlet with the monogrammed initials at the center. Her sister said she had to stay so Bella couldn't steal the silver and the jewelry. So my mother took all the knives from the kitchen—the carving knives and the cutting knives and the service for eighteen with the fleur-de-lis pattern—and she went into my room and together we lay down on my bed and waited the night out for the policeman to come or Bella to leave. At first my mother was crying. I was hungry, but she wouldn't let me go into the kitchen to get anything to eat. There was a deck of cards in my room and we played gin rummy and she taught me hearts and when I got tired of cards she played solitaire alone and then she played hangman with me and a game where you see who can make the most small words out of large words and I was drowsy with pleasure in these unusual circumstances that had brought her to spend so much time in my room with me. Only when I looked at the pile of sharp knives at the end of the bed did I remember to be frightened.

In the morning my mother, rumpled in her dress, makeup streaked across her face and smears of lipstick left on my pillowcase, went to check on Bella, who was still in the bed, now singing hymns about eternal grace. The police arrived just as I was leaving for school. Bella was gone by the time I came home and a new maid was living in the maid's room.

Several months later we got a postcard from a hospital in the middle of the East River. The front was a picture of the Statue of Liberty and on the back was scrawled this message: "They have stolen my body. Help me get it back." Two years later we got another postcard. This message said, "I cannot leave this hospital because they won't return my body. Get me a lawyer."

I thought of Bella the last time I went down to the Western Union office to wire Andrea some money. Some in the line waiting to receive money were wiping runny noses, talking to unseen companions, banging fists against the walls. One woman was holding her hands to her ears to block out the sound that was coming from within her head. They were waiting in line for money from some relative, obligated, concerned, helpless to change events, protective or angry, who kept a job, a home, somewhere else. On line I saw an army of the unrooted, a world of people whose minds and bodies had been arbitrarily separated. A young man carried a sleeping bag and he had not shaved for days. He wore a button on his T-shirt. "Do it to them before they do it to you." I thought of Andrea at the waiting end of a line like this one.

"Does she have identification?" the pockmarked man behind the counter asked me without raising his eyes to mine.

Andrea had lost the birth certificate I had given her. Andrea had no driver's license. I had written her Social Security number out for her on a card, but she had lost that months before. "She may not have identification," I said.

"Test question, then?" The man had his pencil poised over my form.

"Mother's name," I said. "Answer?" he asked without inflection, as if everyone's child traveled without identification, and everyone stood in line in small offices with paint chipping off the walls, with graffiti scribbled by harassed customers like Laura from Utah who thought David was a fag and had used a red Magic Marker to record her opinion.

"Annie," I said as he turned toward his computer. An asylum was meant to be a sanctuary, but for the insane there is no asylum.

DEAR MOTHER, I am wearing the new skirt that Mrs. Cohen has made for me. It is very long and full and when I turn around I feel the skirt turning with me. It is dark blue and with it I am wearing a long-sleeved white blouse. I can cross the courtyards in our section and people nod at me and say, "Shalom," and women look at me carefully and sometimes ask Mrs. Cohen about me. I am not so much a stranger here anymore. I can recognize many of the children who live nearby. It is a duty of Jewish women to have many children, not just for Gd and for the Jewish nation, but to replace the millions we lost. You should have had more children to increase our strength but I suppose you didn't think of it that way. Ronite, who came from St. Louis and lived three years at the yeshiva before she married, comes often to visit with us in the afternoon. She has just had a baby and yesterday I held the child. A boy! He stayed in my arms and looked in my face, right into my eyes. My breasts suddenly felt full as if I had milk and I blushed red. Ronite says I will make a good mother and she will help me at first because there are many things to learn about babies that women must teach each other.

A wonderful thing. Last night after dinner as we were saying the final prayers of the day I looked into the window above the table and because of the lights I saw my own reflection. I liked my face. Right away I felt as if I had really been speaking to Gd, as if He had heard my prayer and allowed me to rest, to sit at the table in calmness, and just in that moment I thought everything was good, so good. I know you don't believe that Gd listens to each one of us thanking Him each night after dinner. I don't know if I really believe that, either, but something did happen at the table, that I certainly promise you. Mrs. Cohen says that if you talk to Gd long enough, if you live righteously, if you understand what is important and what is artificial, faddish and valueless, Gd will one day signal you that He has come into your life. I think I have been signaled. It is so amazing. Love, Sarai.

BELLA WAS signaled by God. What else was all that praying about and the crossing and the hymns! And the millions who died in innocent circumstances that Andrea wants to replace, did they not believe, many of them, in a just God who would reward virtue and punish sin? Did they not pray after dinner and in the morning, and did their righteous path prevent the disaster? There on my shelf is the picture of the rabbi of Vilna standing waiting to be shot. His head has been pushed through the wooden Star of David that had once been a decoration for his synagogue. His beard has been torn off and the raw skin is bleeding onto his black coat. Did he believe, after a lifetime of a pure heart, of study and ritual, that God was signaling him? What was God signaling him? Andrea was taught that the heavens were silent but that human responsibility was great and our possibilities wondrous. She sits at a table and thanks God for her food, so short is human memory, so little can we tolerate an empty sky. It seems to me that she is really becoming one of those whose bodies are being held elsewhere.

DEAR DR. ARNOLD ROSE, I write, I am wondering if we did something to our children to cause them to become so frightened of freedom. I am sitting at my desk looking at Riverside Drive and watching the young mothers push their babies in strollers under the trees that are now losing their leaves. Are they doing something wrong that I can't see? Are we all contaminated and passing social diseases on to our children? I am teaching a class of young women, one of whom said to me that oppression is economic and when women control the means of production, then they will be equal. But of course when women run the banks and own the Fortune 500, then men will be oppressed and we won't have equality, either. My student said that would be all right with her. She wears baggy sweaters in dark colors and her sneakers are always untied. I have an impulse to take her home and brush her hair till it shines. Teaching is not a substitute for mothering. I am at least a good teacher even if what I teach is an open-ended question. I believe in nonanswers. I feel safer without answers. Do you feel about Michael's absence as if a bomb had fallen and left a crater in your house?

* * *

LETTER RECEIVED:

Dear Mrs. Johnson, I can take any crying baby and hold it on my shoulder and in seconds the baby's body will relax and fold into mine. I am not the source of pollution for my children and I don't think you are, either. We are both victims of social confusions or maybe genetic weaknesses, or perhaps the world is going mad. Did you see the pictures of all the Iranians with raised fists praising Allah? Some days I think we atheists had better get passports to another planet before they round us up and do us in. I gave a paper at our hospital on diabetics under the age of three and the effects of diet on their illness. The rheumatoid arthritis man, a member of our club, an old golf partner, asked me about Michael. I dropped my charts and avoided the answer. I am not proud of Michael. Thank you for writing me. Arnold Rose.

LETTER RECEIVED:

Dear Mrs. Johnson, My husband tells me that he has begun a correspondence with you about our children. I want you to know that Michael is, was, the most considerate and sensitive child. He learned early what it was to be hurt, probably because his older brother did some natural bullying. He always defended any child who was picked on. He was not peculiar at all and we are totally surprised at the turn of events. I stayed home with the boys for the first six years. I do not think they were neglected. I made them my first priority. I made them Jell-o with marshmallows and took them ice-skating and played a thousand games of Clue and Parchesi. I am not a bad mother. I don't understand why this is happening but I do not want Michael to marry in this

yeshiva because if he does I am afraid he will never get out
and rejoin the real world. I do not want him to be one of
them forever. I am a teacher of the deaf. Perhaps I didn't
hear my own children well enough. Arnold says you are a
woman who will understand irony. I hope so. We need a
friend. Best wishes, Gloria Rose.

DEAR MRS. JOHNSON, I have had further word
from my son that this marriage is under serious
consideration. I feel that we must take immediate action to
prevent it. I have of course no objection to your daughter
and this is in no sense personal, but I am horrified at the
fact that the potential bride and groom have not yet met, that
they did not select each other, that they are virtual prisoners
of a bunch of lunatics who haven't noticed the century they
live in, so busy are they tripping over their own beards. My
wife and I share our sadness with you. This is not a
marriage we could celebrate with pleasure. Here I am, in
my fifty-seventh year of life, as bewildered and angry as I
was at seventeen. It seems unfair.

I am planning to visit my son in a few months' time and
see if I can shake him up and out of there. I have hopes that
when he sees me and his mother he will return to his senses
and ask us, maybe even beg us, to take him back to
Cleveland, where I believe he can begin his life again with
all forgiven and fast forgotten. I will never again imply in
any way that I want him to be a doctor. I will allow him to
find his own path as long as it is here in Cleveland and
doesn't require the support of anyone's orthodoxy. I want
Michael to be a free man. On my way to the hospital the
other day I listened to our local rock station. I really like the
music. It seems honest and its loudness is a sign of vitality.
I would rather he play the drums than worry about spilled
crumbs in his sofa. Michael wrote me that at Passover time

he and his friends crawl all over the house with feathers, removing any microscopic bits of yeast from all the crevices in the rooms. He says this is the physical version of what he is doing with his mind, removing the last bits of secular distraction as he learns more and more how to devote himself to God. Imagine grown men going around on their hands and knees with feathers! Even my grandfather didn't do that, I don't think. If he did, no one ever told me.

I am writing to ask you to protest to your daughter. Protest vigorously to the Yeshiva Rachel. Don't let them think this will be easy. Do not agree or appear to agree to this marriage. Stall them. Don't provide any documentation: proof of Jewishness, birth certificates, etc. My son had lost his passport before entering the yeshiva and I have instructed our embassy not to issue another until they hear from me. A child is not like a lost dog that breaks its leash and disappears into the night. We will pursue. I assume you share these sentiments. One of the pediatricians on the staff here has been very active in raising funds for the Cleveland pro-Israel lobby. He has contacts in Israel and in Washington. He has promised to help us. I will keep you posted.

Gloria took your book on Spinsters of New England out of the Shaker Heights Library. I haven't had time to read it yet, but Gloria says it's a fine piece of work. We both send you our best. Arnold Rose.

I RETURN to Dr. Wolfert, not because he knows something I do not or because I have any hope that his theoretical mysteries can unravel the messages in the bottom of the teacup better than mine, but because I cannot keep to myself any longer. I tell the story to my mirror again and again; each time another detail surfaces, shimmers among the others, and then sinks to the bottom. I look at my face without kindness. I am always surprised by my reflection. I need to talk about Andrea with Dr. Wolfert, who will register it all as follow-up on a patient, not his first or his last. His calm, his distance, will drain the tale of some of its magic, I think. I am considering telling him my dreams about Rabbi Nachman. A therapist should be able to make bad dreams vanish, or do I exaggerate professional skills?

I remember the night soon after Andrea's eighteenth birthday. I had a dinner party and had invited three couples and a professor of Romance languages who had been making subtle overtures to me at faculty meetings but seemed to need some help in bridging the gap between wish and reality. Before the guests arrived Andrea and I had a fight. She had been fired from a job in a supermarket at the checkout counter. I was furious that she had not tried harder. She was furious that I expected her to work at such a dull and demeaning task. She wanted money for her evening out. I was afraid to give it to her because I wanted her to become independent. I told her she was a parasite. She told me I had always hated her. "Not true, not true," I called out as she ran into her room. But as I stood over my veal blanquette, adding the last of the rosemary, hate flushed through my body, heating it up, pulling apart each cell, making me dizzy. It is hell to hate someone you love.

We were sitting around the table. I had just served the veal and poured the wine. The conversation was noisy and my professor, sitting on my right, was complimenting my dress when the phone rang. It was Andrea's friend Michele.

"Andrea has just taken a whole bottle of Benadryl," she told me. "She changed her mind. She doesn't want to die."

I did what had to be done. I explained to my guests that my daughter in another room had just taken some pills and that I would have to take her to the hospital. They were welcome to finish dinner at their leisure. I found Andrea on her bed, conscious but closing her eyes and waving her hands oddly. My professor helped me push her, drag her, to a cab. I thanked him and said good night.

At the emergency room they took her away from me. I sat in a small straight chair and waited. They pumped her stomach. It must have been unpleasant. I hoped it was unpleasant. When at last they let me in to see her she was pale as a ghost. Her hair was matted and her lips were almost blue. I wanted to hug her, to sit down on the floor and rock her in my arms. I wanted to kiss her face. They insisted on keeping her overnight. They had her interviewed by a resident psychiatrist, who asked questions about suicidal ideation, depression, drug and alcohol abuse. Andrea gave him florid descriptions. He had entered the room half-asleep. Now he was wide awake. He suggested follow-up care. She already had a therapist. Dr. Wolfert arrived in the morning just as I did. I waited outside her room for him.

"An adolescent gesture," he said to me. "Not a serious attempt," he added. "Don't worry, hundreds and thousands of adolescent girls make suicidal feints. Only a small percentage of those repeat and succeed."

I am left standing in the hospital hall hoping that Andrea will be among the failures, those who never succeed at their task. "Why?" I asked Dr. Wolfert.

"Does seem stupid, doesn't it?" said Dr. Wolfert.

"What should I do?" I asked.

"Hold on," he said. "Hold on tightly."

"Thanks," I said.

"What could it be?" I asked my friend Elaine, whose son was in a Phoenix House drug rehabilitation program.

She asked me, "Do you think everything you believed must have been wrong? Do you wish you had married a hardware store owner and lived in a small town and joined the PTA like the family in *Happy Days*? Do you see yourself as a despoiler of virgin land, a setter of forest fires, a dumper of toxic wastes into the streams?"

"Yes," I said, "exactly."

"I know," said Elaine.

"But that is not rational," I interrupted.

"You're a newcomer to this nightmare," she said. "After

a while you'll see that rational and reasonable and sensible and proportion are useless words. Welcome to the Dark Ages.''

"Do you remember," I said to Elaine, "how it started? How much we wanted to do better than our parents? Do you remember how we worried over teething and toilet training, the right age to begin reading, the correct moment to have a sleepover; do you remember how we thought our justification, our real justification, for taking up space on this planet lay in our children, in the future we were building?''

"I thought you were always a feminist," Elaine said.

"I was a feminist, I am a feminist, but I believe all that about the children, and the future too. I thought we were changing the world through our children.''

"I remember," said Elaine, "when there were bad girls and good girls and I even knew which one I was."

"Which one?" I asked.

"Who cares?" said Elaine. "It turns out both kinds get their just deserts.''

"You know what I wish?" I added. "I wish there was a store, a great Bloomingdale's in the sky, where we could return all the damaged goods, the things bought on impulse, the things that shrank or wore out or made us look lumpy.''

"Are you angry at Andrea?" Elaine asked. I was silent.

"Come on," she said, "you can tell me, are you angry?''

"Yes," I said, "I'm angry enough to kill her." Elaine was not a comfort, but talking to her was comforting.

When I brought Andrea home from the hospital, I put her in my bed and made her almond tea. "I'm sorry," she said. "I thought it wasn't worth it anymore. I was frightened that nothing would ever get any better." I sat in the chair beside my bed and looked at my pale child. "It would be so peaceful to be dead," she said.

"I don't think so," I said. "Nothing is what you imagine it to be.''

"Nothing is what I am," said Andrea. But two days later she was all dressed in her black leather pants and a purple shirt and off to a party in the East Village. She was singing in the bathroom and borrowed my rhinestone earrings that I save for New Year's Eve. I gave her money for a cab and for the evening and she planted a kiss on my face, leaving me to grade my papers wearing a lipstick-stained clown's nose.

Dr. Wolfert did not want to discuss Andrea's intended marriage. "What happened?" I asked. "Why is Andrea having such a hard time?"

"Doesn't sound so terrible," he said.

I corrected myself. "I meant why did Andrea have such a hard time?"

"You think I know?" said Dr. Wolfert. "How should I know? There's genetics, of course; each baby is a different bundle of nerves, a mess of its own DNA, and then each life is met with separate props, stage effects that are woven into the fabric of soul, and who can tell which circumstances met with which particles of mind to form the solutions, the misdirections, the convoluted shapes of Andrea? Who knows how the outside world, the TV, and school, the values of Mommy, the absence of Daddy, the effects of climate, the fallout of thought, created its own atmospheric pressure that swept Andrea off to her own Oz? What about luck—maybe Andrea was just unlucky in her birth, in her body, in her vulnerability. Maybe she was flaky because she had red hair. How should I know what made Andrea. What do you think I am, a witch doctor?"

Dr. Wolfert seemed annoyed. I didn't want him to be angry with me. I thought I would tell him about Rabbi Nachman. It should soothe his feathers; a real dream to analyze.

"Last night," I said, "I had this dream in which Rabbi Nachman of Bratslav appeared."

"Who is Rabbi Nachman?" asked Dr. Wolfert.

I explained. "In the dream I was on my way to the cleaners and I had in my arms a pile of old sweaters and heavy winter clothes that smelled of perspiration and the back shelves of unopened closets. Rabbi Nachman appeared and walked beside me. 'I have to tell you a story,' he said, and he told me this tale.

"Once in a far-off kingdom there lived a Queen who had a baby daughter who was born with a strange birthmark on her shoulder. It was the shape of a hand and as red as blood and raised off the skin like a burn. The Queen called in her healers and each tried to remove the mark from the baby's body. Each in turn failed and was exiled from the kingdom.

"The Queen was very sad and stopped going to the nursery to see her baby. 'Let the wetnurses care for it,' she said, and covered her face with her handkerchief.

"The King called his ministers and they sent deputies to foreign lands to find a healer who could remove the hand from the baby's shoulder. A famous surgeon came from afar and cut off the mark and the baby screamed for days and when the bandages were removed it was apparent that the hand had grown back larger than before. The surgeon was sent home without his fee. A woman who claimed she had magic herbs gathered from the center of the forest came and rubbed her ointments on the baby, but the hand just grew larger and now stretched across the infant's entire back.

"The Queen was very sad. This mark was a sign of judgment. She knew her own beauty was flawed and that her body would one day decay. She would not have this reminder living in the castle and so she ordered her loyal knights to carry the baby off to a distant wood and kill the baby under the stars and bury the body under a rock. The king was told that the baby died of pneumonia and he held a grand funeral in which the coffin held a chicken instead of his child, but he didn't know that. The king wept till his eyes were like rubies.

"The Queen became pregnant again and the court rejoiced and the King woke up each morning with a smile and he rewarded all his courtiers with promotions and donations from the treasury. The Queen went into labor at midnight and gave birth at noon. When the midwife saw the baby, she fainted. When the assistant midwives saw the baby, they screamed. Across the face of the newborn lay a large red hand swollen and full. It covered the infant's entire face as if it would smother him.

"The Queen took an infection and died and the King, whose hair turned white as snow, gave up his kingdom and became a woodsman living simply in the forest."

"Rabbi Nachman told me this story and then disappeared."

Dr. Wolfert said, "Yes, so what does this dream make you think of?"

"I want to know what it makes you think of," I pressed.

"Do you think," said Dr. Wolfert, "that the hand of God is on Andrea?"

"No," I said, "I don't."

"Tell me," said Dr. Wolfert, "about Rabbi Nachman. Did something about him remind you of me?"

"Do you think," I said, "that you are some descendant of the Hasidic master, a lost branch of the family, a reincarnation of his divine soul?"

"Maybe." Dr. Wolfert shrugged. "After all, it would be a fitting punishment for a mad Hasid who was always making up stories to be reincarnated as a doctor who must listen to stories for his livelihood. In this city we are the new masters and our disciples become our patients and we tell inscrutable stories about the soul and we too try to bring about reconciliations with demons. It seems very probable that you were dreaming about me. Also, perhaps you had forgotten to take your winter clothes to the cleaners this year."

"Dr. Wolfert," I said in my most appealing, gentlest tone. "Please tell me why I am dreaming about Rabbi Nachman now."

"Maybe," said Dr. Wolfert, "Rabbi Nachman is the Messiah and he is announcing his coming through you. Had you thought of that?"

"Dr. Wolfert," I said, "I am serious. I have lost my daughter. I am bereaved."

Dr. Wolfert stood up, smiled his crooked grin that made a tragedy–comedy mask out of his irregular face. "Have you tried the Missing Persons Bureau?"

I looked at the venetian blind pulled down to abort the curiosity of passersby. "Look," he said, "I deal in inner conflict, the disharmony of the internal parts. You have a real-life problem."

"And inner conflicts," I sniffed at him, "never connect with reality."

"Of course they do." He looked down at his shoes. "But that's where you lose me. You have always overestimated the powers of psychotherapy."

On the way home I remembered my mother's tarot reader, who seemed to live in a restaurant in the east fifties called the Little Club. The decor was red-and-white-striped walls and great ferns and black china plates. My mother had lunch there at least once a week. Madame Yvonne, who was bulbous and covered with black lace and silk shawls and had harlequin glasses with little chips of silver flashing in the frames, would, after the coffee was cleared away, deal the cards. I saw her reach across the table and hold my mother's hand, squeezing the diamond ring and the sapphire ring into the flesh of her finger.

"Darling," she whispered, "you must change your life before you die."

My mother wiped away a mixture of tears and mascara. "How?" said my mother. "Please tell me how."

Madame Yvonne picked up her cards and, shuffling them in a great arc, returned them to her huge black purse that was made of ostrich feathers and snake skin. The headwaiter brought the check, on which was included the fee for Madame Yvonne's reading.

Leaving Dr. Wolfert's office, I saw a figure in a black coat and a round fur hat with his pants cut off above the ankles and black stockings running high on bony legs. His face was turned away from me. First I thought it was a fragment of my dream, a shadow of Rabbi Nachman come to haunt on the Upper East Side where Dr. Wolfert's office nestled among the other traders in the misfortunes of mind and body. But of course it was just a normal Satmar or Lubavitcher come to consult a fancy doctor whose food he wouldn't eat but whose medicines he might tolerate.

Why do I continue to believe in the power of the unconscious? Why, in fact, has psychiatry as a healing discipline seemed more attractive to me than the acts of faith and redemption that religion sets out with such tempting theatrical display? Why have I always rejected the divinity that wants me to say thank you each morning and thank you each time I eat and wants me to atone and be pure of heart and free of trespass and who seems to need constant praise the way my geraniums need water?

The unconscious is described as a neutral force, like the rivers or the oceans that rotate around the globe. It carries within its turbulence our fury, our small neediness, our lust, our hatred, our obsession. Also, but not as an afterthought, our love, like an atom in constant fission, burns and sends light through the system. Our unconscious appears where we can see it, in code, in symbol, in dream. This I can believe. Maybe because it comes dressed in the uniform of science, because it depends on reason, because it makes no claims as to first causes or ultimate ends, but confines itself to describing daily workings. Perhaps I accept Freud's vision only because it's the offer of last resort. If all of psychoanalysis proves as effective as Madame Yvonne's tarot cards, then what will become of us, bending down in abject confusion, crawling about, begging for scraps of meaning, as we turn to the babblings of madmen and the whinings of lost children? I believe in the division of mind into ego, superego and id, because without some kind of trinity we become victims of chaos. Dr. Wolfert on the other hand is about as convincing as a Ouija board.

* * *

DEAR MOTHER (a letter arrives), At last it has happened. I have been allowed to meet at Rabbi and Mrs. Cohen's suggestion with a young man named Micah Rose. Don't be afraid. No one is forcing me to do anything. The final choice is mine and his. Imagine how excited I was when at the breakfast table before the Bracha, Mrs. Cohen asked me if I would like to take a walk in the afternoon with a young man from the yeshiva who is considered very suitable and just right for me. I blushed right in front of everybody and Ronite and Hadassah teased me about it. I felt excited but also very frightened all morning. It seemed to me possible that Micah would not think I was attractive, perhaps he would not think I was smart enough, or educated enough; after all, I have only been learning for the last eighteen months. I worried about my Hebrew and I tried to conjugate all the verbs I know. I rehearsed what I would say. I know this must sound strange to you because after all, I have been with men and I know how to make them think about me when I want. But this is all different; it is serious. It is not just about being liked and having a good time or even about love; it is about how I will stand in the world and be counted and who the father of my children will be and what we will make together of our life for good or for evil. It is not just me, Sarai, and him, Micah, meeting. It is the whole nation waiting for us to decide to come with them.

You can see that this is very important. My body has stopped being simply a means to a quick fix. My body is also intended to serve Gd. Mr. Cohen says I no longer look like a chicken bone. My periods are coming regularly and they never did that before. Mrs. Cohen says that the periods are set in tune with our prayers and move in cycles toward fulfillment of womanhood. I know you won't like this but I believe that my body is like the earth, rhythmic and fertile. At least I hope I'm fertile. I told Mrs. Cohen about the abortions. She says that was before and now is now and Gd will not punish me for the accident of my birthplace and the ignorance that came with it. She says I have good hips for childbearing but I must gain some more weight. She thinks that the cigarettes destroyed my taste buds and now that I am not smoking anymore they will revive and remind me of the goodness of food and the needs of my body. She puts extra spoonfuls of honey on my bread. I know you didn't believe that we should mix up food with love, but it seems to me you separated the things that belong together and mingled the things that should be separated, like dairy and meat. The world without covenant confused you.

So in the afternoon, instead of going to study group I met in the .courtyard with Micah. His friend Avram Berg was there and introduced us. Micah is very tall and he wore the black pants and the tsitsit under his jacket. That I expected, but then there was a surprise. He has red hair! Can you believe it? Not as orange as mine, but definitely red. He felt just as shy as I did and at first it was hard to talk at all. We used English after all so it didn't matter about my verbs. We went for a walk in the quarter. He is so tall he had to bend down to hear me clearly because the streets here are not quiet. We went to a park and sat on a bench and I told him about you, and your books, and then he told me about his father, who is a pediatrician in Cleveland, and his mother, who teaches the deaf. He knows sign language because she taught him when he was a baby. He was supposed to be a doctor but he hates blood and he distrusts science. He says science brought us Auschwitz and the atomic bomb.

I didn't want to tell him too much about me because I thought he might be appalled by some of it, but then he looked me right in the face and said that he had taken dope in high school and I knew it was going to be all right. We did not touch hands. We just looked at each other and I got this feeling in my body that was very good, that made me sigh a long sigh, but we didn't even brush shoulders against each other. He said he was going to make me a necklace in her jewelry shop. I wished I had something to give him in return. While we were walking a cold wind came out of the Judea hills and we walked faster. I couldn't quite keep up and he turned and stopped. He said, "I will have to learn to go slower for you." Wasn't that a beautiful thing for him to have said?

It is not planned for us to see each other for five days and then we will go out walking again. By the time you have received this letter I will have seen Micah twice, but already you know that I can do nothing but think of him. We will certainly have redheaded babies. Of course he may change his mind and decide that he doesn't like me after all. Mrs. Cohen says if that should happen I must not despair but must accept that this was not intended by Gd and that a better match will come along. She says that despair is the work of the evil one and that if we keep our hearts open to Gd we will accept even the difficult things that are put upon us.

Micah has long fingers and a mole over his left eye. He wears glasses that pinch his nose. His beard is not so full but it is red too. He says his father is angry with him for being in the yeshiva. How is it possible to be angry with a boy who is reaching toward Gd? I will let you know what happens next. Aren't you glad I went to Europe with David, because if I hadn't found myself in Jerusalem none of this would have happened and I might right now be in Acapulco growing pot on a farm with Kevin, who asked me to go with him just at the same time David appeared in my life. The Bal Shem Tov says that all the falling stars are gathered together and replaced in the sky by the angels of Gd, who gather them from the earth in their season. Love, Sarai.

AND NOW I had two fears. The first was that Andrea would be married in Jerusalem to a boy she hardly knows in a language in which she can barely request a dozen eggs, much less call out for help, tell a friend a long story or report to a doctor the exact nature of a particular pain. I was afraid that this marriage would seal her into this place where I could not follow, where my grandchildren would be strangers speaking a language in which I could not even ask for a glass of water, following rules I believed the invention of the human mind, petty, bizarre, and self-righteous. These grandchildren would not extend my mortality and I would die completely at my death. The door would be shut and the story of Andrea done, predictable in its ever-after. Assuming political disaster did not undo the state of Israel and send its inhabitants back into slavery in her lifetime, everything would work for her on schedule as planned.

This was a worry. Equally I was now frightened that something would happen and this Micah Rose would turn out not to be a good boy after all. He would have a change of heart. He would catch a glimpse of Ronite or Hadassah and prefer one of them to Andrea. He would prove to be impotent and be hiding under his black coat a dislike of women or a drinking problem that would erupt again and carry him off to unknown parts, leaving Andrea weeping on a foreign shore. Had his drug-taking days left him with brain damage? Had Andrea's? Was he too dull to get into medical school—would that explain his flight? Could Andrea tolerate marriage to a man whose mind was stunned? What was wrong with this suitor that he had become a religious freak; fine parents or not, he was a freak! So was Andrea. I did not want Andrea to be hurt anymore. It seemed to me that she had suffered enough. I could not bear for her to be in pain again. My two fears canceled themselves out and I waited, numbed, for further word.

DEAR ARNOLD, I wrote (by now I assumed we were on a first-name basis), Andrea tells me that she has met your son and that she likes him. I am not sure if this is bad or good news. If things continue they will certainly arrange this marriage. Do you think we have any means to stop it? I will write Andrea that I insist she waits. Please write Michael the same. Time is still on our side. I think. Yours in friendship, Annie Johnson.

ONCE WHEN Andrea was about seven I had received a call from her teacher. Andrea did not keep her papers togther. Andrea did not do the assigned problems in math. She drew pictures and clowned around and jumped up and down in her seat. This was not the portrait of my child I wanted to look at.

"Andrea," I said as we were driving up to the country that weekend, "your schoolwork is very important because when you grow up you will need all the things that you have learned. Perhaps one day," I said, "you will be a doctor, and take care of people who need you to help them. In order to be a doctor you must study hard and go to school for many years. You must be able to work seriously if you are going to be a doctor."

Andrea was coloring in a book in the backseat. "I could be a nurse," she said. "Nurses help people."

"Yes," I said, "but you want to be in charge, to have power, to be the one to make the important decisions; you want to have respect."

Andrea began to chant: aspect, bespect, despect, espect, fespect, mispect, nispect, etc., and her chant continued for ten miles until she tired of it and lay down on the backseat, sucking the trail of hair that she habitually pulled into her mouth.

Later I talked to my friend Elaine. "You know," said Elaine, "if all the daughters of feminists who are pledged to medicine or law actually enter those professions there will be no room for anyone else."

"Ridiculous," I answered, "there was room enough for all the WASP boys from prep school, there was room enough for every Jewish boy who desired it from Brooklyn, why should they suddenly slam the door, return the quota, when it comes to feminists' daughters?"

"I don't see it working out," said Elaine.

I had Andrea tested for a learning disability. The tests took two days and the psychologist was uncertain at the end. Perhaps it was a left-right modality confusion or perhaps it was not. She might have a minimal amount of brain damage, but then again she might not. She was original in her responses, hard to pin down, a terrible speller, interested in jacks and jump rope and showing no signs of small motor disturbance. I sat on a child's chair as the psychologist ran over her test results. On the wall were pictures of tigers and bumblebees. My hands were sweating and I couldn't look the woman in the eye. I didn't want her to see my expression. It was possible that Andrea would not grow up to be a doctor.

DEAR ANNIE, We also heard from Michael. He likes your daughter. She has red hair like he does and he finds this coincidence proof of their destined connection. He is thinking like a primitive bushman who feels he made the sun come up by knocking the right sticks together. He says he will see her again and they will soon make wedding plans. I don't think we can sit by any longer. I have arranged for a colleague to take over my practice for a while. The clinic will have to do without me. Gloria and I are traveling to Jerusalem next week. We are not going to let Michael make this kind of mess of his life without a real attempt to save him. We will be at the King David Hotel on

July 6th. I urge you to join us. We have certain contacts to help us in Israel but your presence would give strength to our side and bolster our troops. They have a huge anthill of black coats over there while we will arrive armed only with our parental memories and our deep commitment to a return to normalcy for our son. Yours, Arnold.

DEAR ANNIE, I hope you are coming to Jerusalem. I have told only one friend about our trouble. She kept asking me if I was hiding a drinking problem or a marital problem that had caused Michael to run away. I feel alone and would be so happy to know you. At least you must understand that if we did do something wrong it was not intentional. My marriage is a good marriage. Lately, of course, we have been less close, but that's because each of us looks at the other wondering if the blame belongs over there. I need your friendship. We could go sightseeing together in Jerusalem. Best, Gloria.

I SPOKE to my friend Helen, who had the friend who knew all about yeshivas, and I told her that they planned to marry Andrea to a boy named Michael. "So," said Helen, "what are you going to do?" Helen's son had dropped out of the University of Michigan and was building solar houses in Utah. Her daughter was studying veterinary medicine at Cornell. "Separating the dishes, playing a little I Ching, looking for the perfect oom, or primal screaming, or hugging the person on the seat next to you, or telling every drugstore clerk that you're okay, it's all the same, don't you think? It means," said Helen, "that when you walk with reason, you walk on air. Since no one can walk on air, you fall down and you stop using reason as your pavement.''

"It's easy enough for you to say," I said as lightly as I could, "you don't have a child who has become a Yahweh freak."

"You know what the difference is between solar energy and the eternal light—you tell me."

Helen was not comforting. I decided to comfort her. "Your daughter will at least be a good vet," I said.

"I'm allergic to cats," Helen said, "my air passages close down if a cat comes within fifty feet of me. Melissa is working on a cure for feline leukemia so that more cats can survive and multiply in this world. Count your blessings. If Andrea wants to pray a lot, at least it won't affect your breathing."

I called a travel agent, made a reservation on El Al and canceled my summer class at Bennington College. I needed to see my daughter.

I CALLED UP Dr. Wolfert and told him I was going to Israel. "What do you hope to accomplish?" he asked.

"Peace of mind," I answered.

"Oh, no," he moaned, "another religious quest."

"You could at least wish me luck," I said.

"I'll tell you what," he said. "Put a little note in a crack in the Wall for me."

"You really want me to do that?" I asked. "You believe that God picks up those scribblings and takes them back to the heavens to read through at His leisure?"

"No"—his voice sounded whiny—"but my mother did and as long as you're going it wouldn't hurt to make my mother happy."

"She's still alive?" I asked.

"No," he said. "It's a serious neurotic problem of yours to insist that everything should be reasonable."

"I'll do it," I said, knowing I wouldn't. I would not enter the segregated women's area even if an angel of the Lord were holding out his hand for my message.

I had an appointment with the rabbi of the synagogue my mother had attended. I was trying to get the right documentation to prove I was Jewish. I was aware that in other times on other continents I would have had to prove I was not Jewish in order to save my life. I felt imposed on. I was offended at this matter of papers and signatures that spoke about me without hearing my voice. I entered the synagogue and took the elevator to the office floor. I passed a small room where a young boy was practicing the Torah portion for his Bar Mitzvah. His voice had not yet changed and the sound was high, innocent and clear. He tried to put in the nasal moan of his elders but it still came out like a love song, like a hand caressing a sick child. The Hebrew chant floated down the modern hall. I held it in my mouth. For a moment I froze with yearning. For God? For a Bar Mitzvah boy of my own? For the sound of the Hebrew that sat at the top of my head and reminded me that I too needed to be taken care of?

I entered the rabbi's office. Here was a sane synagogue in the midst of an American city. It made no excessive demands on its congregation. It allowed them to attend infrequently. It supplied services for weddings and funerals. It was a discreet synagogue with a board of trustees and a monthly bulletin and a sisterhood that had luncheons twice a year. This synagogue was not pushing its way into the daily life of its congregants, separating them from the others, confining them to certain streets, denying them the pleasures of philosophy and Hollywood.

The rabbi sent his secretary through the back files. I sat in an armchair and waited. After a while I was given a photostat of my mother's application for membership in the synagogue and a list of her family names and a letter from the rabbi saying that he knew the family. This last was not quite true, but he was willing to extend the facts to accommodate my need.

"What do you think of Rabbi Nachman from Bratslav?" I said to the rabbi as I was leaving.

"Wonderful storyteller, precursor of Kafka and Max Brod. I have an excellent commentary on him by Steinsaltz; gifted man but crazy, of course."

"Of course," I said, shaking his hand and walking to the elevator without deliberate haste.

DEAR RABBI COHEN, I am writing to tell you that I am on my way to Jerusalem to speak with my daughter. I am bringing with me the documentation that you requested. However, I am not certain that I wish to support this marriage you propose. I am not certain that my daughter is clear in her own mind about her decision to stay with you. After all, only a little more than a year and a half has passed since you found her moping about your streets. I have not seen her in all that time and have received only one phone call. Of course I am anxious to talk with her and will be clearer in my own mind after we have been reunited. I will be arriving next Thursday and will, after recovering from jet lag, come to the Yeshiva Rachel. I will be staying at the King David Hotel. I trust that you will hold to your word and there will be no wedding without my approval. I realize that Andrea is not a minor and I do not have the final word in this matter, but I expect you to honor her parent as I believe your commandments encourage, if not demand. Further, I expect to be able to meet with my daughter without any member of your organization, any relative or friend of yours or hers, being present. I would like to have her stay in my hotel room with me for a few days. I assure you I am only interested in finding out what Andrea really wants and seeing who she has become. I am also lonely for my daughter. This I am certain you can understand. We have not had an easy relationship over the past several years, but despite everything I am still her mother. Yours, Annie Johnson.

I TOOK an El Al flight. I watched the Jews in tallith and black hats rise and stand against the exit door, and facing the sun whose light was just a warm glow at the edges of the pulled-down shade, they prayed, with the words written in a little box wrapped around their foreheads and laced up their arms. I watched the babies sleeping in baskets and the ooze of milk and candy, bread and lettuce, chocolate and wine, as it sank against the chairs as heads rolled back and forth on little pillows that rode through the sky like so many puffs of cloud. I tried to identify the undercover agents: the large burly man who is reading John le Carré, or is it the young girl who does calisthenics in the aisles from time to time?

I could not sleep even when the movie was over and my seat mate placed his fourth Scotch and soda in the pouch in front of him and began to snore gently. I lack faith in the airplane. It stays up, of course, but I feel as if I must concentrate in order to keep it up. I don't like to leave the responsibility for my survival in the hands of technicians. I know that professionals make serious mistakes. It is best to be on guard. So I stay awake listening to each lurch, each unexpected bang of a locker door closing, each downward sag, each tilt of the wing, each little bell that sounds through the darkened airplane. I must believe that alertness itself can avert disaster, that consciousness can fly a plane. I must believe that it matters if the plane continues on course or plummets into the ocean below like a seagull stricken with a heart attack.

Somewhere in the early hours of the dawn I admitted to myself that I was sad but I did not want to die. I wondered if the dark couple in front of me were Arab terrorists or Moroccan Jews in the knitwear business whose carry-on cases held samples from a Seventh Avenue fair they had attended. I knew that I should save my fear for the real thing and not wear myself out with imagined disasters. I took an aspirin. I watched the couple who had been visiting relatives in Brownsville and were returning to Israel with a micro-wave oven, a Cuisinart, a compact disc and an Atari computer. Her wig fell off during the night and I saw her close-cropped hair lying flat against her head. I listened to the men who again rose to pray and blocked the lavatories. I could not tell beneath their beards if their mouths were kind, if they listened to their own words, or if they just mumbled and repeated. I pulled up my shade and saw the sun on the clouds. I felt like a ghost adrift in the universe. I was coming to haunt my daughter.

THIS MORNING I woke up in my robin's-egg-blue room in the King David Hotel. I went out onto the balcony and looked across the clear turquoise swimming pool surrounded by garden chairs draped with long red towels at the wall of the old city, rose-colored in the early-morning light. I could see the cypress tress on the hills and the strange white stones that fall down the slope like pieces of old bone bleached in summer storms. Standing on the balcony framed by the French doors and the soft curtains that rested on the mahogany end table with its gold-leaf handles, I felt like an imperialist, a voyager from an alien country with a chronic interest in swimming pools and tall glasses of iced tea, a person adapted to servants and to rule; a person used to the heat of the wind that blew off deserts, who covered her face with the appropriate creams and scarves. Whatever extravagance had made me choose this hotel? I did not belong here. I belonged in a small pension on the other side of town. Had I felt I had to keep up with the Roses of Cleveland or had I been lured by some magic in the name King David that might work to protect me in this ancestral home that was not my home? Any small boy with a slingshot who stood by my side would please me. I remembered that I should call Arnold Rose and his wife, who must have checked into the hotel the day before.

When the transfer bus had arrived at the hotel I had been so exhausted that I can hardly remember registering, finding my room, tipping the bellboy or falling into bed. What I do remember is a dream in which Rabbi Nachman came to my bedside and tried to put his hands on my breasts. I pushed him away. I told him this must be a sin, a carnal venal horrible sin for which he would be sent down to Gehenna for all the rest of eternity.

He looked at me sadly. He did not seem frightened. "Gd will not count what I do with you," he said. "You are only a fragment in my dream, and I will punish myself for my dreams. I know I am impure and unworthy and have thoughts that I cannot banish from my sleep when I lose control, all control." He came after me again and I sat up in bed and began scratching at his face.

Then I looked at him and he was just a little boy trying to get up onto the bed and hardly able to reach. I picked him up and set him down on the spread next to me. He played with the long payess that came down to his shoulders and he put the payess from the left side in his mouth and began to suck it and I began to sing to him, "Hush, little baby, don't say a word, Mama's gonna buy you a mockingbird, and if that bird should up and die, Mama's gonna buy you an apple pie." I sang and sang, using every rhyme I could think of, and then I saw he was asleep and I took the cover and folded it over him.

* * *

AT A consciousness-raising meeting in New York many years ago, an activist friend of mine once suggested that the Israeli feminists should organize a fence-breaking party and they should invade the area before the Wall and rip down the wires that separate male and female. "Can you just imagine the astonished faces," she said, "of the beards and the wigs when they see their divine law of difference is no more than the sort of barrier that keeps the cows out of the corn?"

"It's their tradition," I said. "You can't just go in like the Catholic church burning voodoo dolls."

"Don't let them hide behind tradition," said my friend. "There is nothing sacred about cruelty to half the people on this globe. We don't have to respect every tradition: cannibalism, slavery, clitorectomies, facial scarring, burning of witches, wives to the funeral pyre, flagellation, hairshirts, binding of feet, worshiping of ancestors, infanticide and on with the list. I have no great respect for tradition."

"As a political action this snipping of wires is sure to create havoc, backlash, fury. It seems unwise," I added.

The question was academic because there were no Israeli feminists in the room and a moment's reflection told us that American feminists could not cross the sea and knock down other women's walls; that was imperialism, colonialism. I thought of that evening now as I passed by the hotel on my way to the Yeshiva Rachel. It was not yet eleven o'clock and there were a few men in black hats and long coats rocking back and forth on their heels in front of the stones that had once been the retaining wall of the old temple. What is the difference, I wondered, between praying to stones and praying to golden calves? Is it not a slippage, a sneaking back of the idol, to make the wall a sacred place where prayer should reach God anywhere or nowhere? All of Jerusalem was a hot place, everyone's God seems to have had a tabernacle on the mount or at least to have died nearby; an accident of geography, another example of Jews at the root of disturbances, metaphysical, political and otherwise?

Between the gray stones of the wall a few green weeds sprouted. A small purple flower drooped downward on its stem. Standing outside the fence watching the women seated on little folding chairs, I wanted to feel the rush of prayer, the release of tightness that might follow the thought of being heard, of being protected. Oh, God, help me, I thought. I heard my words echo in my head. This was only imitative behavior, a grasping for straws, a mere posturing. I was not so humble or so defeated yet that I expected God to help. I considered overlooking my feminist scruples and leaving a message for Dr. Wolfert in the Wall. But I decided against it. I already felt foolish enough.

THERE WERE a few American teenage boys awkwardly holding prayer books that had been offered them by solicitous bearded volunteers. The boys wore Reeboks and Nikes and their T-shirts boasted of baseball teams and carried the names of towns on Long Island. They took pictures of each other looking embarrassed. On the women's side, I could see old women sitting on little chairs, their hair covered in scarves, their faces dry from the sun and heat. They seemed to be talking to each other. A few younger women stood by the Wall. The women's section was a third the size of the men's and they seemed crowded together. The women held prayer books and some just closed their eyes tightly. Their bodies were covered with thick stockings, long skirts, heavy shoes and long-sleeved full blouses. Their hair was covered by dark scarves or tucked under berets. Some of the women wore stiff wigs that did not move with their bodies or lift and fall with the breeze. Why were they here at the Wall? Was a child sick, a husband indifferent, was a mother failing or had a lump been felt in a breast? Not Andrea, standing at the Wall mumbling into a prayer book, rocking back and forth on her sensible shoes; not like this, I thought.

I went on to the Yeshiva Rachel, which was in a court-yard in the center of which one small orange tree sat in a stone pot. I could hear the men's voices raised in discussion through the open windows of a building on one side and as I knocked on the wide pine door of the yeshiva I saw a group of little boys, with payess, yarmulkes and long black pants run through the courtyard. Some turned around to stare at me, a stranger, a woman from a distant planet. An old woman in a shabby dress with her stockings rolled down about her ankles and teeth missing from her mouth pulled at my sleeve. She shook a little box at me, and seeing I didn't understand, she pointed at my pocketbook and held out her hands. Then she reached up on her toes and kissed the silver mezuzah on the doorpost. The door opened. The old lady disappeared into the street.

Mrs. Cohen was younger than I had imagined, with a baby boy on her hip. She led me into the study, where she told me in a strong Brooklyn accent sprinkled with the rhythms of Yiddish what a wonderful daughter I had, how sweet and kind and quick to learn she was. Mrs. Cohen's wig was blond and sat straight across her forehead as if it were a crown. Her eyes were alert and her clean-washed face made her seem like a girl herself, a tired girl who had been up too late the night before, one who might have used a little orthodontics.

She offered me some tea and a biscuit. The biscuit had been made by Sarai several hours before, she told me proudly. I looked at it as if it were a hand grenade found in the streets the morning after a battle. "Try it," said Mrs. Cohen. "Sarai has turned into such a good cook."

"No, thank you," I said, "I've had my breakfast."

"Just pick it up," said Mrs. Cohen, "see how light it is."

I held Andrea's biscuit in my hand. Mrs. Cohen looked at

me, expecting a response. The baby reached out for my biscuit and jokingly she scolded him. I broke my biscuit. I gave half to the baby and the remainder I began to eat. I had crumbs on my chin when Rabbi Cohen entered the room.

"How nice to have you here. How glad we are to have you visit," said Rabbi Cohen. His skin was puffy and pale. The hot Jerusalem sun that had baked the stones gray and rose had not touched him. He too spoke with Brooklyn's rasp, the sound of subway track, semi-attached houses, transplanted shtetl echoes that bounced around between the commas.

His beard was black with flecks of gray. His eyes behind his thick glasses were tired blue. His chest was wide and rose like a mountaintop off his full belly, which stretched against his white shirt, nearly bursting the buttons. His short legs moved across the room with authority, as if his body were only an appendage of his mind, which knew its way absolutely through any thicket or road block that might suddenly appear. His black velvet yarmulke only partly covered the bald spot that shone with perspiration. "More biscuits," he said to his wife, who nodded at him and disappeared from the room.

"So," said Rabbi Cohen, "let's get it all out on the table. What do you really think of us?"

I was not prepared for the direct question. I was silent.

"Perhaps," he said, "you think we are anachronistic, unrealistic, shut off from the source of light that you find in your universities and coming from your TV. Perhaps you think we are all mad or belong in a museum?" He laughed at himself and smiled disarmingly at me. "Come now, tell me what you are thinking or we can never say anything of truth to each other, and that's important for your daughter, I believe."

His bookshelves were filled with old books in leather bindings marked in gold-leaf titles. The map Andrea had described of ancient Israel banged against the door. On his desk rested a velvet sack in which he kept his tefillin and his

prayer shawl. All over the floor were discarded pieces of
paper with writing on them. He noticed that I was looking at
the papers.

"I am trying," he said, "to write a description of our
yeshiva to some friends in America, who will, as soon as I
find the right words, rush to send me the money I need to
continue my work. It is like this in your world too, I
believe; all good deeds take money and people who should
be out doing are instead home writing letters pleading for
funds. Yes?"

"Yes," I said, "that is true."

"So tell me now, what do you think of us?"

I was going to answer. I was going to answer fully, but
just at that moment a young woman burst through the door
and screamed at Rabbi Joshua Cohen in Hebrew. He rose
immediately and tried to put his arms around her, but she
pushed him off and sat down on the floor, tears pouring from
her eyes, her nose bright red with grief. She began to tear at
her dress and ripped open the neckline, exposing a slip and
the straps of a bra. Her heavy breasts heaved as she sobbed.
Rabbi Cohen called for his wife and she and other women
appeared and there was a great commotion in the study.

"Where is Andrea?" I asked. "We can talk later," I
assured him.

He didn't hear me. The little study was filled with sound;
the loudest sound was the woman whose sobbing did not
stop. Three or four children, girls in ironed dresses and boys
with payess and yarmulkes, appeared between the other
bodies. A child began to wail, the teapot on the desk spilled
onto the rug.

I walked out of the study and down the hall. The men
were now in the courtyard walking about in pairs, in groups.
They made a tremendous noise. I found the stairs and was
about to go up when Mrs. Cohen grabbed my elbow. "What
happened," I asked, "what happened to that woman?"

"Very sad, very sad," said Mrs. Cohen. "The rabbinical
court has taken away her children."

"Why? What had she done?"

"It is the law," said Mrs. Cohen.

"Is the law always right?" I asked Mrs. Cohen.

She looked at me, bewildered, and then explained as if she were talking to a slow and inattentive child, "The law comes from Gd, it came at Sinai, our rabbis look into their own hearts and minds and give us rulings that reveal how it was meant to be when it was given. The law is from Gd and keeps us righteous."

"Sometimes the law seems cruel," I said, leaning against the banister of the stairs that led to a place where my daughter must be waiting for me.

"Only," said Mrs. Cohen, "to us in our ignorance; the wise ones, the rabbis, they understand what is right and just. We must do what Gd wants, don't you think?"

A little girl came to her side. "Ima," she whimpered. As Mrs. Cohen bent down to pick the child up, her breasts, large as if they were always swollen with milk, pushed against her high-necked cotton blouse, and on the nape of her neck I saw the soft downy hair of a brunette. She smelled of soap and baby powder. As she bent over her child and her shoulder sloped downward, she looked for a moment like a clothed Ingres, like a Fragonard or a Boucher. I gasped aloud.

"Are you all right?" she asked.

"Fine," I said, "just fine."

She held the little girl in her arms and began to wipe at a stain on the girl's mouth. "I am not what you think," she said to me. "I am not anyone's slave. I have chosen my life. I am a very good chess player also." She glared at me as if I had challenged her to a game.

"How wonderful," I said.

"Yes, I am a level-one master."

"Where did you learn?" I asked.

"My father taught me."

"Do you play in competitions?" I asked.

"For you, everything has to have a purpose. You have to

have a prize to enjoy something. I play against myself, that is enough.''

"That's good," I said. She was ready to fight, like my students who either believe that the entire world was enslaving them because of their gender or that inequality was an idea invented by maniacs in Washington Square Park who were trying to subvert the American system. I was tired and wanted my daughter. "Please," I said, "where is Andrea?"

"Come," said Mrs. Cohen, "come with me into the kitchen. We are just now preparing lunch. You will join us for lunch, I hope."

I followed Mrs. Cohen and her baby down the stairs into the large, clean kitchen with scrubbed pine tables set neatly for the next meal. The little girl stirred a bowl of dough and began to shape cookies and place them on a metal sheet. Two old ladies, their heads covered with long scarves, talking away in Hebrew, paying no attention to my arrival, were cutting onions on a board. Mrs. Cohen began washing salad in the sink. I felt a sudden pain in my hip. I sat down at a table. "Is Andrea coming to the kitchen?" I asked.

"Rabbi Cohen wants to speak with you before you meet with your daughter. That is our way."

"Then I will go back and speak with him now," I said.

"He is very busy just at this moment," said Mrs. Cohen. "He will see you after lunch. Perhaps you will help me with the salad?" She smiled at me and I walked over to the sink and began washing the greens.

"You do not believe that women should cook for the family?" she asked me. Andrea had obviously prepared them.

"Men and women both should cook for the family," I said.

Mrs. Cohen smiled shyly at me. "Those clumsy oxes," she said. "We would eat like donkeys if they were allowed in here."

The doors swung open. Fifteen or so girls came rushing in. One began to pour milk, another to take raw vegetables and arrange them on a plate. I looked for Andrea. "Where is Andrea? I want to see Andrea," I repeated.

The girls all stared at me. "Sarai is out on a walk with Micah," said Mrs. Cohen, and the kitchen filled with giggles and shoves and knowing looks.

We had yogurt and cucumbers and salad and bread, and I sat by Mrs. Cohen's side and counted her children. There seemed to be at least five. "I am pregnant," she said to me, "the next will be at Hanukkah. Why did you only have one child?" she asked me.

"Why do you have so many?" I countered. It was very hot in the kitchen. I was perspiring through my blouse and I could feel my skirt sticking to the chair.

"We do as we were intended," said Mrs. Cohen. "I like being pregnant." She was telling me the truth. Her smile, with overlapping teeth, convinced me. "You are just the way Sarai described you, sharp with questions, almost like a man." Was she complimenting me or not? "Do you play chess?" she asked.

"Not well," I answered.

The girls ate lunch silently, staring at me openly. At the end of the meal they passed around a small pamphlet and began a Hebrew prayer that went on and on for at least ten minutes.

"We are thanking God for our food and our homes," said one of the girls, showing me where they were reading on the page.

Then there was silence, a kind of peaceful quiet in the room; even the babies were still. The old ladies who had joined us at the table began a song with a lot of thumping in it and at a certain point each girl hit the table and sang a verse. It lasted a long time. The sound was squeaky.

"We like to sing together," said Mrs. Cohen. I smiled at her.

Rabbi Cohen had taken the sobbing woman somewhere else. He had not returned when it was time to say the prayer after eating. He did not return while I helped Mrs. Cohen and the girls clean up the kitchen.

"I will come back tomorrow," I said. I had changed my mind and was no longer in such a rush to see Andrea.

Mrs. Cohen saw me to the door. Her baby pulled at my beads and waved bye-bye to me, an encouraging sign that we all speak the same language.

WHAT DOES Andrea look like now? When she left home she was so thin her collarbone was almost an offensive weapon. Her legs were spindly and when she raised her arms you could see her ribs under her shirt. Why did she have to be so thin? What was so disgusting about the rounded shoulder, the full arm, the bodice that announced itself? I was at a NOW strategy meeting with a group designing a campaign to counter abortion clinic bombings when someone in the room asked how many of our daughters had had abortions. All over the room hands went up. I asked how many of our daughters were either grossly overweight, or underweight, or threw up their dinners in the toilet each night. There was a shocked silence and then hands went up, a forest of hands. One woman who did not raise her hand called out, "I have only sons, but my niece is in the hospital being force fed."

What is it? I asked. We are the ones who freed women from the beauty parlor, from waxing their legs, from doing their nails, from feeling that their worth lay in conformity to some model who was shown in soft focus on a magazine cover. We were the ones who said you shouldn't squeeze your stomach into a merry widow, you shouldn't have to mince around in uncomfortable shoes. All by yourself, as a natural woman, you are beautiful whatever the shape of your nose or the color of your skin; that was where we began, but look at our daughters. They diet, they diet too much and end up on the psychiatrist's couch or in the hospital. They gorge and they binge and they hate themselves and they vomit till their teeth fall out. This abortion issue is just the tip of the glacier that's coming to run us over.

Someone shouted out that I was off the subject and so I was. But I'm still thinking about it. There is something in the air that makes women unable to accept their shape, that makes of puberty a nightmare, that makes so many girls hide their breasts in folds of fat or diet them out of existence, or exercise them into flat muscle. Is it still a shame to be female, does it promise so little or offend so greatly? We underestimated the problem. We were romantic in our belief that men would accept women if women would just like themselves. Maybe, like a dog in heat, the female of the species changes her chemistry to attract men. Women, our daughters, do not like their natural selves any better than we did. Perhaps equality was never the real issue. We talked of opportunities, ignoring the roar of biology, the odors of sexuality that could neither be banished nor harnessed for our lofty purposes.

DR. ARNOLD ROSE invited me to his room. He was a stout but large man, with graying hair that had receded to leave a high forehead. He wore bifocals that slipped on his nose and his shirt was half-opened and his tie was pink with a pattern of leaves and bears in trees. He looked like a man who could no longer touch his toes or do ten pushups. He looked like a man who wouldn't mind if your baby spit up orange juice on his pants.

* * *

GLORIA ROSE was a heavy woman with auburn hair now dyed to imitate what must have been its original color. Her eyes became moist behind her owl-framed glasses the instant she saw me.

We sat on the balcony and watched the last of the afternoon sunbathers pick up their towels and head for their rooms.

"I took Michael and George every winter to Florida to stay at the Boca Raton Plaza," said Gloria Rose. "It's a hotel just like this one with palms and fans and shops with gold jewelry in the lobby. The boys played miniature golf and swam in the children's pool. My mother had retired down there." As she spoke her tears dried; when she paused they returned.

Arnold Rose gave me a glass of vodka. "To our children," I said, and lifted up my glass. It seemed the appropriate thing to do. Gloria Rose stared at me. The sky was turning to watery milk and Venus, the star of deception, appeared where the globe began to slope down.

"Tell me more about Michael," I said to the Roses, mother and father. I was avoiding telling them about Andrea. How was I to explain the snake tattoo, the high school degree that never was, the East Village, the Never Ever Cafe where Andrea had held an honored spot at the bar; why was I shamed? Years before when I had first been a graduate student and fallen in love with misbegotten poets, I had thought that good, respectable people like the Roses were responsible for the dulling of thought that was spreading like marmalade across the country. They were the people in gray flannel suits, the Babbitts and the bigots whose search for decency had strangled them in conventionality. But now I sat with them on this balcony and felt ashamed because Andrea was my reproach no less than Michael was theirs.

Gloria Rose reached out her hand for her husband's. He pulled his chair closer to her. "This has been very hard for

Gloria," he said. "She's an excellent teacher. She won the Cleveland Handicapped Teacher Award two years in a row." Gloria blushed and she looked out the window.

"What is it like, to teach the deaf?" I asked.

Gloria straightened up. She was taller than I had first thought. "People think deaf children are different from other children but they're not. They need to be held and cuddled and to believe that you like them. You hang their drawings up on the bulletin board and you serve juice and cookies and each one of them will learn. The hard part is when they understand they are deaf and they are different and they always will be. Then their eyes turn so dark and they sometimes won't sign even to me for weeks and they stop playing and each time it happens I feel rotten. It makes me sick to the core that a child should have to feel that, know that. Some of them, the smarter ones, take it hard, very hard. But then they return as if they have mourned their ears long enough and they begin to fight back and to giggle and to sit on my lap and we go on. I would never want to do anything else but each fall meet a new class of five-year-olds who can't hear but will not give up. We don't let them give up."

Gloria's glasses misted over as she was talking. I leaned toward her as if I could absorb her into my skin. "Teach me a sign," I said.

"Here"—she made a motion with her hand—"the sign for friendship." I copied it.

An awkward silence followed. "Did you come from religious families?" I asked.

"My daddy," said Gloria, whose face had regained its shape, "was a socialist and a union organizer. He was a printer and he wrote pamphlets encouraging the workers in Yiddish. My mother worked in the sewing trade till her children were born and she always made our clothes herself. She made me the most beautiful dresses right from the Vogue patterns. But boy, did my parents not believe in religion. My daddy would buy a pound of bacon every Yom Kippur and all day long he would fry it in front of the open window so all the neighbors had to do was breathe and they could smell his position on God." Gloria smiled at me. "Arnold's parents wanted us to have a rabbi when we got married, but my daddy put his foot down. We had to get married in City Hall. My daddy was the leader of the first strike at the Cleveland *Plain Dealer*. He said that someday all the workers in America would unite and drive the bosses into Canada, where they could freeze their bottoms off. We went to an all-night vigil when they killed the Rosenbergs. My mother and father cried and told us never to forget what happened. I told Michael and George. I wanted them to share everything with us.

Arnold put his hand on his wife's shoulder and squeezed it gently. I put on my jacket. The day had been so hot and now the air was growing cold, or had I just experienced the absence of a mate like a sudden chill?

"Tomorrow morning," said Arnold, "I'm going out to the Hadassah Hospital. I want to see what they are doing in juvenile diabetes over here. I got a colleague to set it all up. I might be able to learn something and I might have something to offer. It seems it's a real problem here." Arnold turned to me. "Do you know about juvenile diabetes?"

"She doesn't want to know," said Gloria. "She wants to know about Michael."

"There's no reason to go over the past. What we have to do is deal with the present. I understand that the yeshivas that are holding our children are planning on going ahead with this wedding. We have been asked to give them our approval and we have withheld it. I have spoken to the American Embassy and they cannot offer us any help because both Michael and Andrea are over the age of eighteen. The guy at the embassy, some fifth-level diplomat named O'Reilly, suggested this was my fault for buying Israeli bonds. I've written a letter about him to our senator which should settle his hash. My colleague, a hematologist whose wife gives a lot to good causes, put me in touch with the Israeli CIA. I have an appointment tomorrow afternoon with a fellow I'm supposed to meet in a cafe on Ben Yehuda Street. I got the feeling the meeting was set up to pay off some favor. My phone contact suggested that I should be pleased that Michael had not become a Jesus freak or joined a Hare Krishna group. Thanks a lot.''

''At least you have George,'' I said. Gloria's nose turned red and she closed her eyes. ''What has George done?'' I asked.

Arnold Rose looked very uncomfortable. He got up to fix my drink. Gloria blew her nose. She pulled herself together and looked me in the eye. She had decided this was no time for evasions.

''George,'' she said, ''dropped out of medical school, Case Western Reserve, in his second semester. He went to California and now he is the maître d' at the hotel on the beach in Baja. He says he likes to watch the pelicans and go fishing on his days off and that he thinks we're crazy to go through the winters in our overcoats and work each day. He says he wants to live like a sand crab, just grabbing whatever is in front of him. We don't even talk to George on the phone much anymore. It's hard to find anything to say. That's why Michael had so much responsibility. When he was pre-med we thought he would really do it. Lightning can't strike twice in the same family, we thought. But it did. Lucky us.''

I TOLD the Roses about Andrea. All about Andrea. I told them about my visit to the Yeshiva Rachel. Arnold Rose took out a yellow legal pad and took notes on my report. We went out to dinner in a restaurant in east Jerusalem, recommended by Arnold's hematologist friend who visited Israel twice a year. We sat on a terrace overlooking the stone houses, the cobblestone streets, the tethered goat at the end of a lane and the marketplace with its jumble of carts nestling together under the lamplight. We ate hummus and stuffed grapeleaves and drank wine and clinked our glasses together. We looked at the moon over the walls of the old city and sighed. Arnold said to me that he would not let Andrea be taken by the body snatchers. He took the check and as we left he put one arm around his wife and the other he put around me. It was a welcome gesture. No one seeing us would have believed that we had been strangers just a short while ago.

Finally, as we walked through the dark, near empty streets on our way back to the hotel, following the directions Arnold got from a map he kept pulling from his pocket and referring to on each corner, I learned about Michael. He played the flute and the piano. He won the silver cup at the club's junior tennis championship five years in a row. He was a backstroke medal winer on his high school team. He was a Latin scholar and an American Civil War buff. He had always wanted to be a doctor like his father and summers he had worked at his father's clinic in the inner city and he had learned how to do injections, how to hold a squirming child and how to comfort a crying baby. When he was in first grade he made his mother a picture frame out of cookie dough and he once made his father a tie rack in shop. Here obviously was the son-in-law of my dreams.

"What happened?" I asked.

Gloria's eyes filled up again. "His senior year of high school he changed. He spent all his time in his room and he stopped joining us at the dinner table. He refused to go to the club with us on weekends. He stopped playing tennis. He was listening to all this strange music, Bob Dylan and the Stones and you know. We just thought it was kid stuff. When I gave him a stereo for his birthday he wouldn't open it. 'I don't want anything from you,' he said. That seemed normal enough. George had left for California. He knew we were upset. It was strange in the house. Michael didn't bring friends home anymore. He was just in his room with the door closed and he pasted up a sign that said, If you enter I'll kill you. We talked to our friend who is a psychiatrist. He laughed at us for worrying.

"We belonged to the Jewish Community Center because Arnold's parents had wanted us to have the boys Bar Mitzvahed. They each went to classes on Wednesday afternoons for two years and then we did it. No big fuss, my dad was no longer with us and my mom had a good time. Even old socialists can enjoy a good party. When Michael started to act strange, I talked to the rabbi about him. He suggested Michael join their youth group. Michael said I could drag his dead body there if I wanted.

"It was lonely in the house with Michael treating me like I was a nothing, an invisible person. Arnold and I took a trip together to Hawaii and left Michael alone. Maybe we shouldn't have done that. When we came back there were cigarette butts and beer cans in all my plants and I found a big pile of Scotch bottles behind the rhododendron. Michael wouldn't talk to me at all, not about school, not about who his friends were or what they were doing. It was as if I had betrayed him and he wouldn't tell me how.

"Michael went to college but everything was wrong from the beginning. He didn't like his roommate. He didn't like the professors, he called them a bunch of ass lickers. He didn't like the girls on campus. He said they were all out for one thing. He took up the jazz trumpet and that seemed to make him happy for a while. When we called he'd tell us what he was learning to play. I asked him once, 'What do you want Michael?' and he just sneered at me. 'You couldn't imagine,' he said, 'what I want. It's beyond your capacity.'

"He was taking chemistry and physics, but he didn't seem interested. He wasn't working hard. I guess that's when I started to put on all this weight; you know how it is," Gloria said without looking at me, "when you feel bad and then you eat and you feel worse. I didn't used to be so fat, not at all."

It seemed that Michael had dropped out of college early in his sophomore year. He had come home and cashed some

bonds that he had been given when he was Bar Mitzvahed
and he took the contents of his mother's jewelry box and
raised enough money to travel to Europe.

"I could have had him arrested," said his father. "I
probably should have had him arrested," he added.

Gloria let the tears run unattended down her cheeks. "I
still love him, he's my son," she said.

"All right," said Arnold, "I didn't have him arrested. I
didn't do a thing to your precious son. He's at liberty in
Jerusalem, driving us crazy with this new scheme of his to
mock everything, to destroy everything." Arnold Rose pulled
the map from his pocket and stared at it.

I held Gloria by the elbow. "You're not fat," I said.

"Jesus," said Gloria, "what would my father say if he
could see Michael with his payess, his beard and his black
coat?" She giggled. I joined in.

"I APOLOGIZE for disappearing yesterday," said
Rabbi Cohen when I was again seated in his
study. "I have certain obligations in the community. Now
tell me, what do you think of us, here at the yeshiva?"

Mrs. Cohen brought in tea and cookies and departed
quickly. I said nothing.

"You look sad, Mrs. Johnson," he said. "You traveled
here all alone, I take it. You have no family who could
have come with you?"

"No," I admitted, "I am quite alone."

"That must be hard for you," he said. "Here we are
always enveloped in our families and we look after each
other because all of us are one family."

"I would like to see Andrea as soon as possible," I said.

"Of course, of course you do. Did you bring me the
papers I had written to you about?"

I pulled out the envelope from the synagogue and gave it to him. "I would think you should take my word," I said.

"I do, I do, it's just that others might not and we must be careful in this community, not everyone welcomes strangers as eagerly as I and we don't want any question of illegitimacy to spoil things. We must at the Yeshiva Rachel be quite above reproach; you understand, I'm sure."

"You mean Andrea is not accepted by everyone in your group?" I asked.

"Well, your child, you understand, is tainted, affected by her years in the secular world, late to knowledge and always far behind those of our children who have followed the law from the earliest moments of their infancy. Many of my people are afraid that the taint of these strangers who have joined us may rub off on their own. They may speak of ideas or of experiences or of taboo matters in a way that tempts our own away from us. They come from an unclean place and it is possible that their memories may contaminate the rest. It is not unreasonable to be wary, but that's all right. There are now a substantial group of these returned and many of us treasure them dearly. They are proof of our ultimate victory over the modern style. The Greeks have been vanquished. These children are our war spoils if you will, taken from the outside, the unbelievers. Their condition when we find them confirms us in our knowledge that the ways of the world are without mercy and forgiveness and that we alone can be counted on to maintain the rule of the righteous till the end of days."

He spoke so softly and stared into my eyes so deeply that I felt touched by his words despite the messages they were leaving in my head. I could feel that he was ready to receive my burden, to relieve my isolation, to arrange my life in a better way. This made me impatient. "Now, Rabbi Cohen, I must see my daughter right now."

"You are as impatient and impetuous as she was when she first came to us. I had such difficulty teaching her the simplest things, such as the alphabet. She wanted to know some ultimate truth, some reason for this or that. It took a long time to teach her acceptance. At first she always demanded that everything fit into a pattern and follow in logical order point by point. She needed us as much as we needed her or else this would never have worked. Now I have to tell you she is a star. She learns whatever we wish to teach her. She learns ahead of many of the others. She can cook a full meal. Mrs. Cohen has taught her how to handle herself in the kitchen. She can keep the kashrut, and she can clean up after herself. I will tell you at first I thought she might be the one Ba'altshuva who would always need a servant in her house. But now there is nothing she cannot do. You should be very proud of her, Mrs. Johnson.''

This was the first glowing report I had ever received on Andrea. It consoled me without being quite consoling.

"Who takes care of you?" I asked him.

"My wife, naturally," he answered.

"No," I said, "who gives back to you all the energy that you give out? I am a teacher. I know you can't go on giving forever."

He looked at me, startled. "I suppose," he said, "I am like a desert well. When I run dry the nomads will move on and I will be no more than an empty hole in the sand."

"Then you will feel like me," I said.

"Don't be so sure." He smiled at me. "I come from a long line of rabbis. Ten generations of Cohens have been rabbis. My sons will be the eleventh generation." He jumped up and pulled an old picture from the wall. In it I could see an old man with a fur hat sitting at the head of a large oak table. Posed alongside of him were other men with long coats and beards. "This photo," he said, "was taken in Prague, when my father was just a baby. It is my family. Rabbis of the district came to do my grandfather honor. You see I am not alone in my work. I belong with the others. We are a train, a continuous train that leads to the end of time, to the repair of the world and the return to peace for all men. I come from a long line of learned men. That is why I can be so strong." He looked at me with pity. "You have no one to follow and no one came before you; that is why you cannot carry a heavy load."

"Andrea would follow me if you had not taken her," I said to him quietly.

"You know that is not true." He looked at me. "I would like to Xerox for you some manuscripts. I think you do not understand your Judaism. You have rejected what you hardly know and that is not intellectually honest. Let me give you some pages to read." He began to search through his papers for just the right pamphlet.

"No," I said, "please, I don't want to read anything. I want to see my daughter."

As he searched through his desktop, he revealed the Xerox machine, shiny white and modern on his desk. "I can Xerox for you in a moment the words of Maimonides that will bring you comfort."

"No," I said. "I don't want to read Maimonides. I want to see Andrea."

He leaned back in his chair. "I thought you were an intellectual?"

"All right," I said, "I'll read what you want. But where is Andrea?"

He began immediately Xeroxing a pamphlet for me. "Look how clear it comes out," he said. "My grandfather was a scribe. It would take him two years to write what this machine can do in three minutes."

"So you don't reject the modern world," I said.

"I pick and choose wisely," he said. "We are not ignorant here. We are merely cautious. In your world you are ignorant and without caution."

I accepted the pages he thrust into my hand. "Andrea?" I asked again.

"Do you accept this marriage?" Rabbi Cohen pulled his chair closer to mine and stared into my face as if he could read my answer there.

"I must see Andrea before I answer," I said. "I must see Andrea."

"No need to get excited," he said. "Soon, soon we will bring Sarai to you. Do not alarm her with tales of your grief. Do not try to make her feel guilty about what she is doing to you. We have forewarned her and she is prepared. Greet her with love and allow her to choose her own future. That is what you believe in, is it not—freedom? Individual choice?"

He was laughing at me. He was teasing me as if I were a small child. It annoyed me deeply but at the same time it was not entirely unpleasing. "When do I get to see Andrea?" I asked.

"Come back this evening, at six o'clock; we can arrange it then." He showed me to the door.

Outside in the hall a group of young women waited. I searched for Andrea. She was not among them. Mrs. Cohen was at my elbow. "Do you mind," she said, "when you come back, could you wear a dress that is more in keeping with our taste? We also prefer you to wear stockings."

After I left I walked through the narrow streets of the section. Men in black hats and beards turned their eyes away from me as I approached them on the cobblestones. Younger boys would flatten themselves against the buildings as I passed as if expecting me to reach out and touch them, arousing, inciting, inflaming, contaminating. I am an older woman, still of possible interest to men of the right age but surely not a threat to the virginity of puppies or the morals of the already attached. I had noticed as I walked along Broadway with Andrea in New York, several years back, that she was the sexual magnet and I was her unseen companion. I have never been one of those feminists who thought it possible to remove casual sexual vibrations from the street. I'm not even certain I would want such a scraped-out world where all fantasies about bodies were kept hidden behind doors. There I accepted my altered position as natural. Here on these streets I was returned to

the status of an adolescent temptress. Here I was a dangerous stranger, a female who might be oozing in any number
of forbidden ways. I felt embarrassed, misunderstood.

On every corner a person, blind or old, in a wheelchair,
wrapped in an old sweater, pushed a little box at me and
shook the coins inside. I stopped by a store window and
looked at the brass menorahs, the silver mezuzahs, the gold
earrings, the candlesticks, the knife with an engraved handle,
and far inside I could see the man behind the counter. He
had no customers. His hat seemed dusty and the rim was
shiny with wear. His head was bent down over a leather-
bound book. His fingers played with the fringes of his
beard. He picked up his head, caught my eye and quickly
turned away and went into the back of his shop.

Two women came up the street, one carrying a baby in
her arms and the other pushing a stroller. A small girl hung
behind them, hopping on one foot. The women stopped at a
store window to look at the tablecloths that were displayed
there. The baby, glancing over her mother's shoulders,
smiled at me. I smiled back. The baby had big black eyes
and tiny pearl earrings in each baby ear. She had on a pink
dress with puffy sleeves. Suddenly the other woman noticed
that the baby was smiling at me. She said something in
Hebrew to her companion, who turned the baby's face away
from me abruptly, and the women hurried down the street.

It took me a while to find my way out of the quarter. It
was very hot and I had perspired through my dress. I was
thirsty and my feet in my sandals had swollen and a blister
was rising on my left heel. I reached Ben Yehuda Street,
where everything again seemed recognizable, music blared
from the stores. The girls were wearing sundresses and their
hair flowed loose behind them. Men and women touched
bare skin against bare skin. Here among the godless ones,
no one noticed me at all. But I noticed Arnold Rose sitting
at a cafe with a man in shirt-sleeves and dark glasses.

He saw me, called me over and introduced me to Aaron
Kaplan, his connection from the "Israeli government."

Spread out on the table were four color photographs of
young men with glasses, wide-brimmed flat black hats and
beards. Down the sides of each face ran tightly curled
ringlets. They were all redheaded. One had a mustache.

"All right, Doctor Rose," said Aaron, "here are four
boys in the yeshivas for Americans. We have taken their
pictures without their consent for our own purposes. One of
these boys is your son. Point him out to me, please."

"It's been two years since I actually saw Michael,"
Arnold Rose mumbled. He picked up the pictures and stared
at them. "Michael doesn't wear glasses. I would know
Michael's nose anywhere, his eyes are blue," he said. But
the boys in all the pictures had blue eyes. "You should ask
my wife," said Arnold finally. "A mother always knows her
own son. I have so many other things on my mind I can't
possibly be expected to identify my child's face when it is
disguised, masked."

"My point," said Aaron, "is that you cannot identify
your son now because he has changed. He is no longer the
boy of the picture you gave me." He pulled out of his
pocket a photograph of Michael Rose in his high school
yearbook. Michael had omitted a quote under his picture,
but his classmates had called him a mystery man. I stared at
the nose in the picture, trying to place it on the bearded
faces of the other photographs, but I could not. "Your
son," said Aaron, "as you knew him, is gone. In this
country we lose many of our sons. The enemy is killing us
all the time. It is a part of the pleasure of being an Israeli
man, this honor of dying. You have lost a son, too, and I am
sorry for you as I am for any parent in such a situation, but
you understand I cannot waste my time over the dead. Our
work is to protect the living. I suggest you go home to
Albuquerque or Detroit, or is it Cleveland, and do what
Israeli parents do: we get on with it."

"Is one of these pictures really my son?" Arnold Rose
sat hunched up at the table.

"Yes," said Aaron, "taken the day certain phone calls were placed from your hospital."

"Which is his son?" I asked.

"It doesn't matter, does it," said the government man, picking up the photos and replacing them in his pocket. "If you cannot recognize him, you cannot claim him. The cemetery for our war dead is out just beyond the Knesset. I suggest before you return home you take a trip out there and see for yourselves how many we have lost."

"Just a moment," said Arnold Rose, rising to his feet. "I have been promised assistance. I have certain friends in Cleveland who have been important to the Israeli government and they expect you to cooperate with me. Do you understand?"

Aaron sighed. "Without you Americans, we would never have made the desert bloom? Is that it?"

"More or less," said Arnold, a doctor unwilling to abandon his patient even though all the lines on the monitors are running straight. "I want you to throw my son out of the country. Use a trumped-up charge, drug trafficking or spying. Throw him out."

"Give my best to your friends in Cleveland," said Aaron. "Tell them that we are keeping their safe haven for them in good condition; should they need it, it will be here."

BEFORE I LEFT for Israel I had called Andrea's friend Michele. "Tell Andrea I miss her," said Michele.

"What are you doing these days?" I asked.

"I waitress down at the Never Ever Cafe. When they can afford to hire me."

I laughed with her at the failure of the Never Ever to assure steady employment.

* * *

AFTER MY MOTHER DIED my father married an
old mistress of his, who was in fact not so old.
Although she came from Budapest as a young girl, she
behaved like a geisha and I think my father was as satisfied
as he could ever be with his new arrangements. He took my
mother's money and moved to Boca Raton in a high rise
that was placed on the edge of the beach and blocked the
view of the sun and ocean from the red-roofed Spanish-style
buildings across the drive in whose courtyard orange trees
bloomed and whose ceramic tiles felt cool underfoot.

I visited him there. His wife did not wake before noon
because she believed that sleeping prevented wrinkles. She
then had a daily massage and watched the afternoon game
shows. She did not go out on the sand that bordered the
building or down to the pool that blinked like a turquoise
eye in the center of the cement patio. She believed the sun,
the daylight, was bad for skin and so she stayed indoors
behind drawn curtains, readying herself to dress for dinner.
Her daughter bred Doberman pinschers in Arizona. Her son
was successfully engaged in transporting illegal substances
from Miami to northern points. She told me that the woods
outside her childhood home were full of pine trees and
elves. Boca Raton had a limited supply of both. She looked
in the mirror and applied creams to cure her homesickness.

My father liked to walk along the beach and I walked
with him. We went down the elevator in the huge high rise
and listened to the Muzak that made conversation unnecessary. We walked past the old men in bathing suits listening
to the stock market reports on special radios in a lounge
downstairs and out to the sand and the sun. My father wore
white pants and a blue shirt. He stood against the edge of
the water, not wetting his white canvas shoes, and told me

that he had invested badly in a few ventures but that now he intended to put all his money in an oil rig in Louisiana.

"You're a handsome man, Daddy," I said.

"Am I?" he said, and looked out to sea like an admiral surveying his fleet.

The oil well didn't work out. He lost the money within two years. His wife went to work at the local Saks Fifth Avenue, selling lingerie. He never invited me down to see him again. I think he forgot about me. When I called to tell him that Andrea was born, he told me to find a husband of means and then he never called again or returned my calls.

In the days when women would get together and talk about their fathers and the sexism they had learned at the hearth, I was always hesitant to talk about my father because I felt foolish, as if I had been in love with a movie star who had sent me a shiny copy of his picture with a fake signature in response to a fan letter.

BEFORE ANDREA had gone to Europe, while she was living with friends on the Lower East Side, the year I was working on the Commission to Investigate Comparable Worth set up by the Foundation for the Humanities, funded by tax deductions afforded to several national banks, at four-ten in the morning, the phone rang. The operator asked, "Will you accept a collect call from Andrea Johnson?"

"Yes," I said.

"Yo, Mother!" she said. Her voice had the high timid quality of an eight-year-old.

"What is it?" I said. My nightgown was suddenly soaked in perspiration. Brought from a stage of sleep where even dreams can't reach, nevertheless I could hear the beat of my heart and the throb of my pulse, and the sound of a car speeding along Riverside Drive, and the wind blowing over a litter basket.

"Mother," she said. "I've lost my keys. I need to come home tonight. Now."

"How did you lose your keys?" I shouted. "You woke me up. I have to go to work in the morning."

"I was just robbed," said Andrea, her voice quivering, whispering.

"Where are you?" I asked.

"In the subway. In Brooklyn at the Atlantic Avenue stop. Three guys with a large knife took everything. The toll booth woman lent me this quarter to call."

"Were you hurt?"

"No, no everything's cool. They just took my bag with fifteen bucks, my keys and my cigarettes. Will you wait up for me and let me in?"

At five-thirty, as the sky began to lighten and I could see the dawn bleaching out the sky, the doorbell rang. Andrea's heavy eye makeup had slid into dark circles under her eyes. Her T-shirt was ripped, but I believed she had done that herself for style. Her black pants were stained with some dark substance. "Morning, Mom," she said. "Thanks for waiting up."

"What were you doing in the subway at four in the morning?" I said. "You could get killed, you could have been raped. You must never go into the subway late at night alone." I could hear my voice, the wheezings of an old harpy, a nag, talking to herself on the street.

"Don't worry, Mom," said Andrea, "next time I'll call my limo and have it pick me up."

"This is not a joke," I said with steel in my voice, "you must have been scared."

"Yeah, Mom," said Andrea. "So what? I'm scared all the time, aren't you?" On her thin wrists she wore black leather bracelets with silver studs in them. "What's to eat in this house?" she asked, and headed for the kitchen.

"I'll make you some eggs," I offered.

"I'll take care of myself," she said.

My God, but how? I thought as I went back to bed and waited for my alarm to ring.

I LAY on my bed in the King David Hotel, exhausted. I had gone to the old city with Gloria, who had needed to buy souvenirs for her nieces. We had carefully examined the endless array of dangling silver and brass, the ornate bulbs and the tiny hands of Fatima that hung off loops and beads. The Arab boys badgered and cajoled till we had bought dozens of hanging earrings that would soon lie lost at the bottom of bureau drawers, caught in the sleeve of sweaters, forgotten in the backseats of cars. Gloria and I walked together down the narrow path that had once been the route of Roman soldiers, of temple priests, and we smelled the oil and the incense and the perspiration of the crowds and the stale smell of money changing hands amid the pots and rugs and embroidered blouses being wrapped and unwrapped, accompanied by the cries of children who played at the edges of the stalls. We bought an orange and we shared it together.

"It would have been better," said Gloria, "if we didn't have children."

"Don't say that," I said.

"I mean," she continued, "it would have been better if everything had stayed the way it was before, before we got married and friends were the most important people in our lives."

It would have been better if Sarah had not asked Abraham to send Hagar out into the desert. It would have been better if Moses had not smashed the tablets. It would have been better if the first boatload of slaves had revolted and no others followed. It would have been better if Truman had become a Zoroaster and decided to win the war through meditation. It would have been better if Stalin had choked on a bit of toast when he was five. It would have been better if the Jews had gone to Australia instead of to Europe in the early years of the Byzantine Empire. "It would have been better if" is not a useful thought. But Gloria and I walked along thinking it nevertheless. I bought a pair of dangling earrings with red stones in them for Andrea, though I knew she would not wear them in her present condition. I bought them for later, for afterwards. Gloria bought twenty-four wooden camels, one for each child in her class.

In the hotel the air was as thick as oatmeal and through the open window I heard the sound of splashing in the swimming pool. I fell asleep and dreamed that I was again a child at the country club in Westchester where my mother played cards and my father played tennis. I am sitting in the club dining room at a big table all by myself, staring at a great bowl of shrimp cocktail that topped a nest of ice. I am about to pick up the little fork that I found at my place when Rabbi Nachman comes into the room, his black coat dragging along the floor, his black hat tilting as if it were too big for his head. The other diners, in golf pants, in pinks and greens and blues, do not turn their heads as he hurries past their tables and joins me. He settles himself in the chair next to mine.

"Don't, do not under any circumstances, eat that shrimp," he says.

"Why not? My mother ordered it for me and I like shrimp very much, especially cold with cocktail sauce," I answer.

"It is forbidden to you to eat shrimp." Rabbi Nachman glares at me.

I put my fork down. "It's forbidden to you but not to me," I reply, and pick up my fork. "Go away, I don't believe you're a member of the Quaker Hills Golf Club at all," I add with relish, a child's pleasure in exclusivity.

"It is forbidden you," he begins to chant, "to eat things of the sea without scales and fins. It is forbidden to you to eat the pig that rummages among the dead, it is forbidden to you to eat the ostrich and the armadillo, the crane and the snail. Do you understand, young lady''—he pulls his chair even closer to mine—''what it means to be forbidden?'' I look for the waiter, who might chase away my uninvited guest. ''It means,'' he says, ''that our Master, our Holy One, our Redeemer, has issued a command, has bound you within His covenant and demanded of you that you follow His laws. He separates the good from the bad, the unclean from the clean, the holy from the profane, and with these separations He teaches us to make distinctions, to understand that the world is under His law and follows His order and His rule. Who are you, little girl, to disobey the One Who created all beings, Who divided the waters and planted the trees and gave life to creation?''

I hold my fork in the air. ''God does not want me to eat this shrimp cocktail?'' I ask my guest. Through the windows of the dining room I see the golfers coming round the fifth hole, which is right off the patio where on Friday nights in summer the club holds dances for its members and Chinese lanterns are strung and the musicians play on the bandshell. I put my fork into my shrimp and stare at Rabbi Nachman defiantly. ''I do not believe,'' I say, ''that God will know what I had for lunch if I eat it very quickly.''

Rabbi Nachman reaches over and grabs my hand. He holds it so tightly that he hurts me.

''Careful of my wrist,'' I say, ''I have a tennis lesson this afternoon.''

Rabbi Nachman speaks very softly. ''If you take one bite, just one tiny bite, He Who Guards the World will know that you have sinned, the ancient sin of denying the peoples, denying the Word, rejecting the sound of Sinai. You will be cast out and you will sink like a stone in the ocean, never again to be found; your soul will disappear like last night's tears. We, the People of the Book, will be there when our names are called, and you, unworthy one, will be no more than fungus at the bottom of the sea, eaten by some shrimp descended from those who sit on your plate this moment.''

I put down my fork. "Where is my mother?" I ask politely.

"Eternally dead," says Rabbi Nachman, and I wake up with my hands curled into fists.

IT WAS five o'clock when I started out for the Yeshiva Rachel. It was Friday and Jerusalem was quiet. The stores had closed and the women who had earlier been out shopping for their families were now behind doors preparing. The Wall was crowded with tourists and others who were praying devoutly. Tour leaders were calling out trying to round up stragglers onto the buses. A small Arab boy brushed past me carrying an armful of T-shirts that read in English, "Jerusalem, the Big Apple of the Mideast."

I asked a man in a black coat if he could direct me to the Bratslav synagogue. I wanted to see the chair that had been brought piece by piece from Poland and reconstructed, an empty throne, in the old city. The man I asked spoke no English. I tried again a few blocks later and was waved to the right and the left. I followed.

I realized suddenly that the streets were almost completely empty. Everyone was home with a family or the men were at shul or on their way to shul. I could hear my own footsteps on the stones. I wanted to see Andrea. I wanted to sit down at a table with Andrea. I wanted her to smile at me, be pleased to see me, to say to me, maybe secretly, "Take me home, get me out of here, I want to go home with you." I wanted to sit next to Andrea on the plane flying west and have her tell me amusing stories about her friends the way she used to when I would pick her up unexpectedly after school and we would go have an ice cream in the park or shop along Broadway for some item she needed. I had lost interest in the Bratslav synagogue. I dressed with care. I hoped Andrea would like how I looked. I put on perfume. I wore a covered dress and stockings and I had bought a scarf for my hair. I did not want to embarrass Andrea in this most delicate of situations.

"ANDREA gone religious on us, has she," said my friend Lionel, who had once been my lover and then had transformed himself by some process neither of us could quite remember into my friend. "Should keep her out of trouble, I would think," he added.

"This is trouble," I said. "This is the moment when her brain turns to cream cheese and her independence drips down her chin."

"You have always overrated independence," said Lionel. "You might have made a fellow a nice wife if you hadn't gotten so stuck on independence, and what is it, after all, only a license issued by your support group to be alone a lot."

"That's unkind," I said. It was unkind and I considered retreating to the bathroom where he could not follow.

"After all," said Lionel, "Andrea has made an independent decision not to be independent in the same way that you were independent, but on the other hand her independence is independence from you and yours was independence from everyone else, so it seems fair to let her try it her way."

"Lionel," I said, "do you understand that those people know that they are right on every issue, they have had the word from Sinai, they have no doubts whatsoever. That makes them dangerous. You know that. They not only want everyone else to live under the law but they are going to end up carrying the state of Israel right back to the fourteenth century when it didn't exist and it won't. Every mass disaster of this century has been caused by people who had the truth, ideologues of the left and right. We alone, we secular humanists, are not responsible for cemeteries the size of a continent.''

''We have never had power,'' said Lionel. ''Just give us our chance.''

MRS. COHEN opened the door. She had on a yellow silk dress with ruffles at the neck and the sleeves. She wore no makeup but her round face was shining and she had changed her wig to one with brown curls that clung to her cheeks. She was carrying her baby on her hip. He was wearing an embroidered bib, and a tiny velvet yarmulke was attached by a clip to the wisps of soft hair on his head. She led me upstairs to a room where many girls were gathered around a wooden table covered with a white lace cloth; at the center sat the brass candle holder with Hebrew letters raised in relief at the base. The candles were not yet lit. It took a moment for my eyes to adjust to the dim gray light that dusk was sending through the narrow window. There were whisperings in English and in Hebrew. I realized everyone was looking at me. I felt light-headed, as if I needed to sit down, but there were no chairs in the room. I took a deep breath and felt the tension in my shoulder blades run down my spine, ending in a sharp pain in my hip.

I saw Andrea, a young woman unmistakably Andrea, but not Andrea exactly, at the other end of the table. She looked up at me and her face turned red. The mole over her left eye stood out darkly, her face was round and her red hair was carefully tied in a bow. She was wearing a shapeless blouse that buttoned to the neck and a long skirt. In her eyes I caught the flash of Andrea, the excitement that was always about to spill out, the hunger that was Andrea. I could not

look at her for more than a second. I wanted to hold her and
have her hold me, but the room was filled with young
women and a few older ones. Some were carrying babies,
and a few little girls with hair carefully curled and gold
earrings in each ear chased each other around the table legs.
I stood in place.

There was a silence as everyone in the room shifted about
and found a private stillness. Then Andrea, picking up the
matches and leaning over the candles, sang the blessing in
Hebrew. Her voice had not changed. It had that same high
restless quality it had always had.

When she was finished she looked at me. "How amazing," I said, and it was amazing. It was the shape and the
sound of words my grandmother and great-grandmother must
have said. Andrea had sounded as if she had an angel
trapped in her nasal passages; the strangeness of the sound,
the way it floated to the top of my head, made my hands
shake. Our past had caught up with us, overtaken us and
pulled us back into a moment when the valor of women
burned with the Sabbath candle and we thought of ourselves
as covered with jewels, wandering down from eternity,
dispensing favors, waving gentle hands like the Sabbath
queen bringing rest to the weary.

Then all the women except me joined in the ancient chant
and suddenly my hands were grabbed by two young women
and we were in a circle around the table and there was a
song in Hebrew whose melody was about the breaking of
hearts whatever the words may have been. The woman on
my left kissed me. "Good Shabbes," she said.

"Good Shabbes," said everyone in the room, and there
were smiles and giggles and I stood still waiting for Andrea
to come to me. After all, I had come so far she could cross
the room, at least. Everyone seemed busy with a task. They
were setting tables and platters of food were appearing on
the sideboard. I saw Andrea with a pitcher of water. She set
it down on a small table and looked at me uncertainly. Her
eyes looked wary. I walked over to her and put my hand on

her arm. I could feel how hot my fingers were as they touched her cool wrist. "You came," she said, "you came for me."

"Did you think for a second that I wouldn't?" I asked.

Rabbi Cohen and several other men arrived. They were introduced to me. We sat at several long tables in the dining room. For an hour before the meal was served there were prayers read from a leather prayer book that lay open at each place. Different girls took parts praising and entreating God and welcoming the virtues of the Sabbath.

"I praise you, O Lord My Gd. I thank you, O Lord, Gd of my Fathers, for all the Lovingkindness that has been bestowed on me and the members of my household. O King of Kings, command Your angels, servants of all High, that they should remember me with compassion and bless me as they come to my home on this holy day because I have lit the candles and made my bed and changes my clothes in honor of the holy Sabbath day. Hear our Words, O Lord, O Gd, and Gd of our Fathers. Forsake us not, shame us not, break not Your covenant with us, may You be praised for ever, great and holy Gd, Who has brought us out of the Land of Egypt, out of the Land of Bondage, Eternal King of the Universe."

I glanced at Andrea as Rabbi Cohen translated the words for me. She was following the Hebrew, her eyes fierce with concentration, her finger on the page before her. The glasses on the table were filled with wine and we drank after the blessing. Andrea took a quick look at me and smiled a small tight smile. I would not embarrass her. I would not ask any questions that should not be asked. I tried to reassure her with my eyes. She looked away.

Rabbi Cohen read at great length. He washed his hands in the pitcher of water placed on a side table. The men got up from their seats and followed him, and each in turn poured the water and rinsed his hands. At the table he passed around a long silver box filled with spice and as it came to me I took in the unfamiliar smells and felt again light-headed and uncertain that I would be able to sit upright through the entire meal. Andrea sat at my side. I wanted to reach under the table and put my hand on hers, but I was afraid that would not be considered proper.

When at last the food was served, kept hot by an Arab woman who came to the kitchen for the Shabbes meal, I turned to Rabbi Cohen and asked him how he had come to found the Yeshiva Rachel. He explained that he had been born in a DP camp nine months after the Liberation. His family had managed to join relatives in Williamsburg and so he was raised an American citizen. But a man with such a birthplace, a man who is the tenth generation of rabbis in one family, had an obligation to go to Israel, didn't I think? I agreed. He had brought his wife to Israel. She was the daughter of a well-known scholar, a man who had memorized the entire Babylonian tractate and had done his own translation of it into modern Hebrew. Rabbi Cohen jumped up from the table and disappeared. He came back and placed in my lap a large leather-bound book. "This," he said, "is written by Hannah's father. It's a collection of Jewish legends that came from the period of the Roman occupation, including all the known material on the martyrdom at Masada."

I cradled the book in my arms. I smelled the binding. I opened the pages and turned them. "It's beautiful," I said. "You must be very proud of your father," I said to Mrs. Cohen.

She nodded and excused herself to go into the kitchen.

"One day," Rabbi Cohen said, "as I was nearing the end of my own yeshiva studies, I had gone to visit the graves of our mothers in Hebron, and as I was waiting in the bus station for the return to Jerusalem I saw a group of young people smoking and sitting with their bare arms around each other, and one of the young women came over to me and asked me for money to buy a sandwich. Her eyes were glazed. I gave her the shekels and she bought her sandwich and came back to sit beside me. We started to talk and I

brought her home with me. I discovered that every time I
went out into the city I could come back with another who
sought refuge from the confusion of the temporary world,
the savagery of the place that is deaf to His voice. It has
become my work, to bring women to us who will become
the mothers of a new generation, who will repeople the
earth with the righteous instead of the condemned."

"Your parents," I asked, "they had no trouble accepting
the law after the camps?"

"The Nameless One spoke to Job in a whirlwind and we
know that is true because it is written. 'I am what I am,' the
voice spoke. I do not pretend to understand Hashem. I have
only to follow His ways. I understand this is hard for you.
You have adopted the habit of skepticism. You have lost the
gift of acceptance. You have become so proud of your
cynicism that you have not noticed how it has blighted your
mind, filling it with useless facts, hiding the truth that you
secretly long for. You deprive yourself of the water that
would quench your thirst.

"My father had nightmares. In the early hours of the
morning he would wake with a cry so terrible it could only
have come from the bowels of Gehenna, and when I would
run into the room I would find my mother fled in tears to the
bathroom. I would take my father's hand and kiss his face
and he would say to me, 'You are proof of Gd's mercy.'"

Rabbi Cohen smiled deep into my eyes as if there could
be no question that I would see his point, accept with him,
follow him. It was the seduction of certainty. He was sitting
at the head of the table. I could see myself as a child at his
table and one who had become eager to please. "After the
Shabbes meal," he said, "you may go into my study and
talk with Sarai. She has many things to tell you, isn't that
so, Saralee?" He winked at her. She looked uncomfortable.

At the end of the meal there were more prayers, more
thanks and more entreaties, and then at last the table was
cleared and I followed Andrea into the kitchen, where she
was stacking dishes in the sink. Her friend Hadassah was by

her side. "When your husband jumped off the roof," said Hadassah, "didn't you feel alone, didn't you need the comfort of Gd?"

"I managed," I said, "to comfort myself."

"Didn't you need your people? If it happened to me, I would not want to be without the nation. I would want to sit shiva and cover the mirrors and rend my clothes. I'm sure that would have helped you."

"I managed," I repeated.

"Perhaps you were sad for so long," she continued, "that you neglected your child. That happens, you know, to people who are depressed and have no one to support them."

I looked at Andrea, who was smiling at her friend as if to say Isn't she clever, just like I told you.

"Everyone here knows everything about you, I gather," I said.

Andrea looked at me directly. "I have no secrets anymore. I used to have so many secrets, I never told anybody the truth. I trusted no one. There was so much I didn't even want to tell myself. Now I have no secrets from anyone."

I didn't believe her. A person who has no secrets is a liar. We always fold ourselves away from others just enough to preserve a secret or two, something that we cannot share without destroying our inner landscape.

But perhaps that was exactly what Andrea wished to destroy, the privacy and singularity of her landscape. We went together into the rabbi's study. "Andrea," I said, "tell me the names of Mrs. Cohen's children."

"Sarai," she said. "Mother, you must call me Sarai or I can't talk to you. I am Sarai."

"Sarai," I said, "tell me the names of Mrs. Cohen's children."

"Ezra, Nehemiah, Rachel, Leah, Amos, Shmuel, and the baby, Isaac," she answered. "And when I get married I will have many children, too, and each one will be like a tree in the forest replenishing our land, replacing those who were stolen from us like Rabbi Cohen's grandparents and Mrs. Cohen's aunts and all her cousins.''

"It is hard," I said, "to have so many children, it will leave you time for nothing else. You will be a baby machine, a diaper changer, a cook, you will not have time to know any of your children well if you have so many."

Andrea looked at me coldly. "I will take good care of my children because that is all that matters to me."

"What do you remember, Sarai," I asked, "about before, about before you came here?"

"I remember," said Andrea, "waking up in the morning and needing something or someone to grab me because I used to think I would fall and break my bones if I opened my eyes and tried to get out of bed. Sometimes I would have nightmares that the door was detached from its hinges and was coming toward me and was going to crush me in my bed. I remember a lot of men touching me."

"You didn't have to let them," I interrupted.

"What difference did anything make? You just wanted me to go to school and do something you could boast about to your friends, something I didn't want to do. You used to tell me I could be anything I wanted. Well, I didn't want to be anything at all, before."

Andrea sat on the leather chair opposite me beneath the map of ancient Israel, and I recognized the sullen tone in her voice as it crashed off the walls of the room. I remembered that I didn't always like her. I didn't like her at all. "You didn't have to take drugs," I said, "nobody made you take drugs. They gave you the nightmares, Dr. Wolfert said they gave you nightmares."

"Dr. Wolfert," said Andrea. "That jerk kept wanting me to think about myself. The problem was I was thinking too much about myself. You paid that moron to pretend he cared about me. I think he's a kind of prostitute; he gives love for money."

"You didn't try without drugs," I said.

"Mother, I wasn't wasted. You should know how people get. I wasn't a real junkie. I just fooled around like everyone else. I'm clean now, absolutely clean."

"If you stay here, if you get married and have babies, do you know what you are giving up?"

Andrea looked at me as if she had never seen me before. "A wonderful life like yours?" she said.

"Not like mine." I fought down the irritation that rose in my voice. "Better than mine, the point was always that your life should be better than mine, I always wanted that. If you live in the real world you could be an artist or a singer or you could have a farm with horses"—I remembered when she loved horses and kept an album of photographs of stallions and mares that she cut from magazines—"or you could live in Paris or Rome or Estes Park, Colorado. So many things won't happen to you if you stay here. I could take you back to my hotel with me tonight and we could be on a plane back to New York in a few hours and this whole experience could be a memory, a good memory, of course."

Andrew jumped up and moved to the door. She leaned back against the door as though for support. "If you weren't so selfish you would never ask me to leave here," she said. "I want a cigarette now," she wailed, "just because you came I need a cigarette again. I never think about cigarettes and now I want one because of you."

We were quiet for a while, just standing looking at each other in the rabbi's study. She had gained weight and the fullness of her face, the line of her chin, the slope under her eyes, made me think of Botticelli, or was it Vermeer, a desk top, a bowl of fruit, a wooden-framed window, a woman leaning forward, her face like a mirror to the afternoon light, her skin promising never to decay? Through the door we could hear children running down the hall.

"Do you want to get married?" I asked her.

She looked at me again. Her face was clear of anger. She shrugged and turned away. "Micah," she said, "is a wonderful man. He is like me. We were needing each other, we were needing our Gd, we were needing our past, our place. He is the other part of me. It will be a good marriage, don't worry."

"How often have you seen him now?" I asked.

"At least four times alone and twice with Rabbi Cohen and Avram Berg."

"You have seen him only six times and you're ready to marry him?" I asked. "I can't believe that."

"Six times is enough," said Andrea.

I moved next to her. She moved to the door. "Would you like to see Jerusalem from our rooftop?" she asked me shyly. I nodded. "Wait for a minute or two," she said, and left me alone.

When she returned she had brought me a thick white shawl, an old lady's wrap. I put it over my shoulders and she led me up the back stairs and pushed open a hatch and we were standing on the roof and all around I could see the black silhouettes of chimney tops and a few TV antennas and then the dome of the mosque loomed in the distance and beyond that I could see the outlines of the far hills of Judea and Samaria lit by the three-quarter moon that hung low in the sky.

I stood shivering in the night air, hugging the shawl close, and listened to the Muezzin calling out the hour in the Arab quarter, and the bells of the Armenian church, whose cross could just be identified under the stars, lowed like a cow in the field. The sound of Hebrew chattering came through an open window and a radio in the far distance carried the voice of an urgent announcement. Looking down, I could see in the courtyard an old couple walking together, their covered heads caught in the moonlight. I saw through the curtains of a small window a young boy sleeping in his chair, his hands covering the pages of the book he held in his lap.

"I like it up here, don't you?" said Andrea. "I come sometimes to think by myself. I feel close to Gd up here and each time I come I promise to obey His laws so that He will always watch over me. When it is very hot sometimes we all come up here with our blankets and sleep under the sky." Andrea turned to me with a tentative smile. "Don't you see, it's good I'm here, Mother," she said.

I reached out and touched her hand. I put my arms around her shoulders. She touched my hair. "You are looking very tired," she said. "Are you worried about me?"

"Yes," I said.

"I love you," she said.

I had to turn my face away even in the darkness.

"Are you crying?" she said. "Please don't cry."

As we went downstairs I realized that Andrea's teeth were clean and white. When she smiled I had noticed a gold molar on the left side. She had gone to a dentist.

ARNOLD AND GLORIA ROSE had been to see Michael. A message was waiting at the desk of the King David for me to call when I came in, whatever the hour.

Gloria Rose answered the phone. "Come and see us, we need to talk."

Strange that our children should have brought us so close together, as if we had known each other for years. They would under other circumstances have made good in-laws. I would visit them. They would stay in Andrea's old room when they came to New York. I would go with them to the museum and take them to lunch in Soho. I would write them letters and send them copies of my articles. I would learn all there was to learn about juvenile diabetes. I would join an organization that works for the deaf. As it was, our bond was born of disaster. We were three parents peering down the rabbit hole after our vanishing children.

I entered their room and saw Gloria lying on the bed watching a rerun of *Dynasty* that was broadcast in Hebrew.

"I've seen this one," said Gloria, "so it doesn't matter
about the Hebrew."

Arnold was drinking. He had been drinking for a while.
His face was pink and he had not wiped away the wetness
from the corners of his mouth where his last sip had
splashed awry.

The Shabbat meal at Michael's yeshiva had been all right.
The chicken was rubbery and the noodles stuck together, but
that didn't matter. The wine was sticky sweet, "perhaps the
blessing takes the bite out of it," Arnold suggested. Rabbi
Goldstein's wife had lit the candles. She had given Gloria a
long beige scarf to put over her hair. It had silver threads in
it and hung almost to her waist. Gloria had felt peculiar
wearing the scarf. The prayers had been said. The prayers
had been sung. The spice container had been passed around
the table and Rabbi Goldstein and all the males had washed
their hands and dried them in a blue bowl with an ancient
engraved pitcher at its side. Michael had read a long passage
in Hebrew and Arnold Rose had worn a yarmulke at the
table as he had been asked to do. He had no trouble
identifying his son, who had the same bend to his head he
always had, moved his long arms across the table just as he
had in Cleveland and looked directly into his father's face,
reminding the father immediately of how he had picked him
up when he was six years old and held him on his shoulders
so he could see the Little League game his older brother was
playing in at their local park. He had no trouble recognizing
the child he had fed strawberry ice cream to in the hospital
when he had his tonsils out, the child who showed him his
math homework papers and who pestered his father endlessly
until they bought a family dog who was immediately run
over by a hasty neighbor and replaced by the collie who had
only two years ago died of old age in Gloria's arms. Gloria,
who hadn't liked dogs in the first place, had placed eyedrop-
pers full of medicine in the back of the dog's throat for
months before the end.

After the meal, after the last prayers, Arnold had asked

his son to go for a walk with him. Michael, who insisted upon being called Micah, had refused the father's offer of an immediate escape to the King David, a plane ticket home. Micah had declared his intention to live the rest of his life under the Jewish law as he had learned it here at the yeshiva. He patiently explained to his father that following the Halacha (the laws of observance) would hasten the arrival of the Messiah, bringing to an end the suffering of humankind.

"Michael is no longer afraid of death," said his father. "He told me that I have wasted my life and if I do not change my ways I will rot in my grave for all eternity, whereas he will survive, if not exactly as himself, as a part of the nation, as a line into the future. God damn," said Arnold Rose. "He has turned into a self-righteous prig. He knows the answer to any problem or he can find a rabbi to tell him.

"He says that medical knowledge is vainglory; that the Torah contains everything worth knowing; that observance is better protection against disaster than vaccination. He says I never had time for him when he was growing up. He claims he never knew I loved him. He lies. He looked right at me and lied. I loved him too much, not too little. The Mishnah, he says, everything he needs is in the Mishnah. He offered to teach me how to read Talmud. The god-damned arrogance of it."

Arnold Rose opened the doors to the balcony and watched the lights of the old city wall. "This is the ugliest city in the world," he pronounced. "It's all about dead gods who have been nailed or swept off to heaven with a camel, whose prophets have been flayed alive or thrown into pits of fire or whose children were marched off into slavery. What does anyone like about this city? It is nothing but a calamity waiting to happen again. Look at it"—he waved his hand across the King David pool "—nothing but death here, under every stone another stone that once housed a living person whose memory spooks you even if you're only a

tourist. Give it to the PLO, I say; the place hangs on modern
men like an albatross.''

Gloria turned the TV up louder. "Redemption, my ass,''
muttered Arnold. "Michael accused me of antisemitism. He
accuses me of being ashamed of being Jewish. I am not
ashamed. I am uninterested. I am a man of my time. He is a
relic from a little town with mud-packed streets and sewage
running down the alleys; someplace filled with plague where
little children died of earaches and a splinter was fatal and
childbirth had a thirty-five percent chance of ending in
maternal death.

"I am not ashamed of being Jewish. How dare he accuse
me of that! I'm not a traitor. I simply prefer Mozart to
prayers whose notes rock back and forth like they're trying
to saw you in half. You should have heard my son snoring
out music. It was appalling. He used to play Bach fugues on
the flute. I'm a doctor of medicine, for Christ's sake. I've
been practicing for thirty-two years and now he mocks
everything I've done. The wisdom of man, he says, is like a
message whispered in the ears of fifty men, garbled at the
end, confused and erratic. 'Dad,' he said—to see that
creature with those payess and the black hat and the shirt
that's so white you could grow a germ-free culture on it
calling me Dad!—'everything here makes sense. Everything
we do has a symbolic meaning and a moral meaning and is
related to something that happened in the past. These aren't
made-up rules to inconvenience people. It's all about truth.
For example, when we go into the Succoth and we hold the
herbs as we pray we are holding the four kinds of Jews in
our hands and so we pray for all Jewry. Each plant repre-
sents a different kind of Jew. Isn't that spectacular?' he said
to me.

" 'No,' I said, 'that is not spectacular.'

" 'We eat bitter herbs at the seder to remind us of the
suffering in Egypt. The rabbis wear white on Yom Kippur
because the priest of the temple wore white as he made the
sacrifice for the people. Everything has a reason and the

reason echoes into our history and makes each of us part of the whole. You see, nothing is just itself, everything is connected to the past; every law has an argument that was made for it a long while ago, and we don't improvise our lives and group our way as if we were walking in the dark on a precipice. Everything has already been designed. It is all written before, it's all tied together. The law doesn't change. It stands outside of history, cradling us in its arms.' "

Gloria looked very pale. She stared at the TV. Arnold paced the floor. "It makes no sense to me," he said. "I can't make any sense out of it. Michael said to me, 'You have mistaken your hospital, your clinic, for the inner sanctum of the temple, you have made a mortal error.' You understand, my whole life, my work, the money I earned to give him his education, his food, his ten-speed bike, his flute lessons, it's all worthless, hollow, meaningless in his eyes. I am beneath contempt and he respects only those myopic, fossilized rabbis who have the important know-how when it comes to footnotes in those crumbling books."

"Stop it, Arnold," Gloria called out. "You're only upsetting yourself. You're a wonderful doctor and Michael knows it. He's just confused now."

"It's not my fault," said Arnold. "You were always telling him about earthquakes and floods and wars. You let him go trick-or-treating for Unicef and you told him that he should leave the earth better than he found it."

"You told him that too," Gloria said. "You took him to your clinic when I thought he was too young."

Arnold sat down. "It can't be wrong for a boy to see his father at work. That can't produce a fanatic."

"Annie," said Gloria, turning off the TV, on which an elf was doing a soft-shoe on top of a giant container of yogurt, "we're going in circles."

"Maybe," I said, "when they put the words over the gates at Auschwitz, 'Work shall make you free,' all over the globe people stopped wanting to be free. Some of our

children just can't make it. They're not strong enough."
The room was silent.

"My stone-deaf sister," said Gloria, "is married and has
two hearing children who seem perfectly normal."

"We should have done better," Arnold said, "we should
have."

I walked toward the door. "Don't go," said Arnold Rose,
his voice barely audible.

"Yes, don't go," said Gloria.

I accepted a drink and the three of us sat down on the
chairs on the balcony. I realized I was still wearing the
shawl Andrea had lent me.

"I just can't bear to think of Michael wasting his life like
that," said Arnold. "I don't believe for a minute that some
fucking voice in a burning bush wants my son to spend his
days making gold earrings for lady tourists, eating like some
paranoid who expects to be poisoned by his neighbor, and
praising a creator who is either sitting up there in the clouds
devising dramatic ways to annihilate him or who may not be
there at all. What I hate most is the humility. The Almighty
God, the all-powerful God, the One Who writes in the book
who should live and who should die; it makes me sick to my
stomach that my son can't stand up and say, I'll do what I
want, I'm a man not a worm. Your son"—he turned to
Gloria—"has turned into a worm."

Gloria ignored him. "Michael says he wants to marry
your daughter. He wants to take care of her, to have children
with her, to build a life in Jerusalem, near the yeshiva, with
her. He made me this necklace in his jewelry shop." Gloria
leaned toward me and I saw a silver chain from which hung
a green stone set in the Star of David. Its design was not
original. "He explained," said Gloria, "that the catch is
not quite right. He is still a novice at this craft. He said to
be careful when I took it off, but I can't seem to get it off at
all."

I went behind her and tried, but the silver loops would

not respond to tug or gentle pull. "He's just learning," I said.

"I don't want to look at that necklace," said Arnold, and reaching over yanked it hard. It came apart in his hands. He tossed it over the balcony edge and into the bushes below. "Are you going to let this happen? Are you going to let your grandchildren be afraid to eat anything in your house?"

"I don't know," I said. "I don't know."

"I'm not giving up," said Arnold Rose.

"The three of us," said Gloria, "we'll stick together, we'll keep on trying."

"I'll drink to that," I said, and raised my glass.

I woke up late the next morning and had my breakfast on the terrace. At the next table a young American woman was trying to feed her baby from a jar while keeping her four-year-old from running into the gardens below. The father returned to the table and his son sat down and began to eat his cereal. A car was waiting for them. They were going to visit her parents, who had retired to Natanya.

I drank my coffee and stared at the family. How good it would be to have everything ahead, to have just recently created life, to feel that you could, through your decisions— yes to television, no to television, yes to summer camp, no to summer camp, yes to a sleepover, no to an extra package of cookies—shape the future for your children, could give them character with which to protect themselves against the coming events of their personal histories. How fine it must feel to wake and answer the cry of a baby and know that just by fulfilling your trust you are making your child capable of caring for others, of imagining and inventing and learning. You are creating a mind and earning the right to direct that mind; or is that only the illusion that makes the work bearable? Are we in fact in our million ministrations only holding death at bay and our deeds of no more worth than those of the sandbaggers at the edge of the rising river attempting to control the path and ferocity of the waters? I watched the young mother whose hands were now busy with the baby's temporary stomach difficulties. I am ashamed to admit that I enjoyed my knowledge that her turn would likely come when she would taste ash and wonder where her error had been.

The Roses came down and joined me at my table. The waiter brought coffee and juice. The baby at the next table began to cry hard and the mother could not comfort him. She was beginning to look frantic. The screams of her child were knotting in my stomach. Her husband left the table, taking the older child with him.

Arnold went over to her. "I am a pediatrician," he said, "from Cleveland. Perhaps you would let me hold your baby for a moment and we'll see what the trouble is." His voice was gentle, softer than I had heard it before.

The mother silently handed over her screaming bundle and Arnold placed the baby against his chest. He began to croon to the child. "There," he said, "it's not easy to travel to strange places, especially when you don't know your own home yet. There," he said. "It will be fine, you'll see," and his large arms held the small child and his chest turned into a massive pillow.

The baby's sounds changed from anger to grief and then to quieter complaint and then, in the second turn around the terrace, to silence, and above Arnold's shoulder we could see a pair of eyes looking around in contented curiosity.

"There," said Arnold, "now you feel better," and he stood still with the baby in his arms and rocked back and forth under the striped umbrella. In the haze of the morning sun they looked like one large form, man and baby, made of the same material, molded edges flowing one into the other. The mother was smiling at him, expressing her slightly embarrassed gratitude. Arnold returned the baby as the waitress brought cucumbers and milky white cheese to our table.

"How did you do that?" I asked.

"I'm a professional, remember?" He smiled at me, only

the gray pebble-filled pouches under his eyes gave away the excesses of the night before.

I decided to keep my appointment with an Israeli lawyer whose name had been given me by a friend who had attended a conference on battered women in New Orleans and came back with the name of a lawyer in Jerusalem who represented a network of shelters in Israel and was prominent in women's causes. I did not expect much help from the law. Arnold Rose had already exhausted his governmental connections and it seemed unlikely that matters of religious illumination could respond to rules of state, but I had nothing else to do with myself but wait for the evening when I was to return to the yeshiva.

Naomi Shen Lov was not gentle. "Another of those fool kids you Americans can't seem to raise right come to lurk around the yeshivas looking for someone to take care of them, searching for the meaning of life you Americans couldn't give them. It's your materialism, your chaos, your divorce rate, your drug scene, your porno magazines, your cutthroat competitiveness and you're shipping it to us, every crazy Jewish kid whose parents ran out of insurance for the mental hospital takes a trip on El Al and finds God." She glared at me. "We are in need of true Zionists, of people of learning and technology and democratic principles, and what do you send us, your broken, drug-riddled, starry-eyed, wiped-out dropouts. And what do they do when they get here? They breed and make more of themselves, exactly what we don't need, thank you very much."

I reminded Naomi Shen Lov that she had met my friend at the battered women's conference. She asked if I wanted a cup of coffee. "Some of those nice fellows who study the Torah morning, noon and night, you know what they do? They go home and bash their wives about. You think that's not true. We hear it. We get many in our shelters and they tell us about others. Holy means they don't look at pictures of naked women. It doesn't mean they fight beside us to preserve the state. It doesn't mean they never make a woman cry."

The doorbell rang. "My client," said Naomi Shen Lov, "a victim of the law of your daughter's adopted religion."

A young women of about twenty-five entered. She was bareheaded and wearing a flower print dress that marked her as secular. Hebrew was exchanged. The young woman turned to me and explained in English, "I am here because the rabbinical courts have denied me permission to remarry. My husband, the father of my three-year-old son, was killed in Lebanon. By the law of the religious courts, which is here the law of the land, I cannot remarry without the ceremony of release being performed by my husband's younger brother. He will not do this for me unless my family gives him fifty thousand dollars. My parents will have to sell their apartment if I am ever to marry again." The young woman stared at the floor. "I don't want my life to be over," she said, "but what can I do? Should I ask my parents to go into the street in their old age or should I give up and live like a dried-up stick although I am not yet thirty? I might as well have died with Etan on the land mine." She looked at me reproachfully.

Naomi Shen Lov stood up. "This is the work of the holy people who have managed in this insane asylum to become the keepers of the law of marriage, divorce, and child custody. They say the law has come from Sinai and should not be changed by our modern faddish convictions. I will argue this case in front of the rabbinic court. There are no women on the court because no women are allowed to be rabbis and I will lose again. But we keep trying." She shrugged. "And when your daughter gets married and has a hundred children they will all grow up and vote and demonstrate and insist that the rest of us have no right to another code of law, we must live as if the temple had just been destroyed, as if women were better off without too much learning, as if the events of this century had not taught us anything about respect or dignity. These Orthodox are going to turn the Knesset into a shul and all of Israel into a shtetl. We will be armed with prayers when the invaders come."

The young woman opened her pocketbook and showed me a picture of her son and then a photograph of a young man. "He is my fiancé," she said. "Can you help me? Can you tell women in America to help me?"

I wrote down her name in my address book; perhaps a philanthropist would pay the blackmail.

"Are you aware," said Naomi Shen Lov, "that the archaeological digs in this country are constantly in jeopardy because the Orthodox do not want graves undone? They don't want bones disturbed when the Messiah comes to raise the dead. They won't let scientists do autopsies. In the twentieth century, after the smoke of the crematoriums, they prevent us from studying our history, our own bodies. Their girls are excused from the army so they won't be contaminated by the values of the other Israelis who are doing service to keep us all from being driven into the sea. They have eaten up this society with their certainty, their unwillingness to let someone else drive a car, take a swim on the Sabbath. Intolerant, bigoted, fearful of a little menstrual blood, holier than holy, pious but cruel, demeaning women, forcing their truth on everyone else—that's what your grandchildren will do in Israel. Better it would have been if your daughter could have been a Moonie and stayed out of our hair."

"Can you stall Andrea's marriage?" I asked Naomi Shen Lov.

"On what grounds, on what legal premise? She is an adult, yes?"

"Yes and no," I answered. Biology is not everything in human development.

"There is nothing I can do for you." Naomi Shen Lov showed me to the door. "Tell American women to keep their sick children home. That would be better than buying Israeli bonds." She pushed into my hand a pamphlet about her battered women's shelter and I was on the street again.

I sat down at a cafe for lunch. I was too old to have another child to replace Andrea. I was probably too old to find another man who could lie in bed with me at night and pull me safely into the day. I reminded myself that liberation was never intended as a paradise, where contented women could loll under chestnut trees and tell frightening stories of how it used to be. I was now planning to make an appointment with my doctor to find out if they had yet invented a medicine that might prevent dreams.

During the night I had dreamed that I was in Williamsburg. In my dream it appears as if all the women of the Hasidic community are out on the street pushing toward the Jewish center. I am carried along by the crowd. There are a few men on the sides who have handkerchiefs in their hands and their eyes are red. It is a funeral. I have come to a funeral. Whose funeral? I ask, and the ones I speak to turn their heads away from me. From the size of the crowd in the streets I assume that the dead person had been important. Because the mourners appear to be mostly women I assume a woman has died.

As I approach the building I see the coffin being carried on the shoulders of men and placed in a hearse and slowly the hearse makes its way through the crowd. Women put their hands on the black wood as it passes and kiss the palm that touches the hearse. Whose funeral?

I see a knot of mourners behind the hearse. There is Rabbi Nachman surrounded by many children, some quite grown, others still small. The children are trying to look brave. The small ones hold the hands of the older ones. The boys all have glasses and black jackets and the girls wear dark coats and their hair is carefully braided. Whose funeral? I want to look in the curtained windows of the hearse but I can't push my way close enough.

On the corners police cars wait to escort the mourners to the cemetery. I make my way up to the front. "Who has died?" I ask Rabbi Nachman, who seems to be at the head of the line.

"My wife," he says. "The woman who has been my wife since I was thirteen years old."

"I'm so sorry," I say.

"She died in childbirth; our nineteenth will live to give thanks to the Holy One."

"I don't know how to comfort you," I say.

Rabbi Nachman turns to me and holds me by the elbow. "You could marry me," he whispers. "You could take care of my children who will need a mother."

"I couldn't," I say, "I am not a believer."

"That will be all right," nods Rabbi Nachman, "all that will be required of you is to keep kashrut, observe the holidays, keep sacred the Sabbath and you can learn those simple things very quickly. Good deeds, good behavior, will in time turn you into a believer. Marry me," says Rabbi Nachman, "and I will tell you wonderful stories. I want to tell my stories to you."

I try to go to the side or to sink back into the crowd, but somehow I am pushed forward beside Rabbi Nachman, and as we follow the hearse he tells me the story of the kingdom of the purple mountain, where the King became very ill with a mysterious illness that his doctors could not treat. He became very thin and his hair fell out and he was weak and confined to his bed. He had patches of raw flesh on his skin and his fingers curled up and refused to open. Magicians were called from far parts of the kingdom, sorcerers appeared at the bedside and brought him toads pickled in dandelion juice and spiders that were trained to bite and medicines made from tree bark and rodent dung; but nothing helped.

His consort tore her hair and wept to the heavens and prayed with her advisers and pleaded with the doctors to find a cure. The King slept many hours and when he was awake he held her hand and asked her to sing to him because above all other things on this earth he loved the voice of his wife. She sang till he fell asleep again. The food that had been prepared by the most famous cooks in the land sat untouched by his bedside.

The Queen decided to journey to the top of the kingdom's purple mountain and there beg for the life of her husband from the power above. She took only one servant and set out on the treacherous path up to the top of the icy crags that stood above the kingdom. The trip took her four days and four nights. When at last she reached the peak she got down on her knees and promised to crawl down the mountain, to eat nothing but roots and dirt, to pierce her skin with thorns, to let insects sting her face, if only her husband would be healed. She promised to rip out her tongue and never to sing again if only her husband would be healed. She offered to die herself in his place if a death were necessary.

She crawled down the mountain on her hands and knees and they became bloody and infected with dirt. She scratched her face with thorns and sat among the bees till they stung her face. As she approached the castle in which her husband lay upon his sickbed she sent her servant on before her to inquire about his condition. The servant returned to the Queen and reported that there had been no change. So the Queen took her own hands and pulled at her tongue and ripped it bloody from the back of her throat and lay on the grass choking and weeping from pain and fright. The servant ran back to the castle and brought doctors and a cart and blankets to cover the injured Queen.

In the castle the King called for his wife to sing to him. "The Queen can no longer sing," explained the prime minister. The King was grieved but he nevertheless was able to eat a bit of soup that afternoon.

Within days his sores were no longer running and his fingers uncurled and there was no more hair on the royal pillow. He called his prime minister and all his cabinet to a meeting to show them that he was well again. "It may have been the doctors, it may have been the sorcerers, it may have been my wife, who was willing to give up her voice for me; whatever the cause, I am thankful and now I need a new Queen, one with a beautiful voice to sing to me in the evenings when I am tired.''

The old Queen was sent to the country and the new Queen, who was younger by far, came to be loved by all in the kingdom for her songs, which could be heard from the castle windows at all hours of the night.

''I am not a believer,'' I screamed as a group of women in mourning clothes come up to me and led me away. Then I am alone in an empty street. The hearse, the mourners, Rabbi Nachman, his children, everyone has disappeared. I am lost.

A few black children play stickball on the corner; in a garage a truck leans on its side, its tires removed. I see a young redheaded girl dashing toward the Burger King down the block. She is wearing familiar red high-heeled shoes and a black miniskirt. I call to Andrea, I call several times, but she doesn't turn around.

BRURIA; in my profession we are always recovering forgotten women, women whose diaries, whose letters, whose histories, show us, if we turn the kaleidoscope just right, three-dimensional landscapes in which the great theories, the plans of the war council, the inventions, the scientific breakthroughs, the aggressions, the digressions, the ambitions, the stealth, the oppression and the liberation, are set. We see through female eyes the daily human experience; how it felt to be a war widow, a mail-order bride, a factory girl, an immigrant, a debutante, to lose a baby, to bury a son, to plant an orchard, to serve the food, to clean the kitchen, to nurse the baby, yours and someone else's, to be burned out in a revolution, to gain everything because of a revolution.

Women's history is not, as students sometimes think, about recovering the great figures our male colleagues have neglected. It carries a mandate to fill in the empty spaces where feeling pain, ambition, expectation, human experience, belong. Women's history reminds us of the primacy of biology. It is about the seam between the idea and the weather, the weather and human sweat, human sweat and human dream, and always, continually, boringly and persistently it is about giving birth and children dying. It is about mates gone off to sea, to war, disappearing on the road selling or buying. It is always about money and food and shelter and how these needs are affected by lust, by birth and death, politics and catastrophe. It is about loneliness: how we avoid it, court it, ride it straight to the grave. This is as true for Marie Antoinette as for her dairy maid.

And Bruria. She was pious and educated, a contradiction in her time for her sex. She was virtuous but seduced. She lost her father and her children and finally her home. Bruria disappears. She brought about her own destruction by learning too much. Maybe if my daughter learns just a little and stays in her place and does not become conspicuous, does not frighten the others by breaking the rules, she will be safe. Feminism is not an inherited trait.

Bruria, I hope that you went to another city, perhaps to Greece, and there became a philosopher who gathered disciples by your side who wrote down your wise sayings and issued them under a pseudonym, because it was not seemly for a woman to be so wise. Perhaps you used the nom de plume Plato. Maybe instead you made your way to Africa and there a great prince saw you in the marketplace and you became his concubine and because you were so wise you soon replaced his adviser and under your guidance the crops of the land flourished and the merchants grew fat and the beggars were taken off the streets and given a city of their own, which you administered with justice for all. More likely you were captured by pirates and sold into slavery and spent the rest of your days scrubbing the tiled floors of a mistress who worshiped a golden idol and gave you no food but crayfish and pork and so you starved to death in a house of plenty.

The difficult thing about women's history is that we have to imagine so much of it. Are we fortune-tellers, palm readers or historians?

I ARRIVED at the yeshiva after dinner. Andrea opened the door for me. "Come and meet him, Mother, he's here, waiting for you."

Her eyes were wide and alert. The scarf that she had tied around her head was pale pink and from the twist in the back it spread down over one shoulder like a horse's mane. "My scarf," she said. "I am wearing it to show Micah how I will look when we marry." Her hands were trembling. She walked so fast down the hall that I had to call to her to wait for me.

I followed Andrea into the study and there, looking out the window, nervously playing with his tsitsit, whose fringes hung below his black jacket, was Michael, Micah. On his feet he wore the more familiar Nike sneakers. He was as Andrea had described him, tall, narrow, pale, shy. His reddish beard was scraggly and uneven and the ringlets he had grown down the side of his face hung limply as if they had been pasted on or were attached to his black hat, part of the props that must be returned to the costume room when the senior play is over.

"I am pleased to meet you, Mrs. Johnson," he said. "I want to tell you that I will take care of your daughter for the rest of our natural lives and we will fill our days with sanctity, not just on the holidays or the Sabbath, but every day we will share with the One Above in the glory of His creation. I am thankful to you for having brought your daughter to me."

He did not look directly into my face. I knew the speech

was largely rehearsed. It sounded as if it had been given a thousand times before, but then that was the nature of this religion. Everything had been done and said before and there was its value, or its hollowness, depending on your view. Through the practiced words I heard the boy trying to behave well, to do what was expected of him, to still the fright that must have been rising in his gut at such a decisive statement.

"I don't deserve your thanks," I said. "I had nothing to do with Andrea coming to the Yeshiva Rachel."

He looked confused. This was not part of the script. There was a long pause. He looked at me sadly. "I know," he said. "I understand my parents are not happy that I am here, either. It is very hard for them to accept what I am doing." Behind his glasses I could see his eyes blink nervously. Did he have a tic? "Sarai and I hope that you will come to see that our way is the right one and that you will join in our wedding plans."

My daughter left the room, closing the door quietly behind her. She had stood for the first moments of our meeting in the corner, in a shadow. Was that her place?

"Michael," I said, "tell me what it was like for you in the real world."

He stood before me stiffly. "Micah," he said. "You must call me Micah or I don't know who you are talking to." He waited.

"Micah," I said, "talk to me." I caught a tremor in his lower lip as he leaned forward toward the light on the desk.

"This is the real world; the other, the one I lived in before, was an illusion."

"Micah," I said, "tell me the truth, tell me how it was for you, when you were at college, when you were home on vacation."

Michael sat down in a chair and twisted the fringes of his tsitsit around his fingers. He pulled at the red ringlet that hung down the side of his face. He pushed the tortoise-shell glasses up and down his nose and I could see the bluish marks where they pinched him between the eyes. He blinked and blinked. I could see the traces of the acne that must have plagued him a short while ago. "It seems a long time ago now, I don't remember so much." He smiled at me, still not looking in my face, like a student who had skipped the lecture and was hoping to get away with it.

"Tell me what you remember," I asked him.

"I didn't believe in Gd," he said. "No one in my family believed in Gd. But sometimes I would be playing my music and lying on my bed and a feeling would come over me as if I were not anchored to the ground, as if I had no insides. It was very frightening. I was afraid to go look in the mirror. I thought I might not have a face. At school everyone seemed so sure of themselves, they all had plans about getting cars and going out on dates and winning. I thought everyone was going to win something but me. I didn't want to let down my mom and dad, but what could I win? My brother George said he had found the meaning of his life on the beach in Baja. But that made Dad crazy. I visited George. He gave me coke. He had a girlfriend who had a rash from the sun and kept itching all the time.

"I decided to take some dope to block out certain pictures in my head. It was hard, you know, I could have been any number of things and I just couldn't make up my mind. My dad wanted me to go into medicine, of course, but I thought maybe I wouldn't be so good at it because I'm not the same sort of person my dad is. I'm not curious about the insides of people. I don't want to know how anything in the body works or doesn't work. I didn't want to do it. Dad just seems a natural with sick kids but I felt peculiar around them. I wasted a lot of time on dope. I kept thinking there must be something else out there, something to do besides just grow up and die. I didn't want to die. I thought about becoming nothing and nobody caring and I thought if I took the car and drove it into a telephone pole I could get it over with, and I thought about that a lot."

Andrea returned. She brought in tea and cookies and

poured a cup for Michael, who smiled at her quickly as if he didn't want me to catch him in such a bold and intimate gesture. My daughter poured me a cup and I was amazed. With the teapot in her hand, with the full skirt she was wearing brushing almost against the floor, the scarf on her head, she looked calm, almost like a Cezanne apple, rosytoned and solid. I felt as if I were part of a composition: books, curtains, map of ancient Israel and girl serving tea. She was the woman and he was the man and I was the mother. Everyone and everything in the room had a weight and held to the ground.

As we sat in the study talking I noticed the flash of a silver necklace hanging against her blouse. "A pretty necklace," I said.

Andrea moved next to me so that I could see it more clearly. "Isn't it beautiful? Micah made it for me. I am never going to take it off." Since I knew something about Micah's jewelry efforts this seemed a good decision. As I looked about the room everything appeared in order; only my expectations fit rudely into the scene.

"I came to Israel," said Michael, "with two friends of mine who had bought this van we were going to drive all the way to New Delhi. I had been out of college a while, knocking around. I didn't want to go back to college. I thought about moving to New York and becoming a musician. But then I knew I would end up waiting on tables and playing my flute on the streets hoping someone would throw change at me. I wanted something great, not to be ordinary, not just to take up space. I wanted to make a mark. But how? What was the point of studying? What for? It didn't mean anything to me. I was hoping to switch from pre-med into history. But history was another joke. Each term we studied another war and the collapse of yet another empire. Where was it going? What was the point? All that killing for what? I wasn't a pacifist or any other kind of political kook and there was nothing happening on the campus; I mean, you couldn't demonstrate against Wall Street, especially if you thought you might want a job there one day. I did a little for divestment, but what was it? A night out on the library steps, singing some old songs with people who didn't remember my name two days later. I came to Israel because my friends asked me to go with them. Sometimes Gd reveals himself in the most ordinary and casual of ways.''

There was a long pause. I waited for him to continue. He thought he had spoken enough. "Tell me the rest, Micah," I asked. "Tell me how you changed."

"We were the three of us sitting around in the parking lot of the Rockefeller Museum. We had some dope and we were just sitting on the van and taking in the sun when this bearded man came and offered us a night's rest in his yeshiva. 'Come and see what we do while you're in Israel,' he said. 'You can have a shower and we've got a great cook.' We spent the night. My friends left the next morning. I decided to stay a while. Here I am.''

He looked at Andrea is if for approval. She immediately said, "Micah has told you everything. This is enough third degree. You can see how special he is, can't you? You can see that we will be good together.''

"You like making jewelry?" I asked. "You will really be content to make jewelry, to work with your hands for the rest of your life?''

"It will be a good job for me," he said. "There are many tourists who come to our quarter and they will buy our jewelry and so I can pay for my wife and children. In the evenings I can study. Study of the Talmud is the real purpose of my life. It brings me closer to Gd. I will never be a great teacher or a famous scholar because I started so late and I will always be behind, but each day I can understand something else. I can go on learning till the end and that is all that is wanted of me, all that I want of myself. I can read Hebrew now well enough so that I can follow the best students in our yeshiva. I will make jewelry so that I can serve Torah. My dad doesn't understand that

Gd doesn't want everybody to go to medical school. I have found something that will make me far happier than he is, don't you see.''

There was another long pause. I waited. He said, ''I will make you gold earrings with a little pearl in them if you like. I have just today learned how to do that, to set the pearl in the center of the earring. It is not so easy to get it just right. I would like to give you my first pair, the ones I made today.''

He looked at me now directly. His face was so open, so eager, that I could only tell him how much I looked forward to having those earrings, to take them back to America with me and telling everyone that they were a gift from a friend in Israel.

He looked worried. He blinked again several times in a row. ''The pearls are a little off center in these earrings. Maybe I should give you the next pair I make, they will be better, I'm sure.''

''I like earrings with the pearls off center,'' I reassured him. ''Why are you wearing sneakers?'' I asked. All religious men seem to go about in black pointy shoes and high black socks.

Andrea said, ''He is not yet ready to give up his sneakers. He needs, I think, to remind himself of where he has run from.''

''These sneakers,'' said Michael, ''have a smell to them of everything before. I can't just put them in the trash can. But when they wear out I will not buy another pair. I will buy the black shoes then, I promise.''

''The sneakers,'' said Andrea, ''they are like my tattoo. Rabbi Cohen says that one day, when I am ready, we can have it removed by a surgeon. But for now I should carry it as a reminder of how I was and what side I was on. I can feel the tattoo sometimes as if it were burning or itching on my shoulder. It is tempting me to wicked thoughts. That is good, though, because I resist and become stronger.''

''Has Micah seen the tattoo?'' I asked.

They both looked embarrassed. "It is not like it is in the world you live in," said Micah. "Here we do not touch our women, even to hold hands, until after we are married. It is not right that man and woman should excite each other when their minds should be on other matters."

I looked at Andrea, who was staring into her lap. "You really believe this?" I asked her.

There was a flash of panic across her face. I felt I had a hold but then a second later she was composed. "You do not understand that love is more, well, special, when you save it for the right time. Here we have learned how a man and woman can keep their love for each other new as the monthly cycles repeat themselves. It is a better way than yours. We are patient and we are rewarded."

"What are you learning?" I asked. "What is this you study all day?"

Michael looked at me to see if I was teasing or testing or taunting him. I wasn't. He leaned forward, his features now settled into an intent line. His flush faded, and behind his glasses his eyes were focused clearly. "Listen," he said. "Today we studied in the Talmud about the destruction of the temples. The rabbis told the story that before the second devastation a famous rabbi held a party and told his servant to invite Bar Kosima, and his servant got confused and invited instead a man named only Kosima, who was an enemy of the host. When he arrived, the host asked him to leave, and he begged the host to let him stay. He did not wish to be humiliated in front of the others gathered there. He offered to pay for half the party, but the host said no, he must leave. He offered to pay for the whole party, but still the host said no, he must leave, and he took him by the arm and made him go. The unwanted guest was deeply ashamed. This, the rabbis said, was an example of Causeless Hatred, and this was the reason that Gd let the enemies of the city of Jerusalem triumph. Gd saw that the hearts of the men of the city were filled with Causeless Hatred. We are studying

these passages because we will soon mourn for the city and
its inhabitants again." Michael paused and looked at me.

"You are saying," I said, "that an entire city was sacked
because one man did not let another stay at a party?"

Michael smiled at me, as if I were a difficult but charming child. "You misunderstand," he said. "The story from
our rabbis is meant to instruct us that each of our acts, each
of our gestures toward our fellows, becomes part of the
history and the fate of our people and of the fate of the
creation itself, and that each moment of life, even those that
are not sacred or marked as holy, must be lived in the spirit
of His Path, His Way. If we all had done so, we could have
saved the city."

"But you weren't there," I said.

"We have learned," said Michael, "that in Hebrew the
tenses of all the words in the verses of the Book of
Lamentations are fluid between the past and the present and
the future. One disaster echoes and foreshadows the next
and the one that went before. Time is like a river that flows
in circles, and we pick it up where we stand on the bank,
but the water has been everywhere. Even the grammar of
the scripture tells us this."

Here was the kind of conversation a colleague of mine
once referred to as varicose vein thinking, the kind of logic
that caused her to wear support hose in class.

"See," said Michael to me, his face alight and his eyes
still steady. "This is what I want to do with my life, learn
and understand. Everything, the verb tense, the story of the
rabbis and the party, the destruction of the temple, everything is woven together, and I am a part of the tale, of the
way the words are written, of what has been said and what
will be said. Of course, I don't know very much yet," he
added. He looked at Andrea and began blinking rapidly
again. She looked at me, half-afraid.

"It's amazing," I said. "You have learned so much."
Andrea knew I admired learning. She smiled.

Michael said, "Rabbi Kook, the first chief rabbi of the

new Zion, said that Israel will be preserved by Causeless Love."

"And Arms," I muttered under my breath.

The door opened. A man with brown curls down to his neck and a short athletic build entered. He introduced himself as Avram Berg of Micah's yeshiva, Micah's friend. He was delighted to meet me. He had heard from Sarai that I was a remarkable woman.

"You are the painter," I said.

"Former painter," he answered, leaning easily against the bookcase.

"You must miss painting," I said. "You had a gift, after all."

"If a man had a wolf tied to his legs who kept biting him day after day, would he miss the wolf?"

"I don't see the analogy," I said. I wanted him to know he was not talking to one of his gullible children. "You were an artist and the work must have given you pleasure," I added.

"It only kept me even," he said. "I was running hard to stay in place. I fell behind. I could not make a universe as diverse yet as unified as Gd's. I was a pale imitator, a clumsy mime. I wasn't good enough."

"And now?" I asked.

"Oh, now," he said, "I am good enough. I make it from one Day of Atonement to another." He grinned at me. "Your daughter is a brave young woman," he said to me. "This will be an excellent couple."

Was he friend or enemy? Was I? "Will my daughter ever hold a job, talk in public, work in politics, become a leader?" I asked him.

He laughed at me as if I were teasing him, flirting, perhaps. "Here," he said, "we believe that the king's daughter should stay within. She will find plenty to do in the house. Your American women, I understand, spend their time running in the parks until their menstruation stops. Is that so?"

"An exaggeration," I said. "Perhaps even a libel."

"Really," he said. "I am relieved to hear it."

"Mother." Andrea spoke up. "Will you come to our wedding? We need to know if you will come. We are planning in just eight days to have the wedding here in the courtyard with everyone from both yeshivas and you and Micah's parents, I hope. You are happy for me. Say it to me, say you are happy for me."

I felt very tired, as if I had climbed to the top of Mt. Sinai and come down again. "Yes," I said, "I am very happy for you, but you may not have the wedding without me. I am coming."

Did she want me to say yes or did she want me to say no? Was I being permissive when I should have been firm? Was my acceptance given out of the excessive permissiveness that had led her in the first place to bind herself to endless rules and laws that ordered every breath that she might take? I might have been lying to her. She had deceived me often enough. I could lie to her without feeling guilty. Perhaps I really didn't accept this marriage but was only stalling for time, keeping in touch, not losing her to the bowels of the yeshiva, where they were sure to grind her into a kosher offering for the temple of their Lord. But on the other hand, perhaps I meant what I had said. It appeared to be a situation without choice. Andrea always had me with my back against the wall and my feet stuck in cement.

Michael stood up. He was so unlike his father, whose bulk was part of his authority. He glanced at me quickly out of the corner of his eye. "Help my mother," he said. "I want my mother to find peace. Tell her I will play the flute sometimes. I promise. I am afraid she will not come to see me again. Tell her that if any of our children is born deaf, we will love that child the most. She would want to know that." He looked at me and blinked furiously.

As I left the house, the home of my daughter that was not my home, I walked past a room with an open door. Inside I saw Mrs. Cohen sitting at a small table with a chessboard open and a battle engaged. She had no opponent. As we passed Andrea said, "She plays with herself. No one else is good enough."

As I felt the night air on my face, as I moved away from the quarter, I was not peaceful. Why couldn't Andrea stand up without cringing and admit that if you died you were dead forever and if you lived you had to invent the form of your life yourself and give it content and soul through the strength of your own spirit?

On the other hand, none of us do that very well. Often I had thought of Hilary stepping off the terrace and spreading his arms, sinking and rising up again as if he had been on a diving board and we were showing home movies of his feat. It is hard to live with finality and not to rewrite the script, creating a happy ending. Am I a better woman because I try not to flinch, and if I am a better woman, who notices and rewards me or comforts me for my courage?

LAST NIGHT I went with Andrea and the Cohens and all the members of the yeshiva to a synagogue. It was Tisha B'av, the day set aside to remember the destruction of the first temple. It is a very important holiday, Andrea explained to me as we walked to the synagogue. Everyone feels very sad as if it happened yesterday and all the women wear dark clothes and cover their hair with a black scarf.

We were each given a candle as we entered. The synagogue was dark and somber and a black curtain hung in front of the ark. We were sent upstairs into the balcony, where there were not enough seats. The women stood against the back wall; some sat in the spaces between the aisles. There was a whisper of talk through the balcony and the smell of perspiration hung heavy in the air and mixed with the heat that rose to the roof and sat among us.

Mrs. Cohen had given me a black shawl so that I would
not be conspicuous, but my white flowered skirt peeped out
and my shoes gave me away. She had given me a gray scarf
for my hair and had tied it herself in the right way in a bun
at the back of my head, but I did not pass. The women were
looking at me. I stared at the floor, discomfited.

Matches were passed along the rows. We were sitting so
close to one another that I could not raise my elbows to light
my candle. A hand from the row behind reached over and
took my candle and returned it lit. I tried to turn around to
smile a thank-you but I could not move my shoulders.
Downstairs we could see the men lighting their candles.
Their black hats and coats made it hard to distinguish
individual forms and only the shape of beard here and there
made up of individual parts below. It began with a low
singing, a chanting moan from all the men that reached up
into the balcony and started my amazed mind racing.

Mrs. Cohen had provided me with an English translation.
The women did not join in the song. They swayed back and
forth, holding their candles upright. As their flames shifted
with their breath I could see their eyes searching the
benches below for particular men. I could see sweat rolling
down cheeks and settling in the hollows above the lip, under
eyes.

Suddenly a single voice began to sing from a corner
underneath my side of the balcony. Mrs. Cohen reached
over, poking me in the ribs, and pointed on my page to the
English words: ''Her gates are sunk unto the ground, He has
smashed her bars to bits; her King and her leaders are in
exile. . . . My eyes are spent with tears, my heart is in
tumult, my being melts away over the ruin of my poor
people. As babes and sucklings languish in the squares of
the city, they keep asking their mothers where is bread and
wine as they languish like battle wounded in the squares of
the town, as their life runs out in their mothers' bosoms.''

Some of the women had their eyes closed. Others were
staring straight ahead as if transfixed by the horrors of the

description. Different voices came floating up from downstairs, each carrying its own distinctive note of grief and terror. Each singer bore within his own soul the tragedy that had befallen the people and the city over two thousand years ago. Some of the passages were chanted by all the men below and then there was a great swelling of sound like a thunder roll. Not Gd's fault, said the words, the fault of man, who had disobeyed the law, who had strayed from the law and was so mightily punished.

I looked at Andrea, whose white fingers clutched her candle as if it were a lifeline. Mrs. Cohen, whose new pregnancy could be barely seen under the slope of her heavy breasts, had tears in her eyes, tears for the punishment that had been deserved. If the beauty of words, if the power of the human voice raised in supplication, in devotion, begging for pity, for forgiveness, for restitution, could be heard, it would have been heard and the angels would have immediately undone what had been done and the temple would have risen again, an ascension of brick and mortar that would have contented the people, who might never again have drifted from the dots and the lines, the exact demands, of the law.

But it wasn't the peoples' fault, it was history and armies and forces of imperialism and matters of body counts, stockpiles and technological invention, and perhaps all over the ancient world fires burned and cities were sacked and once proud peoples were carted off into slavery no matter how well or how badly they had worshiped their divinities. At least on this religious occasion each year the Jews could pretend it was their own fault and in so pretending maintain a secret weapon that might have been used, but unfortunately was not. In the face of invasions and destructions, inquisitions and pogroms, the power of virtue had never been fully deployed, either, because its use would prove too devastating to the enemy or because this megaton of the last resort might prove useless, and then what would survive?

I looked down at the sea of faces below and searched for

Michael. In the flickering candlelight I saw several thin beards that might have been reddish-colored, but the distance was too great and I could not make him out. I could see Andrea leaning forward, searching the benches below for him. There was something in that blinking of his eyes, the way they darted into the corners of a room, that made me hope he would never find out that obedience to the law of God was as effective a shield as wearing a lead apron during an atomic siege.

There was a sudden commotion in my section. Women were pushing and standing and whispering in frantic Hebrew. I looked over and saw that in the row in front of me several seats down a young woman's scarf had caught fire from the candle held by the old lady behind her. The smell of singed hair mixed with fright as everyone jumped up, and I looked for the exit from the balcony. The crowd of women was on its feet but there was no possibility of movement. The men below did not look up from their texts and their voices rose and fell with the cantillation of each line.

The scarf was ripped off. Women were stamping on it. Candles were blown out and others were waved frantically in the air. The woman cried out in pain and a shawl was placed over her dress. The fire was out. Andrea had not moved at all. She had tears in her eyes but I didn't know if this was because of the destruction of the temple or because she had been so close to a disaster. I wanted to leave. I'd had enough of poetry for one evening, but the row settled back down and there was no exit till the very end.

"Our dancing is turned into mourning. The crown has fallen from our head; woe to us that we have sinned. Because of this our hearts are sick, because of these our eyes are dimmed. Because of Mount Zion, which lies desolate, jackals prowl over it; but You, O Lord, are enthroned forever, Your throne endures through the ages. Why have You forgotten us utterly, forsaken us for all time? Take us back, O Lord, to Yourself, and let us come back. Renew our days of old! For truly You have rejected us, bitterly raged against us. Take us back, O Lord, to Yourself and let us come back; renew our days as of Old.''

At last, after what seemed an hour's wait on a crowded staircase, I found myself out in the street. It was dark and above the flowerpots and between the buildings two or three stars hung low in the crack of sky. I looked for Arnold Rose but did not see him. He had said that he might come to the services too but Gloria had said no, she didn't want to offend anyone but she found all that prayer very boring. She preferred to stay in the hotel room and read her book, *Clan of the Cave Bear*, a really great story when you get into it, she told me. ''I sat through baseball games and soccer games and school plays about frogs and princes and I've eaten medieval feasts and pilgrim harvests and I've been to meetings to discuss the shortage of footlockers in the boys' gym and I've sat through Boy Scout demonstrations on how to read a compass and how to tell the north side of a tree and now I can't do another thing that makes my mind go numb. I've done enough for them and none of it made any difference. It's all been wiped out as if I had stayed home in my bed drinking for twenty years.''

Outside on the street the men walked off without waiting for the women. Their expressions made it clear this was no time for casual conversation. I tried to find Andrea to say good night but she had melted away into the crowd. I did not see anyone I could recognize, so I wandered up the street and turning left followed a hill that seemed to lead up but in fact twisted down. I could soon tell from the signs on the stores, from the smell in the gutter, that I should have turned the other way. I found a small hotel with a single light bulb dangling from a socket in the lobby. A few American dollars persuaded the sullen half-shaved concierge to call a cab.

I stood on the steps of the hotel looking as self-assured as possible, my borrowed black shawl hugged tight about my shoulders. I knew I had wandered into the wrong part of town, where the reasons to snatch my purse were more than

mercenary and the stones above my head were pockmarked
with bulletholes from a battle that had too recently passed
by. My daughter had joined her fate to those who made
poetry and music out of catastrophe. Here were a people
who knew how to appreciate disaster. They had practice in
secreting the spirit and carrying it off, with the ink still wet
on the pages of a scroll or a diary, right under the nose of
the victorious conqueror. In the abstract this is a matter of
pride and self-congratulation, but in the flesh, in the here
and now, when it was the vulnerable form of my daughter
Andrea bound on the same altar as Isaac, I would have felt
better had there been more rams in the thicket and less
blood on the stone. I would have felt better if Purim were
the only holiday in memory, if someone else's spirit was
given the opportunity to show its brave inspiration in the
face of military collapse and Andrea and Michael could
walk among the spoils choosing for themselves whatever
struck their fancy. An Arab cabdriver took me back to the
King David. I was too exhausted to walk or to think
anymore. If the city of Jerusalem were a loved one the way
it was written, then what of the rest of the harem: Warsaw,
Chernovitz, Vilna, Polnar, Lvov?

IN THE LOBBY of the King David a group of
benefactors of the Hadassah Hospital were just
checking out to take the evening El Al flight back to the
States. They carried shopping bags full of pottery, rugs,
menorahs, prints, and in their bags, sealed in cellophane,
were countless silver chains laced with the green stones that
were said to come from the rocks below Eilat. They had
visited the children's playroom their fund-raising efforts had
purchased and they were returning home with pictures of
themselves in front of Chagall's chapel or arms about each
other, smiling bravely into the sun on Mt. Scopus, that their

grandchildren would one day toss into a box destined for a rummage sale.

As I waited in line I took off my shawl. I felt self-conscious in such a gloomy and unfashionable wrap amid the porters carrying bags and the party of French journalists who were sitting about a marble table drinking to each other's health. Reaching the desk of the hotel, the reassuringly grand mahogany desk with its silver bell, its clerks in green jackets and white shirts, its rows of cubbies and its telephones attached to computers, I felt reassured. There was a message for me from Arnold Rose. It was handwritten. "Come to our room, immediately on your return. We have made an interesting purchase today."

I took the elevator to the third floor and walked without desire toward the Rose room. I wanted my bed. I was even willing to dream. I felt a pain in my hip that made me drag my body along as if it were an unwanted bundle I was forced to carry.

In front of room 313 were two large men. They were Israelis for sure because they were smoking nonfiltered cigarettes. They were large and muscular and wore white shirts with open collars and blue pants. I walked to the door prepared to knock. They blocked my way. "They are busy in there," one said. "You cannot go in."

"What's happened?' I said. "Are you hotel security?"

"We are security," said one. The other laughed.

"I am a friend of Dr. and Mrs. Arnold Rose. I'm sure they would want me to come in."

"Eh!" said the one who had spoken first.

"What has happened to the Roses?" I raised my voice; I could hear how shrill and scared I sounded. I thought they might have been robbed. I thought that Arnold might have collapsed under the strain and had a heart attack. "Tell Mrs. Rose it's Mrs. Annie Johnson out in the hall, just tell her I'm here."

The men did not move. "I'm going down to call the

manager," I said, and started back toward the elevator. A hand was on my arm pulling me around.

"Don't be in such a rush, all you Americans rush around like chickens who are dead but don't know it. Wait here and I'll find out what to do about you."

When he turned toward the door I noticed the bulge in his hip pocket that looked like a weapon, but then I thought maybe he was carrying a heavy wallet or a Thermos of iced tea to drink on the job. I reminded myself that just because I had spent the evening listening to the tale of an entire city sacked I shouldn't expect violence in the hotel corridor. "Hotel security?" I repeated my question to the remaining man.

He shrugged. "Security," he said.

The door opened a crack. The face of the first man appeared behind the door chain. He spoke in whispered Hebrew to his colleague. The door was partly opened and I was let in. Both men resumed their post outside.

Inside, the curtains were drawn and only one small bedside lamp lit the room. On the bed on top of the floral spread I saw Michael stretched out, his arms and legs sprawled strangely awry. His breathing was slow and heavy. His eyes were closed. He was sleeping, and in his sleep he was perspiring. Round drops of sweat covered his face. In places they stained his beard dark. His glases were on the table. His old worn sneakers had been placed neatly on the floor. The room had a peculiar smell, somewhere between body odor and feces. Michael's mother was sitting on the bed stroking his limp hand. He looked like a child with a fever, as if he would wake up and ask his mother to bring him a bowl of chocolate ice cream. In an armchair sat Arnold Rose.

"This is a country like any other," he said. "Money gets certain things done that are just impossible if you rely on the usual channels. We have taken Michael back. The gentlemen you saw outside the door returned him to us early this evening. He was on his way to that service and they called him into a side street to assist a man fallen on the walk. Michael had told us that if it was possible to do a good deed he was obligated by his 'law' to do it. On the way to the hotel Michael protested and tried to escape from the car. The men were careful not to bruise him and used some medicine to keep him quiet until we can get him on the plane. We have an ambulance meeting us at Kennedy Airport. We are taking him directly to the Yale Psychiatric Institute in New Haven. It has all been arranged. He is clearly a very sick boy and this is his best chance for a full recovery.''

Arnold got out of his chair and paced back and forth in front of the drawn curtains. He looked tired and there were lines in his face I hadn't noticed before. "I can hardly believe I did this. I just kidnapped my own son, had two guns for hire throw him in the back of a rented Audi and here he is. A mental hospital for my son; I wouldn't have believed it myself two years ago, but now I'm not surprised. He is a loon. After we talked with him I was sure of it; he is without question ready for the loony bin.''

"Don't call him a loon,'' said Gloria. "He's not crazy, he's just mixed up and we're going to help him straighten everything out. Don't call him a loon, supposing he hears you?''

"He can't hear me,'' said Arnold. "He's on another level of consciousness, where in fact he's been for too long. We have to wait twenty-four hours for the American embassy to process his new passport.''

Gloria looked at her son. "We have to shave him. He must be shaved. I can't stand that beard and the side curls.''

She went to her suitcase and pulled out her makeup kit. In it she had a small pair of scissors in the shape of a miniature gold pelican. She snipped at the curls nearest her and they came off in her hand. Michael turned on his side as if to protect his other ringlet. Gently, the way one picks up a newborn, Gloria raised his head and snipped away the remaining payess. She put her hand on his forehead and held it there.

Then she took both ringlets and dropped them down the toilet. I could hear the flush in the bathroom.

"So," said Arnold, "the price is three thousand. If you like I'll help you make arrangements in the good old U.S. The doctor on our staff who arranged Michael's admission has a colleague in New York who would be able to give you some names and make a preliminary contact for you. These guys outside can get your daughter if you want. You don't have to abandon her to those fanatics. The big boys at the door, tank unit with the Israeli army; one of the doctors in the research lab at the hospital had a brother-in-law in the unit and with a few phone calls we managed to borrow a few good men. I have two others in the hotel lobby just in case the holy ones come looking. They want all cash but I'll lay it out for you," he said. "You can pay me back later. I feel like we're in this together. Our kids almost got married, for Christ's sake."

Gloria wiped at her eyes. "I want Michael to get married in our home in Cleveland. I have a ruby brooch from my mother I want to give to his bride."

"What did the doctors at Yale say?" I asked.

Arnold told me, "I spoke with this Dr. Solson, who said he has worked with other cult victims. I got his name from a friend of ours whose daughter was trying to starve herself to death. She was a walking skeleton when we saw her at Thanksgiving recess. She wouldn't eat a carrot. They forced her into a hospital and Dr. Solson was her therapist and she's done fine. She's taking a word-processing course back in Cleveland. Kind of a fat kid now, but I guess that's better than a dead one.

"Dr. Solson said not to expect magic. It's not like removing the appendix. He says it takes time to restore one of these kids who got their minds turned inside out. He told me that there is a special part of the brain, the left anterior lobe, where the latest research has located the source of spiritual hallucinations and religious delusions. They think it's a disease that you can provoke by using the right

electrodes in this certain place. Dr. Solson said these kids
got trapped before they were allowed to complete the
growing process or some such thing. He says it takes a lot
of work on the part of the staff and the patient to put the
pieces back together but that a mixture of psychotherapy
and chemical intervention have frequently proven effective.
Dr. Solson assured me that if Michael is not suffering from
an underlying mental illness, which he can't diagnose on a
long-distance telephone call with a parent, we can expect
good results. He believes that removing these kids from the
tight support system that works like a constant brainwash is
the best therapy; given exposure to reality they mostly come
around. I've always believed that psychiatrists were failed
doctors, the ones who can't stand the real confrontation with
death, the cowards who took a desk job, leaving the fighting
at the front to others. But now I need them. They're
doctors, too. I have to trust them. It probably serves me
right. Over the years I've come down with hubris or some
other Greek disease, I guess.

"It costs a lot, these hospitals, you got coverage?" he
asked.

Gloria had picked up Michael's glasses. "He never needed
these before. I don't believe he needs glasses at all. He just
wore them to be like all the others." She tossed them in the
wastepaper basket that sat under the turquoise French desk
that held the King David stationery and a *TV Guide*.

Without his glasses and with his payess gone, Michael
looked younger. Perspiration had collected above his lip.
His skin was white. "Is he all right?" I asked.

Arnold walked over to the bed and checked his pulse.
"Fine," he said, "just fine." He picked up a washcloth and
gently wiped his son's face. He patted him on the shoulder
and Michael turned and sighed. I could still see the marks on
the side of his nose where his glasses had pinched.

The smell in the room got stronger. Michael's body rolled
on the cover. Gloria went into the bathroom.

There was a knock on the door. Three bangs, pause,

another bang. "It's just the guys," said Arnold, and opened the door.

"We're hungry. Call up room service and get us some sandwiches and beer. The kid smells," he said. "Hasn't he bathed lately?"

Michael was immaculately clean. It was the chemical mix in his body from the drug that was sending something foul into the room. Arnold had obtained some new drug used for intelligence purposes by the Israeli CIA, the Mossad. It was effective but not perfect. The sleeping child was innocent of his odor.

It was now late at night and room service was on half staff and it was going to take a long time for the food to arrive. Arnold yelled at the person who had answered the phone in the far reaches of the hotel. "You are a four-star hotel, you are not supposed to shut down like you were the Holiday Inn in Tulsa." I saw that his hand was trembling when he put down the phone. He had made his decision, but he was as uncertain as I. He kept wiping his face of invisible sweat. "I love my son," he said.

"I don't know," I said, "if I can do this to Andrea." I thought of her body lying in my room with the same odor as Michael's with the same drops of perspiration forming on her forehead. I thought of Andrea back in our apartment on Riverside Drive. What could a hospital do? It was true that she did not love Michael the way the Roses and I understood the word. They had not pledged themselves to one another the way we expect of our couples, but Andrea had given herself in the only terms that had been open to her. Michael was about to become one more loss, one more vanished temporary hand that had appeared to be steady and then turned into thin air as she grasped for it. Would she ever forgive me if I took her home to a psychiatric hospital and let them convince her that all was illusion, her friends were not her friends and her accomplishments just petty scratchings against the existential sky? I told Arnold that I had to think a while and would let him know in the morning whether I wanted his hired help to catch Andrea and bring her back to me.

As I was turning toward the door Michael suddenly groaned loudly and opened his eyes. His mother was right there and with a wet towel wiped his forehead. His arms were floppy and he was clearly weak and dizzy. "Mother," he said with a thick tongue, "let me go back, let me go to the yeshiva. They are wondering about me now and worrying. Let me go back to Sarai. She needs me, Mother. I have to take care of her."

"Hush, now," said Gloria, squeezing her cloth. "We know what is good for you and all we are doing is taking care of you. Trust me; I promise, we are taking good care of you."

"Hey, boy," said Arnold in a tight voice.

I left the room as Michael closed his eyes again and seemed to fall back asleep. Each breath scratched across his larynx as if he had a chest cold. There was no one to protect him from all the people who were protecting him.

I went downstairs and sat in a chair in the hotel lobby. The lobby was now empty of all but three cleaning women with mop and pail and a couple of American students sitting on a love seat under the palms arguing intensely and loudly about the security of the northern border. I saw the other two men Arnold had placed on guard duty. They were smoking furiously and playing cards. The doorman was leaning against the wood-paneled lobby wall and watching the empty street through the glass of the revolving door.

I thought about Andrea when she was about ten and it snowed in New York and I had gone with her to Riverside Park and stood at the top of the hill watching her ride in her sled down to the bottom, my feet freezing in my lined boots and my fingers aching inside my down gloves. I caught a glimpse of her face as she came toward me pulling the sled.

"I want it to be today, forever," she said to me.

"In ten minutes we have to go because I'm too cold," I said.

"I'm not going," she said. "I'm not going."

"Andrea," I said, "you're not going to fight with me now, are you? I'm too cold to argue. Now we are going home."

"No," she said, "I can't go. I like it too much today."

I gave in and we stayed another hour and a half and I watched her red face lit with excitement as she poised on the top of the hill, as she picked up mittens full of snow and smashed them down against her feet. I heard her scream with pleasure and terror as her sled hit a bump and went flying forward. I remembered when I could let everything go and feel the snow on my mouth and the speed of the sled and not think about anything else at all. I watched my child who had what I had lost. Had given up? Was no longer entitled to? I stamped my feet to keep frostbite at bay.

I GOT UP from the large green velvet chair I was sitting in. I walked over to the wall phones and contacted the operator, who while billing the call to my room was irritated with my demand. "Eh," she said, and made me repeat the number I wanted three times as if she couldn't understand English, which I knew she could or she wouldn't be working at the King David Hotel. The phone at the Yeshiva Rachel rang and rang. I could see it sitting in the rabbi's study and the sound echoing into the empty room where I had sat the day before with Andrea and Michael and watched them looking at me, not looking at each other. It was now well after midnight and everyone must be asleep. The pregnant Mrs. Cohen, dreaming of stalemates and checkmates and pawns that must be sacrificed for a higher good, Ronite and Hadassah and my daughter, Sarai/Andrea, were lying in their beds trusting to God, who appeared at the moment to have given the victory to Arnold and Gloria

Rose from Cleveland, whose ethical actions required no verification in the texts.

I hung up the phone. I decided to go back to my room. I had time. I would wait to make my final decision at dawn.

Riding up in the elevator with me was an elderly American couple from the South. They had come to see the place where Christ was laid out upon the slab, to visit all the shrines at Bethlehem.

"This has been the most excitin' trip of our entire lives, includin' the time we went to Hawaii," the woman told me. I smiled at her. "Have you walked the Stations of the Cross yet?" she asked. I shook my head. "Oh, my dear, you must," she said. "This is just the best place in the whole world to suffer His sufferin's."

I smiled agreeably. Her husband looked at his shoes. I suspected his feet were hurting. "Night, you all," she called after me as I got off the elevator.

I lay down on my bed. I could ask the Roses to arrange to have Andrea brought to me at the hotel in the morning. I could ask their help in getting her passport, in getting her on the plane. I could place her in Payne Whitney or in Mt. Sinai Hospital. But she was no longer covered by my faculty insurance plan. She was too old. I could use my savings, the bits and pieces that had come to me from my mother, that sat in the bank gathering interest. I had no greater need for savings than to save my daughter. It would be a long terrible air trip. It would be a horrible ride in an ambulance to the airport, to the hospital. Andrea would smell and sweat and toss in her sleep. I would watch her. But I could manage it if at the end, the end of a period of time, she returned to our apartment, to her old room, ready to begin again, to tilt with her own demons, to tilt with mine, to breathe free air and become whatever Andrea was becoming before the interference of rabbis and their wives and children.

I bothered the operator again. She reluctantly agreed to

place my long-distance call. I waited for her to call me back. It was early evening in New York.

The phone rang. The operator had connected me with an answering machine. I left an urgent message. I lay down on my bed and waited. An hour and a half later the phone rang again. This time it was Dr. Wolfert himself, his voice somewhat muffled by the particles of space, the motions of the sky through which it was traveling.

"Hospital, you say! What do you think they can do for her in the hospital?"

"Don't yell at me," I said. "This phone call is extremely long distance and expensive. Just tell me what you think."

"What do you think?" he asked.

"Tell me," I said, "could a hospital make her forget her loyalties here? Would she ever forgive me for taking her away? Could they give her the strength to get a job, to go to school, to choose a mate who might stay with her?"

There was a pause. "What kind of hospital you got in mind?" said Dr. Wolfert. "Is it the one on the Magic Mountain with the terrific air where they take a lot of chest X-rays or something more modest like a Midas Muffler shop in Queens where they do body rehab as well?"

"Dr. Wolfert," I fairly screamed, "I want to know if a hospital can help Andrea."

"Is Rabbi Hillel talking to her personally from under the bed?"

"Of course not," I shouted.

"Has she any new stigmata since I saw her last?" he went on.

I shouted, in case he was having trouble hearing me, "Can the new drugs that they use in these hospitals help?"

"To make Andrea the person you want her to be, a good daughter, perhaps a Ph.D. candidate in Middle Eastern history? A straight arrow with a bank account, a Social Security number and a MasterCharge card?"

"Essentially that," I agreed.

"Perhaps," he said. "I've seen patients in the last stages

of cancer suddenly buck up and live another four days. I've seen shadows on X-rays disappear, probably because the radiologist mixed up the plates, but nevertheless, miracles are always possible and I would be the last doctor to tell you that occupational therapy, a little clay work before lunch, some afternoon aerobic exercise, along with an up-to-date, state-of-the-art chemical stew that may only make her legs tremble permanently or drop her lip so that she can never again close her mouth and the flies will go in and out as they please, a dose of group therapy so she can see that others are worse off than she is might do the trick. You never could punish her enough when she stepped out of line. You never knew how to set limits, how to be firm in your expectations. Maybe it's not too late to try."

"Dr. Wolfert," I said, "are you telling me that you don't have faith in hospitals, even the best ones?"

"You do?" he asked me.

"They must help somebody." I could feel myself straining to be reasonable. "There are so many of them, they cost so much. If no one ever recovered they'd be gone like—"

"Like Lourdes," he interrupted.

"They have so many patients some must be healed."

"Yes," he said, "many are healed. Most are healed over and over again. There are limits to what democracy can do and will do. There are limits to what education can do and will do. There are final failures in medicine of all kinds. There are limits to how much improvement the environment can tolerate and for each of us there is a limit to our days. Psychiatry has its place but not among the wonder cures, not among the miracle workers. We are not high priests or even low priests. We are simply doctors and while Americans choose to believe in happy endings, what we do best, the thing we are really good at, is listening. That's it."

"If you don't believe in psychiatry," I said, "why are you practicing?"

He laughed. "Couldn't get any malpractice insurance as

an orthodontist. By the way," he added, "did you leave my note in the Wall?"

"No," I said, and hung up.

He wasn't the only psychiatrist in New York. I could try others. I could call a friend and get the name of another. I could get Arnold's contact in Cleveland to put me in touch with a New York psychiatrist. But Dr. Wolfert had seen Andrea. He knew me.

I changed directions. I called the front desk and put in a wakeup call for the first light of dawn and I lay down on my bed without taking off my clothes and stared at the ceiling until I fell asleep.

I am walking along the beach wearing my great straw hat to keep the sun off my face. I am walking close to the water's edge and every now and then the waves carry farther than I anticipate and I am surrounded by swirling froth and my skirt is splashed and sticks to my thighs. I am looking down at the sand, my eyes searching for unusual shells, for the carapaces of crabs that might still be intact, their rose speckles like the patterns on the Chinese vases in the cases at the Metropolitan Museum.

I see a small figure a hundred yards ahead. In a few seconds I recognize Rabbi Nachman hurrying toward me, holding his shoes in his hand, barefoot with his black socks sticking out of his breast pocket. I look to the empty dunes for rescue, but the people and their umbrellas, the lifeguard on his stand, the parking lot with its hot dog carts, are all beyond vision. There is no avoiding Rabbi Nachman, who comes up to me panting, his chest heaving and the fringes of his tallis damp from the salt spray. He is wearing sunglasses but otherwise has made no concession to the natural surroundings. He speaks in Yiddish, but I understand him even though I do not speak Yiddish.

"I have a story to tell you," he says.

"Amscray ownay," I shout at him in some vague hope I can send him back to the shadows.

"Pig latin," he says. "Twice forbidden." He looks at me

disapprovingly. "I must talk to you right now." He says, "I want you to understand what I am telling you."

"Then tell me directly," I shout. "Stop telling me stories."

"It is like the shell you hold in your hand," he says to me. "When I tell you a story, the truth is in it, but if I take the truth out of the story, like the shell you take home from the beach, it dries, it becomes something else, it no longer is the shell on the beach, it is a dead object whose truth you have lost by taking it home, away from the place it belonged."

"All right," I say.

His voice is quiet and gentle, I can hardly hear him over the slap of the waves and the wind that rustles in the beach grass at the back of the dunes. We sit down together. I see him dig his bare feet into the sand and move them back and forth, watching the grains fall beneath his toes. "Once," he begins—

I interrupt. "Why are all your stories 'Once'?" I ask. "What is wrong with today, or now, or tomorrow?"

"Once," he says, "is the right time. Once there was a great and good King who ruled a kingdom so vast that he could not visit all his subjects in one day, not in a month or a year. He built a castle so large and so high that when he stood out on the promontory he could see almost to the borders of his land, or where he imagined those borders to be, right at the edge of the horizon where the sun rose in the morning and sank in the evening. He had a Queen whose beauty and whose grace filled his days with pleasure and his nights with awe. She played the harp and the lute and whenever he was distracted, filled with concern for his people, she would soothe him with song and he would know just what to do to make the crops grow well, the children honor their parents and merchants deal fairly with each other in the market. He had a courier who would bring him messages from all parts of his country and would present him with petitions from the poorest people who lived in the hamlets at a great distance from the castle, and the King always filled their requests and sent the courier back across

the country with carts laden with warm blankets and toys for
the children and tools for the men.

"One day the courier came into the Queen's quarters and
told her of the wonders he had seen in the countryside,
where great waters fell from the mountaintops, where animals with horns on their heads fought with one another for
the privilege of the female, where the men worked bare-
chested in the hot sun and plowed the fields while the
children gathered the grains and placed them in sacks,
leaving some for the rabbits and the chickens.

"The Queen had never lived anywhere but inside the castle
and had not pressed her own clothes, gathered her own
fruit, or folded her own sheets. She listened as the courier
told her how simple people bathe in the river and how
babies are carried in slings held against the bosoms of women
as they knead the bread of the house. The Queen thought
of all the things the courier had told her. Her songs grew
woeful. The King was no longer soothed by her music
and he asked her what was wrong. She said to him that she
was tired of living caged like a canary in his castle. She
wished to travel the kingdom with the courier.

"The King was enraged. He forbade the courier ever to
speak with the Queen again. He banished the courier from
the castle, but the Queen went out one night when the stars
were hidden behind the clouds and the moon did not shine
and she rode on a donkey she had borrowed from her maid.
She left the castle in search of the courier because she
wanted to smell a baby when it was sleeping.

"When in the morning her absence was discovered, the
King grieved. He tore his hair. He rolled in the dust. He
sent out a search party but they came back late at night
without the Queen. They had found no trace of her anywhere. The donkey had been found tied to a tree by a
stream, but the Queen was gone and so was the courier. The
King looked out at his kingdom and no longer thought it
was beautiful. He no longer cared what happened in the
market, what needs the people had in the far hamlets. He no

longer listened to tales of trouble and made plans. He stayed in his room and waited for the Queen to tire of her journey and come back to him.

"Without the attention of the King, the cruel landlords threw their tenants out into the cold. The merchants who could turn profits without giving value began to do so and the hungry increased and the sick had no place to go and the children's schools were closed down because no longer did their King wish them to learn."

Rabbi Nachman pauses. His voice is blocked by tears.

"Go on," I say, "I'm listening."

He lies back on the sand. His black hat tilts and falls off his head, which I can see is beginning to bald, and drops of perspiration have gathered above his forehead. His pate is turning pink.

"You'll get too much sun," I say. "You'd better keep your hat on."

He sits up and replaces his hat, and grains of sand trickle from it down onto his face and stick in his beard. "Then one day a peasant came to the King with a package in his arms. 'I believe, sire,' he said, 'these belong to the palace.'

"In the package was a golden gown with jewels sewn along the neck and in the pattern of stars along the hem. It was the Queen's dress, the very one she had been wearing the night she ran away.

"'Where did you get this?' thundered the King.

"'I fished it out of the river many miles away,' said the peasant. 'My wife said I should bring it to you and you might reward us well.'

"The King was not in the mood for rewarding anyone. Without his Queen he could not remember how he should govern, and in his temper and out of his grief he had the poor peasant thrown off the highest ledge of the castle turret.

"All of the King's advisers told him that the Queen had drowned. How else was it possible that her dress should be found in the river? The King would not listen to his advisers and he called for his master magician to help him find the Queen.

"The master magician brewed himself a potion and drinking it fell to the floor. Moaning and swooning, he spoke of seeing the Queen under the water floating by rocks and speckled fish with pebbles in her eyes. He woke from his spell and told the King, 'The Queen is under the water at the pass where the mountains turn to hills in the south.'

"The King sent his troops to the river and they came back with the golden crown with sapphires in it that they had found in the waters behind the rock just before the great falls that spilled downward toward the sea.

"The King held the crown in his hand and he called the magician to his court and he ordered him to be hung upside down outside the castle until he confessed that he had planted the crown by the rock and invented the whole vision. The magician immediately confessed and the King had him roasted over the coals as if he were fresh-killed lamb.

"Soon word of a remarkable event reached the palace. The river that ran from the highest mountains down to the sea, that crossed through the great falls and whirled past the sharp rocks and trunks of dead trees that had caught in the pools at the bottom, had turned red, the color of blood. It flowed red throughout the kingdom and the people were afraid to drink or to wash or to fish in the river, and they suffered greatly because of this. Floating in the red water they had found the pouch, the leather bag that the courier had once slung over his shoulder and in which he had placed their letters to the King. No one dared bring the pouch to the castle but word of it came anyway to the ministers of state, who heard it from the second-story maids, who heard it from the cooks, who heard it from the gardeners. The King heard the story of the pouch whispered behind the doors of his castle and he clenched his teeth and pulled at his skin until he was covered with sores.

"The King had shutters placed on all the palace windows

and he had the shutters nailed closed and they were not opened morning, noon or night. He put rocks on the road approaching the palace and he hid himself in his chambers."

Rabbi Nachman closed his eyes and I can see tears at the edges of his lashes. I stare out to sea. "I don't want to die," I say to Rabbi Nachman.

"There is a way," he says to me. "If you can find the name of Hashem as it is buried in the writings, as it is in code, waiting for a holy person to decipher it, then there will be no dying, not you, not Andrea, not anyone at all."

"You are afraid of dying," I say to Rabbi Nachman. "You are as afraid as I am. There is no code, there is no Queen, she was always a fiction of the King's imagination, a hallucination of a lonely mad ruler. There is no name to decipher, no number code hidden in sacred texts. We can depend on nothing but our wit and our sense of decency. The rest is a tale to put the children to sleep."

I look over at Rabbi Nachman kindly. "You are dreaming?"

He does not seem to hear me. "The King will stay in the castle until we are all dead," says Rabbi Nachman, "unless you help me find the wandering Queen."

I sigh. The ocean stretches out with all its creatures devouring each other just beyond the shore. The seagulls fly overhead looking for something small to pick up in their sharp beaks and smash onto the rocks. "So," I say, "it will end without reconciliation, your story, the Queen is not coming back of her own free will? The King will sit like a wounded cripple sulking in his castle till the end of time, until we blow ourselves up or dry ourselves out, or sink beneath the earth?"

"I don't know," says Rabbi Nachman, sitting up and brushing the sand off his clothes. "I have no time for melancholy or philosphical speculation. Jews are not interested in theology. I am on my way, I am looking for the Queen."

"I wish you luck," I say, "for all of us."

Suddenly he becomes a child of perhaps a year or so. He

is wearing a diaper and toddling toward me in the sand. On his small head he wears a tiny blue velvet yarmulke with embroidered writing and little red and white flowers looped together with gold threads. His face is lit in smile and he turns toward me. "Mama," he says and laughs. He has small wisps of payess at the side of his head and he carries a yellow plastic pail and shovel in his hand.

I scoop him up in my arms and carry him up the dune. I find a beach umbrella waiting and I sit down with him in the shade and lay him on a blanket and kiss him on the forehead. His skin is soft and his fingers curl in my hair. If I did not know that I would never have another baby and that this one would disappear from my sight faster than I could say Rumpelstiltskin, I would be as happy as the King before the Queen went away. Then the sky turns turquoise and the sands turn white as marble and the tide recedes quickly, leaving a mud flat out to the horizon's edge, and in the mud I see large fish thrashing in brown puddles until drops of blood spill from their eyes. The Angel of Death walks out of the dry bed of the ocean and stands above us with dark wings that blot out the sun and all the sky.

"It is not my choice," says the Angel of Death. "This is not a job I have sought. I am a figment of God's imagination. I have no will of my own. Understand me," he says in the unchanged voice of a Bar Mitzvah boy beginning his address to the congregation.

In terror I watch as the arms of the angel, gently, as if they were of snow, reach down and pick up Rabbi Nachman, who puts out his baby hand, pudgy and dimpled, and reaches for me; but I am too slow and the Angel of Death rises to the sky, taking with him Rabbi Nachman, who calls out to me, "Mama." I can do nothing but sit on the beach as the tide comes in and a young couple begin to play Frisbee at the water's edge.

"Hear, O Israel," says the voice of the angel as he nears the sun, but the rest of his words are too faint to decipher.

* * *

THE PHONE RANG. The operator was calling to tell me that the sun was rising. I felt sour, a sourness in my mouth and in my hair, my clothes were rumpled and the panty hose I had worn to the yeshiva the night before were ripped. I could hear a heavy cart being wheeled down the hall, someone else's coffee, croissant and newspaper went swiftly by my door. I showered, dressed, but I had no other stockings to put on, so bare-legged, in my sandals, with my hair falling wet around my face, I went downstairs and asked the doorman to call a taxi. I was hungry. I thought about stopping for breakfast but felt I had no time to waste. I went to the Yeshiva Rachel and banged on the door. I knew they were up, because the sun was already over the edge of Mt. Scopus and reflecting off the top of the walls of the old city. It was going to be a very hot day and even the early-morning air tasted of desert sand. In other streets of the city, people in beds not necessarily their own were waking up to go to work. Here, everybody would be in their assigned place. Rabbi Cohen had already thanked God for the new day. He had placed the Ten Commandments on his forehead and bound them around his wrists. He had already praised the creation and asked for the blessing of the day. He had raised his voice in ancient rhythms to say the sacred words in the holy city just as they have always been said and would now be ready to turn to the practical necessities of his twentieth-century mission.

I was at his door with news, with a reminder that God does not always protect his own. In fact, the most innocent lambs, standing on the outer edges of the flock, are the ones most frequently devoured by the wolves.

The door opened. I explained to the young girl standing there that it was an emergency. I had to see Rabbi Cohen immediately. She brought me into the building and I waited in the courtyard until Rabbi Cohen appeared, jam flecks in his beard, and listened to my tale.

"It's all right," he said to me. "We will take care of it."

First I felt relieved. I had betrayed the Roses, but I had kept faith with Andrea and with Michael. Then I felt anxious. Maybe I had kept the faith with Rabbi Cohen and betrayed Andrea and Michael. Perhaps I had kept the faith with Andrea and Michael but betrayed myself and the Roses. Perhaps I had been true to myself but had betrayed the Roses and Andrea and Michael.

I wanted to see Andrea. I sat in the rabbi's study and waited. Would my child feel betrayed by me in a few years because I did this or would my child have been betrayed by me if I had not? One of the young girls, a daughter of Rabbi Cohen, brought me a cup of coffee and a roll. I was no longer hungry. Mrs. Cohen came in and brought me a paper bag that contained a sealed package of panty hose, thick and dark and discouraging to the wandering eye; it would mark any leg as off limits, as more the property of a table than a woman.

"They will be about your size, I believe," she said.

"It's so hot," I complained. "Why do you wear these heavy stockings in the heat?"

"I don't mind the heat," she said. "If you are feeling warm take a glass of hot tea, it will cool you down."

Rabbi Cohen came into the room. "Where is my daughter?" I asked. "Has she been told? I would like to be with her now." I looked at Rabbi Cohen. He owed it to me.

"We are organizing at this moment," he said. "We are very busy. It would be better if you went to the hotel. We will do what we think best. We are very grateful to you for coming to us. You are a true daughter of Zion." He pressed a prayer book into my hand. "I would like you to have this as a present from Mrs. Cohen and myself."

"You remember," I said, "about the two additional men in the lobby and the time," I urged him. "The time is going fast."

There was nothing for me to do but to go back to the hotel and wait. I walked through the streets until I came to the shopping section near the Hilton Hotel. There people were breakfasting in the open-air cafes and children were walking to day camps with their knapsacks on their backs. I found a large litter basket and dropped the prayer book in among the old newspapers, the empty cigarette packs and a torn shirt someone had discarded. I reached into the basket just like the matted urine-soaked ladies of my own city and pulled out the prayer book. Respect, aspect, dispect, espect, I couldn't leave it there. I reached into my purse and pulled out the package of panty hose. That I threw into the basket and hurried on, turning like a fugitive at the very next corner.

I was afraid that Rabbi Cohen could not handle it, this teacher, man of prayer, intruder on the American anxiety dream; what could he do against the tank corps of the Israeli army, the connections of Arnold Rose in the embassy, what could he do when he was pushed? How much precious time would he waste praying to God to guide him? Was I insane not to join the Roses and steal my daughter out of this country where disaster lurks under every bus seat and no two people wish the same third person well?

Arnold Rose was in the lobby. He came right up to me the second I crossed the threshold. I saw the Roses' suitcases packed and waiting in the baggage room. He was dressed in a suit and tie. The circles under his eyes had become craters.

"I've just gotten back from the embassy. We are scheduled on this afternoon's flight. I gather you don't want to use my people to get your daughter," he said.

"I'm having a hard time making up my mind," I answered.

"Well, you don't have much longer. The passport should be ready by noon. We're going to move out to the airport immediately. I have arranged a police escort for my very sick son, who will be transported in a private ambulance. If you reach a decision in the next forty-five minutes or so, I can help you with the arrangements. I understand." He put his arm around my shoulder. "It's a terrible decision to make. It even makes me wish I had a God who would tell me what to do."

"Are you sure you did the right thing?" I asked.

He looked at me as if I were a child. "You decide something and then you don't look back. You just keep going. That's the sort of guy I've always been. You should see my office. I don't have time for second or third guesses." He smiled at me as if we were old friends who'd been in the same war, a cookie box full of memories that we might one day sit down and devour together.

I felt nauseous, probably from the heat. I went into the hotel coffee shop, which doubled as a breakfast room, and ordered a cup of hot tea. From my table I could see the comings and goings in the main lobby. I could see the two men in white shirts who belonged to the tank corps whom I had noticed the night before. They were now unshaven and wore dark sunglasses. They were still playing cards and watching the main door. At a nearby table in the coffee shop I noticed a white-haired gentleman with a large mustache finishing off his yogurt and cucumbers. He was reading the Jerusalem *Post* and an attaché case rested by his side. He caught my eye and looked down at my legs. I flicked them easily and crossed them carefully. He came over to the table and asked if he could join me. I told him I was waiting for my husband and he smiled and went back to his seat. Would Andrea's sex burn under her heavy wraps more brightly because of its disguise or would it smother under the dark stockings and the light go out? Too late for second guesses.

Through the main door of the King David came one or two black-coated men of middle years. Following immediately came three or four more and they made a small group under the palms on the side nearest the front desk. The doors turned around again and there were more, younger men, in their early twenties, with strong backs and long legs. They all appeared to be wearing glasses. Their skin was white as skim milk. They looked as if they only ventured out in the moonlight. Their hands were veined and frail. There was now a crowd of them clustered together and they were aware of the fact that other guests in the hotel were looking at them with some surprise. I was wondering if a worldwide association of diamond merchants were holding their convention at the hotel, but it seemed unlikely that they would select the King David with its swimming pool and its bare-legged women as a suitable meeting place.

The front door kept turning around and around and more and more black coats and black hats kept appearing. They were no longer a small group but now seemed to be so many that they blocked the way of the bellhops who were coming out of the elevators, pushing heavy metal carts loaded with luggage. There were so many beards and black hats bobbing in the lobby that it seemed Judgment Day had arrived. Because of the uniform they wore, because of the glasses and the payess and the hats, their faces all looked similar. I felt that twinge of bigotry that makes it hard to recognize one's own waiter in a Chinese restaurant or distinguish one from another the Indians riding on the bluff staring at the passing wagon train. My son-in-law-to-be would soon disappear (except for his sneakers), his individuality squeezed out in the service of God and nation. But only from my point of view. To the black coats that swirled through the lobby perhaps we all looked alike, a sea of bare legs, a patchwork of multicolors, faces that blended into a dangerous organism, capable of any barbarism, called "secularity."

A busload of newly arrived tourists from the Kansas City Methodist Union entered the lobby and were startled to find themselves pressed against men with black coats and beards. Luggage piled up against the walls. The newcomers pushed toward the front desk to check in. The black coats kept their eyes down so as not to see what ought not to be seen. There were now so many of them that they filled the halls by the elevator. They had overflowed into the coffee shop and many were standing on the terrace looking at their feet, not at the pool below.

A man in a green blazer with a coat of arms on its pocket appeared from behind the desk to inquire if he could help the group. I saw Rabbi Cohen talking to him. I saw a wave of black hats move toward the elevators. I saw the two Israeli tank corps men jump to their feet and run up the stairs. They were immediately followed by dozens and dozens of men in black coats. More and more poured through the revolving doors at increasing speed. Three uniformed guards appeared and raced up the stairs with the crowd. The man at the desk was using the phone.

In a few seconds' time the lobby was back to normal. There were no black coats there at all. It was as if a flock of crows had hit on a fence and then suddenly taken flight again and the landscape had resettled itself as if they had never existed. I blinked. The man at the next table paid his check and waved an ironic good-bye to me. I was embarrassed that my husband had not yet appeared.

The waitress was hovering about trying to give me my check. I waved her off. I thought of Mrs. Cohen, who might have wanted to join her husband on this rescue mission but was not permitted, not asked, not even considered as one of the soldiers. Mrs. Cohen was a woman of valor. She was a carrier of the law, a maintainer of the body and the frame of the family. Rabbi Cohen was the mind. He was the one who made the decisions. He was the one who had the authority. His was the obligation to study and to learn. His was the reward and hers was the work. My skin crawled. Mrs. Cohen accepted the separation before God and she hadn't grasped that separation never results in equality but always serves to sweep power to one side or another. She washed away her impurities each month and regarded her body as a vessel for her people, for her husband, for her God. She had turned her back on the enlightenment and the promise of reason and the hope of technology and the laws of causality and she had never heard of Occam's razor or Descartes'

"Cogito ergo sum." I would despise her, I should despise her, except that I know how insane you have to be to stay in my world, how much loneliness you have to bear as you walk among the ruins of other households, knowing that the future may be just as bad as the past. I know how difficult it is to balance when the ground is always spinning and you have to be able to accept losing, most of all you have to be able to accept losing. It is this that I have spared Andrea. Mrs. Cohen could beat me at chess. My king would stand there unable to move forward, back or to the side while her king watched my terminal paralysis from a safe vantage point on the other side of the board.

I heard sirens and through the lobby doors came the police, four or five of them, and they rushed to the desk and then headed for the stairs. The manager came out from behind the desk to reassure passing guests that there was no trouble at all, just a small domestic dispute, no bomb scare, no terrorists in the kitchen, just a family matter that would soon be settled.

The elevator doors opened and a pack of black coats and hats tumbled out into the lobby. The stair door opened and dozens more came running down. They were shouting to each other in Hebrew.

"What are they saying?" I asked the waitress. She looked confused.

Then I saw two large men supporting a limp boy between them. The boy had no hat. He had no payess. He had red hair and he was wearing an old pair of Nike sneakers. He was wearing tan slacks and a plaid shirt. His parents had already dressed him for the trip home. His beard was gone. They had changed him back. He looked like any American boy, except his skin was pale white and he couldn't stand by himself. His eyes were open but cloudy. They had the vacant expression of a blind man. I caught only a glimpse of him for a second as he was instantly surrounded by the others and out the revolving door.

The elevator opened again and more black coats and hats

appeared and moved swiftly toward the door. The police
came down the stairs and shouted at the men to stop. Some
of them did and others did not. A crowd of black coats and
black hats surrounded the four policemen and there was a
great commotion and a lot of shouting back and forth. The
police were trying to clear a path.

A group from Houston, Texas, appeared with each member wearing a white identification tag. They were carrying
cameras, maps and a guide book. The doors were suddenly
clogged with people trying to go out and there was a great
shoving. A British voice called, "These are the rudest
people I have ever seen."

Into the lobby came the four tank corps men. One had a
black eye. One was holding his arm and there was blood on
his shirt. They joined the crowd pushing their way out the
door. They were swallowed up by a group of black coats
and when the black coats had gone, out the door, the four
men lay on the floor, struggling to get up with the police
standing over them.

Gloria came out of an elevator door into the lobby. Her
hair was disheveled, her lipstick smeared. She had tears in
her eyes and her nose was red. "They got him back," she
said to me. "They've stolen him again. There were so many
of them. They just pushed in and the men couldn't stop
them. Arnold has a bloody nose. They took my boy right
away from us. They have no right to him. He belongs to us.
He's our child. They kidnapped him. They kidnapped my
baby." She sat down at my table and her hands were
shaking.

"I'm so sorry," I said. I put my arms around her in a
gesture of sisterhood. This was Judas's country too.

I was in my room. The phone rang. It was Andrea.
"Mother," she said.

"Are you all right?" I asked.

"I'm fine," she said, "but I'm going away. If you want
to see me come right now to the yeshiva. I'm leaving soon.
Guess what?"

"What?" I obliged.

"Rabbi Weiss, the famous scholar, the one who is descended directly from the Bal Shem, who knows more than any living Jew, this morning he requested a visit with me. Mrs. Cohen took me to his house and I sat in his study and he asked me questions. I was frightened I would give the wrong answers. I could hardly hear my own voice. But I remembered everything important and I told him the truth because I knew he would know if I lied about anything. He said I was like Ruth and that he would take me as his own daughter and stand at my wedding like my father because of the joy I brought to him and to all the people of Israel. Can you just imagine that." I was silent. "Do you understand?" she said, and I heard a whine, a cranking up of irritation. It was a familiar sound.

"I'm proud of you too," I said. "Really proud."

As I approached the yeshiva I saw crowds of men milling about. There were so many of them that they spilled into the street and cars could not pass and had to detour around. I wove my way through the crowd. This was facilitated by the fact that the men turned away from me, pressing their bodies against each other and squeezing into doorways in order to avoid any touch of mine. I tried to catch someone's eye, to explain that I was not an intruder but a part of the day's events. No one looked at me as I made slow progress toward the yeshiva.

In front of the yeshiva the crowd was so thick that I couldn't move forward. I shouted in English, "I am Sarai's mother. My daughter is in the yeshiva. Let me through. I am Sarai's mother. I am the mother. I am the mother." I was embarrassed because I was calling into the air. No one was looking at me, no one seemed to hear me.

I screamed again. Now the young man on one side of me heard me. He did not turn around but he shouted something in Hebrew and his words were repeated through the immediate group and a path was cleared and I walked through. I kept my eyes down on the ground. I was a stranger among strangers in an alien land. My head was throbbing and there was a sharp pain in my hip. I needed aspirin. I needed to lie down. The heat of the day was now so strong that my blouse was stained with perspiration and I could feel the beads of sweat on my lip and each breath weighed down in my chest as if it were smoke, as if the sun had come too close to the earth.

All the girls of the yeshiva, Mrs. Cohen, all her children and Rabbi Cohen were gathered in the kitchen. They were sitting at the tables and they were singing together. It was a rhythmic, waving song and they stamped their feet and they clapped their hands and when it was done they laughed and kissed each other. Andrea was surrounded by girls who were whispering in her ear, pulling at her dress and smoothing her hair. Rabbi Cohen explained to me that this was a small celebration because the girls themselves could not go to the wedding due to the special circumstances.

Andrea rushed up to me. Her eyes were light and her cheeks were pink. "I wish this moment would never pass," she said. "I wish I could be like this, like now, forever."

I sat down and mopped my face with a paper napkin; my daughter, caught in bridal fantasies, thinking of happily ever after, made me hope, despite myself, made tears spring to my eyes, even though I was not sad but rather amazed. I felt soft. If I was touched I might fold like a cushion, crush like new grass, as if I were not a matron who knew too much but again a maiden ready to risk all. My hip ached, my eye twitched, but I touched Andrea gently on the arm. "Sarai," I said, "I wish you happiness."

She smiled at me but an instant later was drawn away by a group of girls who wanted to show her some piece of linen someone was embroidering for her.

"We have to send them off, now, within a half hour," said Rabbi Cohen. "The police want to interview Micah and make sure that it is his decision to stay. The rabbinical court will deal with the police and the Rose parents will be stalled. There are some reporters about. We do not want to risk any more incidents, any more kidnappings, so we are sending Sarai and Micah out of the city to a settlement in Judea where they will be well taken care of among our people, and when the Roses have returned to the U.S.A. and the incident at the hotel fotgotten, we will bring them back here. They will be married in the settlement immediately. It would perhaps be better for you, involve you less in matters with the authority, if you returned to your country. We will see that this wedding takes place as it should."

"All right," I said, "as long as Sarai does not think I have run away from her."

Rabbi Cohen looked directly at me. His eyes were so kind that I wished I could believe he was not a tyrant, a remnant of a past that could not survive into the future. "You are a good mother," he said to me.

I turned away because I did not want him to see on my face the lines of gratitude, irony, regret.

Andrea approached the waiting car. There was a driver, a large man whose heavy arms rested on the steering wheel. There was a woman in the backseat, her head covered with a purple scarf attached with metal hair clips. She was not young. There were whiskers of unplucked hair on her chin. Michael was already in the front seat. He had a new hat on and the black jacket he wore seemed a few sizes too large. He did not have his glasses. There was a cut on his cheek where the razor had moved too quickly. His eyes were blinking furiously. He did not look at Andrea but stared straight ahead. As the car door closed and she settled herself in the backseat he blushed, but did not speak. The car inched away from the curb as the crowd of men in the street slowly parted to let the vehicle through. Andrea did not turn around to wave at me.

I ARRIVE after a long flight to find the ficus has withered in my absence. Brown leaves are strewn about the floor. My neighbor either forgot to water the plant or watered it too much. I take some aspirin for my hip, which is grinding in its socket and protested through the night as I turned and turned in my seat trying to find a place to rest.

I go into Andrea's room and look at the poster of Alan Alda that has hung there for years. I look at the bookshelf with the tales of Sid and Nancy, John Belushi and the story of a plane crash in the Andes that introduced a soccer team to cannibalism. I could rent the room to a graduate student or I could seal it off as if it were an ancient shrine with snakes guarding treasure behind a stone slab. I could leave everything untouched and a window open in case Andrea changes her changeable mind and comes back. Is Rabbi Cohen a Jewish incarnation of Peter Pan or was Peter Pan the English Bal Shem? I am not grateful to have been taken out of bondage from Egypt. After all, how did I become a slave in Egypt?

I lie down on my bed with a cup of tea and open my mail. Maybe if I am very quiet I will hear God whispering, explaining matters to me or releasing me from the need for explanations. If reason cannot lead to reconciliation, can I abandon reason? Maybe I am not too old for revelation. After all, Sarah was ninety when she conceived a child. If that happens, will I have found my own way to Jerusalem or will I have joined the ladies matted and scabbed who wander on Broadway looking for a doorway that will shelter them from the cold? On the plane I made notes from a monograph on Rabbi Nachman. I would like to open his life and works to rational analysis. There are biographies in the library. His disciples wrote down all he told them. He is the ideal figure for a study on psychosis and God. Without heavenly visitations I will console myself.

A thought comes: If Israel does not burn down in the next eighteen years—and after all, an eighteen-year pause between catastrophes is not so much to ask for—then I might have a granddaughter who might come to New York to visit me. There would be difficulties about the food, but I could agree to turn the kitchen kosher. I will be very agreeable for eighteen years. In the summers I will go and visit and never challenge even the smallest or most irritating of rules. They can settle in Judea, I won't say a word. When my grand-daughter is eighteen and restless with all she has been taught, I will invite her to visit me. Once she is here I will slowly introduce her to science and math and deductive reasoning and Chekhov and Dostoyevsky, Locke and Susan B. Anthony, and when she is ready I will suggest to her that she become a doctor and stay here and go to college. Don't despair, Dr. Arnold Rose, we may yet have a doctor in the family. She may be the one to find the cure for juvenile diabetes. She can change her name to Jane for Jane Austen or to Charlotte for Charlotte Brontë, to Simone for Simone de Beauvoir, to Amelia for Amelia Earhart. There are so many names that would suit.

Ah! I feel a stab of pain for the grief my daughter will feel when her daughter grabs hold of the pendulum and swings toward me. How quickly that stab of pain subsides as I anticipate the most delicious shape of comforts ahead.

But what if I am simply wrong, anachronistic, a figment of the enlightenment's imagination, wiped out in the coming wave of history that will put women behind veils or under scarfs and men on their knees before deities that promise the moon and as usual deliver the earth on which we do no more than devour and decay as we hurry toward oblivion? Then I have the honor of treading water as long as possible. I have the honor of my intentions.